COUNTERTRADE: A GLOBAL PERSPECTIVE

COUNTERTRADE:
A Global
Perspective

P.N. AGARWALA

VIKAS PUBLISHING HOUSE PVT LTD

VIKAS PUBLISHING HOUSE PVT LTD
576, Masjid Road, Jangpura, New Delhi 110 014

Printed at Hindustan Offset Printers, Delhi - 32 (INDIA)

PREFACE

Countertrade currently accounts for nearly a fifth to a quarter of global trade estimated in 1989 at $ 3,100 billion. The incidence of countertrade is growing and in the nineties is likely to accelerate and has become a global phenomenon in over 100 countries.

I was commissioned by UNCTAD to make an in-depth study of countertrade in Asia-Pacific which I have supplemented by my studies and interface in Latin America/Caribbean and Africa besides East-West Trade and the OECD exchanges in offset and buy back. I have attempted to analyse its practices in 100 countries. My study was deliberated at an UNCTAD Workshop held at Kuala Lumpur attended by 61 participants from 31 countries and has been highly commended.

There is a growing body of literature on the subject but this is possibly the first comprehensive global study of the subject from a professional and practising viewpoint. I had the opportunity to initiate, negotiate and implement special trading arrangements on behalf of India with many leading industrial houses in Germany, UK, Japan, Canada, USA, Austria and Sweden besides my long experience of bilateral trade exchanges and four decades of global experience in areas of international marketing.

I have attempted to share my studies and experiences and outlined the steps necessary to successfully practise countertrade with safeguards to ensure additionality without undue loading of import prices.

I hope the readers will get a feel of the global countertrade scenario and I have analysed the causes, rationale of countertrade and its variants and pitfalls and the U.N. guidelines on the subject have been incorporated.

In the wake of the generally depressed prices for commodities and the current Gulf oil crises, many of the developing countries' exports registered significant declines in the '80s, barring the exports of newly industrialised countries of East Asia which are also slowing down. There was some recovery in 1987-88 but it has petered out in 1989. In real terms the prices are around the lowest levels touched in the depressed 'thirties'. The protectionist measures are severely affecting the exports of manufactures to developed countries through quotas, countervailing and surveillance measures. The Gulf crisis has aggravated the flight of non-oil importing countries and East European economies who are now called upon to pay for Soviet Crude in free foreign exchange. The energy scenario is sombre.

The overhang of the $ 1300 billion dollar debt has placed the Third World economies in a bind, there has been a net resources transfer to developed countries in recent years. The annual interest and amortisation payments amount to over US $ 130 billion dollars. The climate of aid has greatly deteriorated as also the flow of concessional bank finance. The violent Exchange fluctuations have aggravated the crisis in the world economy. There has been a decoupling of manufactures and employment in developed countries as also a decoupling of raw materials and manufactures owing to automation, robotisation, substitutes and synthetics. It is in this environment that countertrade has assumed increasing acceptance. Trading blocs are emerging in USA/Canada, EEC & Asia/Pacific and the Uruguay round has resulted in a stalemate.

In many developing countries practising countertrade, no clear and consistent policy formulation either in the form of legislation or guidelines concerning this form of trade has been established. Responsibilities for policy implementation are divided among several ministries, parastatal agencies and the Central Bank, causing uncertainty and delay in the clearance of countertrade proposals. In India, MMTC had taken a lead in negotiating countertrade deals against fertiliser and mineral imports. The STC also made a modest start. The Ministry of Commerce in India, while encouraging such deals has yet not formulated any clear policy guidelines. The initial reluctance of the Indian Finance Ministry appears to have been largely overcome. In many developed and developing countries, large volume of countertrade deals have been finalised against petroleum imports and offset deals for defence and aircraft purchases.

India's balance of payments position in 1988-89 and 1989-90 has continued to be very difficult with a trade deficit of around 75,000 to 100,000 million. The exchange reserves have declined sharply and barely cover one month imports. The foreign debt stands at over US $69 billion and the interest payments and amortisation amount to 30 per cent of foreign exchange earnings. Countertrade has become inescapable in these circumstances. Similarly, the situation has emerged in other South Asian countries besides the Latin American/Caribbean and African region.

There is difficulty of ensuring that countertrade exports do not cut into traditional markets and that they serve to diversify the country's basket and expand existing exports lines and generate additionality. This requires continuous monitoring of the products and their eventual destination and high level commercial intelligence, besides negotiating capabilities of a high order on the part of executives of para-statal organisations in the developing world.

The control of the ultimate destination of countertrade export could be ensured by mandating either C&F contracts or by stipulating the production of discharge or customs clearance certificates. The objective of product diversification could be assisted by differentiated countertrade requirements depending on the competitiveness of the export goods involved.

Despite the fact that countertrade had increasingly assumed a North-South direction in the eighties, most developing countries have not developed specialised skills on a par with the massive growth of such expertise in the developed countries, where both trading houses as well as banks have accumulated considerable expertise and information in this field, partly based on long experience in East-West countertrade. Developing countries which have large trading houses – generally state controlled – are in a better position to meet the challenge of countertrade. There is need to develop professionalisation and negotiating skills in the State Trading Corporations and the Ministries of Commerce/Finance together with the Banks with foreign branches.

Some countries have decided to create a consortium of trading houses to establish a non-profit trading house along the Swedish Sukab model which has now become parastatal or an association along the French ACECO model, or by a number of commercial banks to establish specialised subsidiaries or branches following the examples of many banks in the industrialised countries, giving them access to knowledge of a vast range of countertrade opportunities. There is need for establishing an apex organisation in developing countries for negotiating and implementing countertrade deals to derive the maximum trading opportunities for export, utilising the immense buying power of the canalising agencies which account for a substantial share of the imports besides the massive defence and aerospace imports. Australia, Canada, New Zealand and West European countries are in the vanguard of countertrade in offset arrangements and buy-back countertrade deals.

There is an imperative need to identify products that are difficult to export in traditional markets and to the non-traditional markets for newer products. Equally important is the need to enlarge the production capacities to augment export surpluses.

In view of the unequal experience of procurement agencies importing under countertrade compared to foreign suppliers making countertrade offers, the danger exists that the underlying (shadow) price relationship of a countertrade transaction, resulting in an undesirable deterioration of the developing country's terms of trade on that account, price surveillance function might be given to the co-originating body to avoid any distortions and loading of subsidies.

. The recent experience has shown that countertrade of developing countries has had a particularly strong North-South bias as contrasted to a small South-South component. The ultimate purchasers of countertrade goods are very often located in other developing countries. The reasons for this are partly institutional and partly of an attitudinal/informational nature. The information and attitudinal barriers need to be overcome in sister developing countries. The recent Kuala Lumpur meet is a step to foster South-South Exchanges.

Countertrade requirements could be softened with regard to suppliers from other developing countries, following the example already practised by Brazil, Yugoslavia, Indonesia, Malaysia, Thailand and Argentina. Countertrade could become an element of the global system of trade preferences (GSTP). Sufficient attention needs to be paid to the problems of risk management and pricing, including shadow prices and public accountability under countertrade situations. Commercial countertrade transactions can be insured in London/Vienna. So far there is not much case law but a legal framework has just been formulated by U.N. General Assembly and is incorporated herein.

Countertrade had emerged as a partial solution to the trading problems of the war torn economies of Central and Eastern Europe. With the economic reconstruction and prosperity, the Western European economies shed this form of trade in favour of free and multilateral trade, while the Eastern European countries have maintained this mechanism to achieve their developmental requirements and conducted their trade within the framework of bilateral payments agreements using clearing account. East European economies concluded a series of bilateral arrangements with developing countries to secure raw materials and dispose off their manufactures and semi-manufactures. Developed countries have resorted to countertrade as a mechanism to enhance their trading capacity in goods and manufactures during a period of slow growth of international trade; developing countries have been considering this method of trade and gradually adapting it to their requirements. It is hard to precisely quantify the volume of countertrade, as no separate statistics are maintained. World trade in 1988 was estimated at US $ 2800 billion dollars and is likely to touch $ 3100 billion in 1989. The growth in 1990 is slowing down in USA, U.K., Canada, Australia and Newzealand.

Countertrade has several variants like counter-purchase, buy-back, offset and compensation arrangements besides the traditional barter and links.

The ratio of counter-purchase required from the foreign suppliers has varied. In Indonesia, it was set at 100 per cent of the foreign element. Indonesia entered into countertrade deals of over US $ 2000 million dollars. A little over US $ 800 million dollars have been implemented. In Malaysia countertrade of M$ 800 million (Malaysian dollars) worth of deals had been entered into upto 1988. These contracts have been mainly for government tender purchases for imports of telecommunication equipment, railway rolling stock, requirements of national electricity boards, PWD, Defence equipment, highway equipments, etc.

In Thailand, the Department of Agriculture and Cooperatives had purchased fertilisers and aviation planes against sale of surplus agricultural products. India had entered into link deals which are akin to countertrade. Bangladesh had entered into special trading-cum-private-clearing arrangements, which were also akin to countertrade. Owing to the weakness of global economy a number of countertrade deals were entered into by Brazil for import of crude with Nigeria and the Gulf countries. Both in Argentina and Uruguay large countertrade deals have been concluded and Mexico has also entered the arena. It is likely to increase in the nineties. The Uruguay Round is making painfully slow progress in liberalising multilateral trading. New trading blocs are emerging in North America with the U.S.A.–Canada free trade agreement and Mexico is likely to join. The EEC incorporating Benelux countries, Germany, France, Italy, U.K., Denmark, Ireland, Greece, Spain & Portugal is integrating to become the single largest trading bloc in 1992.

The EFTA countries are likely to join the Economic European Space-closely integrated with EEC and the momentous changes in Hungary, Czechoslovakia, Poland, Bulgaria, Rumania and possibly in U.S.S.R. in the nineties will form the largest trading bloc. The Asia/Pacific rim led by Japan is emerging with ASEAN, Australia, Korea & Taiwan.

Safeguards

In order to estimate the costs of countertrade, mandatory separate quotations of countertrade costs in government tenders may be resorted to. While countertrade had proven itself to be a most effective tool for market penetration, this did not disguise the fact that there was a built-in subsidy element in it, which led to price distortions. It should be used for short/medium term export promotion of particular products requiring such subsidies, until these had become well-established in the target markets. Developing countries like India with foreign exchange problems often used their buying power for the promotion of their exports through countertrade. In many cases countertrade had been resorted to in order to overcome restrictions placed as a result of international price support and quota arrangements.

Additionality

In giving consideration to countertrade proposals, the additionality of exports has to be given due weight. Countertrade could become an important instrument in promoting intra and inter-regional trade among developing countries. Its incidence is increasing even in OECD countries.

Over 150 banks and enterprises have established specialised countertrade affiliates, while 400 others have set-up specialised countertrade units.

Additionality of exports is one of the primary objectives in conducting countertrade. For countertrade to be an effective instrument of trade promotion, clear government policy guidelines as well as a flexible implementing authority are of primary importance. The scope of countertrade should be extended to include offset operations in defence and aerospace procurement. Countertrade can be used as an effective trading mechanism to promote South-South trade. Developing countries look at countertrade more as an instrument of development, production and long-term export strategy, rather than a mere short-term trading instrument and as a supplement to normal exchanges.

My labours will have been amply repaid if this book is able to generate wide interest in the subject which is becoming of great significance in world trade. Despite the Uruguay round problems of profectionism, indebtedness of developing countries and low commodity prices persist and are likely to accentuate in the decade of the nineties.

P N Agarwala

December, 1990
New Delhi.

CONTENTS

1. Summary and Overview   1

2. Countertrade Variants   9

3. Countertrade in China and India   66

4. Countertrade—Developing Country Practices   76

5. International Workshop at Kuala Lumpur in
    March 1986 on Countertrade   82

6. Compensatory Trade as an International Issue   85

7. Organising for Countertrade   113

8. Assessment of Effects of Barter and
    Countertrade Transactions — A Global View of
    Country Experiences   123

9. The Legal Framework   168

Chapter 1

SUMMARY AND OVERVIEW

Countertrade is not a new phenomenon on the world scene. What is new is the exploding volume of such trade, as well as the growing number of countries that required or practice countertrade. The most recent GATT and 'Economist' estimates place countertrade at 10 per cent of world merchandise trade; the OECD and the Economic Commission for Europe peg countertrade's share of total East-West trade at 15 per cent. Traditionally defined countertrade deals—including barter, counterpurchase, compensation deals and buy-back arrangements, but not switch deals, offset agreements or other export-related performance requirements-account for approximately 15 per cent to 20 per cent of East-West trade and around 10 per cent of global trade. LDCs share in countertrade transactions is growing much faster than that of Eastern Europe.

The countertrade phenomenon will not subside—at least, not in the current decade and beyond, nor through most of the nineties either. Slow and uneven recovery in commodity prices, on-going if modest oil prices increases, relatively stiff real interest rates, stagnant commercial and aid finance, and continued population growth and urbanisation clearly all tend to militate against rapid global economic expansion in the 90s and will thus exacerbate the pressures for countertrade. As long as the fear exists that one or more countries may default on their international debt obligations, countertrade will continue to be seen as a viable option. Crude oil prices continue depressed together with commodities in mid 1990.

Countertrade can be used as a serviceable marketing tool to outperform the competition. Countertrade is also increasingly reaching the realm of the corporate finance and treasury officials. Banks with shaky loans in LDCs and manufacturing companies with huge sums of blocked local currency in various parts of the world are beginning to look at the trading function and countertrade as possible tools to solve basically financial and not their marketing problems.

Many LDCs are now turning to countertrade in response to conditions that closely parallel those of the East European countries in the last two decades; growing service burdens, falling commodity prices, generally worsening terms of trade, declining exports and deteriorating domestic economic performance. The underlying differences between degrees of government centralisation and those of most LDCs—a private sector and different degrees of government centralisation and economic control—make for totally different operating conditions.

The spread of countertrade practices and pressures throughout the Third World—particularly government mandated countertrade requirements in, for example, Indonesia, Malaysia, Columbia, Uruguay or Ecuador—has evoked strong negative reactions from multilateral trade and financing institutions particularly GATT, IMF, IBRD: EEC for many years has focussed on countertrade in East-West trade. It is now trying to relate its experiences with Eastern Europe to the developing forms of countertrade in LDCs.

Most Western governments' stated policies object to the spread of government-mandated countertrade. In practice, many have helped their nations' companies to come to operate more effectively where countertrade is demanded—through facilitating services, export credits and guarantees or joint government/private sector countertrade pools. In some cases they have actually promoted or directly sponsored government-to-government countertrade deals in China and centrally planned economies.

In the US-Commodity Credit Corporation programme was, until its termination in 1973, perhaps the single largest barter facility in the annals of countertrade (reaching a volume of US $ 6.7 billion in its 23 year history). The US Government brokered a number of deals exchanging US commodities for Jamaican bauxite, ostensively for national security and foreign policy reasons. The US Commerce Department has geared up to help US exporters compete more effectively in the changing countertrade climate.

Countertrade encompasses all foreign trade transactions in which an exporter commits himself to take products from an importer (or the importer's country) in full or partial payment. In some countertrade transactions, payments for the goods bought and sold are actually made, in other forms of countertrade, there are no payments at all. There are four basic types of countertrade:

(a) Barter
(b) Compensation (or compensatory deals);

(c) Counter-purchase (also called counter-delivery, parallel trade, or reciprocal trade); Industrial compensation, and

(d) Product buy-back/offset or advance purchases.

These traditional forms of countertrade have dominated the countertrade experience over the past decades, particularly between the East and the West. As the practice spreads to more and more Third World countries—most of which are characterised by either a dominant private sector or a mixed economy—these old forms are taking on new turns to adapt to the different environment.

The long established practice of counter-purchase is taking on new life in the LDCs, which allows firms to accept countertrade goods in advance (a technique known as advance purchase. The LDCs partly tends to be a private firm (although it may also be the government or a parastatal enterprise) with something of value to sell. Companies are not fending off shoddy goods, which in East European experience were often rammed down a company's throat. Firms are taking the initiative in finding goods and getting an agreement to link their purchase of those goods to their sale to, in all likelihood, a totally different party in the same country.

In LDCs, though not in Eastern Europe, hard currency allocation, repatriation of locally generated funds and hedging against revolution are dominant concerns for multinational Corporations. LDCs themselves and MNCs (Multi-national Corporations) dealing in those countries are exploring new ways of discounting LDC trade paper, as traditional discounting and factoring becomes more and more difficult if not well-nigh impossible in some markets. The practice of forfaiting (essentially discounting without recourse to the exporter), becomes an attractive alternative, and one that is proved extremely viable in East-West trade. There are recent attempts to develop a more efficient mechanism to handle commercial countertrade and to overcome one of the most fundamental obstacles to its functioning—the forced bilateralism between buyer and seller—which often forces companies to deal with unfamiliar goods and services. A concept launched in mid-1984 by General Foods Trading Company and the First National Bank of Boston would create an International Trading Certificate—a transferable document guaranteed by the Central Bank of the issuing country. If successful, the mechanism could go a long way towards multilateralising countertrade obligations. Such companies are likely to come up in Miami, London, Vienna and Singapore from indications. The changes in East Europe will make Vienna the centre.

The demand for offset agreements comes largely from the industrialised countries themselves. Offset agreements are not limited to buying or even exporting local products, more often than not, they increasingly take an investment approach. The US Aerospace Industry Association surveyed 143 contracts concluded from 1975 to 1981-82 in over 26 countries. Of these 130, 92 per cent had compensation or offset requirements. Trade involved 113 contracts with a total value of US $ 15 billion of which $ 9.5 billion dollars, or 61 per cent involved offset commitments. Lately these have significantly increased.

Switch transactions, involve a third party making use of a trade imbalance between partners with a bilateral trade clearing and payments agreement. There is a tremendous surge of clearing/payment agreements between LDCs and Eastern Europe. It is no longer quite possible to switch trade imbalances between West and East European countries. There are still around 130 clearing (bilateral payment) agreements in existence between non-market economy and developing countries, seven between OECD and centrally planned countries and another four between OECD and developing countries.

Current global switch trade is estimated at around US $ 4000-5000 million per year, and the trend is rising. Latin American countries alone account for two-thirds of this volume. Major partners in switch transactions are Brazil, Colombia, Ecuador, Bangladesh, India, Pakistan and Syria among the centrally planned economies. Brazil has the largest number of clearing agreements with Eastern Europe. Brazil was offering Western firms its substantial trade surpluses in Eastern Europe at discounts ranging between two per cent and seven per cent.

Just as clearing agreements between LDCs and East European countries offer a significant opportunity for MNCs to make use of switch deals, so also do trade and co-production agreements. Such trade and co-production agreements are intended to serve as frameworks within which individual companies may negotiate specific commercial deals with foreign trade organizations or productive enterprises. Bilateral cooperation pacts commit the signatories to encourage cooperation in a specific number of industrial, agricultural and commercial sectors.

Of the corporate sector (non-trading house) that have taken on countertrade, 12 per cent limited themselves to products they could use in-house, another 22 per cent preferred to take only related products for resale. The other 66 per cent took both related and unrelated products for resale. A major consideration is to obtain greater control of international divisions. A corporate-wise countertrade policy has the additional benefit of improving inter-corporate communication and cohesion.

Most MNCs confronted with the one-shot countertrade deal, inevitably make use of established trading houses and even MNCs with extensive in-house facilities that handle countertrade and firms that provide ancillary countertrade services, such as consulting, legal advice and insurance.

In the context of countertrade specialisation, there is invariably preference for certain goods or territories that the trading house has grown accustomed to handling. In most cases, however, countertrade goods are not disposed of so readily and other means of finding a buyer must be used. These other channels, which a company can seldom duplicate on its own, establish the real advantage offered by a trading house.

Many of the large trading houses active in countertrade are part of international groups that have affiliated brokering, processing and distribution companies. Such a trading house is in a better position to find an end-user of countertrade products quickly—if not within the group then in one of the many other companies with which it cooperates. The smaller independent trading houses lack this flexibility.

A trading house usually agrees to make a specific countertrade product only after it has found a definite buyer. The degree of specialisation of the trading houses that handles the commitment and the extent of its contracts will be the key factors in determining the length of interim financing that will be required.

Many firms find it advantageous to enter into a permanent arrangement for their business with some or all countries in a geographic region, particularly in Eastern Europe. Should a company anticipate only occasional countertrade commitments, it is better to employ the services of a suitable trading house on ad-hoc basis. This allows a company more flexibility—it can work with different houses, depending upon the products and countries involved, and take advantage of each trader's special skills and facilities. If the trading house must shop around, the settlement may take as long as one to two years or more.

A trading house that accepts a countertrade obligation but cannot dispose of the goods on its own will usually transfer the obligation to another trader. In such cases, the commission will generally be split between the two trading houses, with the shares varying from deal to deal. A company should get from the trading house an accurate estimate of the total settlement cost of its countertrade commitment before signing a final commitment contract with a potential supplier of countertrade goods. A global MNC may successfully fulfill a switch deal, but most companies—even big MNCs—seldom have access to the range of possibilities that switch experts have.

There are several ways to organising to handle countertrade operations—

(a) Act as a coordinator without any staff, attached to purchasing, sales, set up the international coordinating department or a corporate staff office. Appointment of a staff consultant for countertrade, who regularly advises all departments faced with countertrade obligations.

(b) A countertrade unit, including product, function and country specialists.

(c) An autonomous trading house, of which the company owns a share and through which it disposes of countertrade obligations.

(d) An independent trading subsidiary or trading house, set-up by the company, to coordinate the countertrade goods that cannot be used internally and to trade on its own account.

The point at issue in respect of setting-up trading units or subsidiaries is whether it should be a profit centre set-up which provides greater incentives for good performance, the latter may be easier to push through in a company with many autonomous divisions headed by strong personalities. Another controversial question which relates to establishing a countertrade organisation is whether the trading subsidiary should be allowed to work for third parties. In evaluating the performance of a trading operation, the company must accurately measure the costs attributable to the unit.

Locating the trading unit within the corporate structure or putting the trading subsidiary in a geographical location that makes both logistic and management sense is a big area of concern for many managements. Proper staffing and compensation of training executives can make or break a trading operation. A trading company's success depends largely on how well its traders develop contacts and use those contacts to generate business.

The countertrade units should be closely linked to top management. The critical factors are the diversity and complexity or products traded and the number of transactions. If a trading subsidiary is aiming for maximum profitability, it should reward staffers for increasing the profit margin in individual deals and should encourage growth in the volume of profitable deals. Traders are remunerated on a salary plus high commission basis. One way to harmonize traders' income with that of other employees and top management is to keep the commission fairly low. Other firms pay bonuses for meeting sales or profit targets, rather than commissions based on each transaction.

Some countries, such as the non-market economies of Eastern Europe and some LDCs such as Indonesia, Uruguay, Malaysia and Ecuador, have clearly spelt-out countertrade rules and regulations; an established institutional infrastructure and varied experience in pushing countertrade on MNCs. Many LDCs are only now turning to countertrade as a means to finance needed exports or in the case of individual private sector importers, to overcome import, currency and investment restrictions.

Negotiating skills are crucial to a company's success. Countertrade requirements will be lower for exporters that take finished industrial products that are difficult to sell in developed countries. East European negotiators, for example, will typically open countertrade talks with a request that 50-100 per cent of the value of the Western deliveries be payable in local products, but would possibly settle for a lower negotiated percentage.

A company should ascertain how payment will be made and whether the countertrade suppliers expects some sort of financial assistance from the MNCs. It is absolutely crucial to determine this point and to reach an agreement, sales price increases will have to cover all costs of disposing off the countertrade goods. Unusually long maturities may imply that countertrade requirements will follow. Excessive prices can usually be reduced after extensive haggling. A surcharge of upto five per cent for countertrade goods over regular exports goods is considered reasonable.

Subsidies vary from country to country, industry to industry, product to product and deal to deal. Subsidies run anywhere from five per cent to 15 per cent depending on a number of factors. The most crucial mistake made by companies that are newcomers to countertrade is to combine the sales of their goods and the purchase of countertrade products in one contract. In many LDCs, 'force majeure' may include strikes, crop failures, droughts, floods, earthquakes, hurricanes and fire caused by lighting of inflammable materials are generally considered in these countries as human error. Most countertrade arrangements include penalty provisions for a company's non-fulfillment of the countertrade commitment. Penalties average from eight to eighteen per cent but they can go as high as 50 to 100 per cent. In compensation deals penalty provisions are usually not applied. The private market, covering some US $ 10 billion in exports, has begun to acknowledge the growth of countertrade and is taking up the slack in insuring against inherent perils. Global countertrade can be handled by an international department without the need of a separate subsidiary.

The public sector organisations in India handling countertrade—MMTC, STC—lack the professional and negotiating skills and the commercial intelligence needed to ensure additionality without undue loading of prices and close monitoring. The new apex trading Co. recently formed has yet to make a debt.

Chapter 2

COUNTERTRADE : VARIANTS

Countertrade is a much broader concept; it encompasses many forms of compensatory trade—including counter-purchase buy-back, co-production, triangular trade and swap. Estimates place countertrade currently at 1/5th to 1/4th of world trade or more than US $ 500 to US $ 600 billion annually. The US Department of Commerce believes that by the year 2000, a third to one-half of all world trade will be undertaken via some form of countertrade. The recent stock market crash in the USA on October 19, 1987 and the sharp downturn on January 8, 1988 and the steep decline in the dollar in the last two and half years will tend to slow down the growth in developing countries. Although the recent package on Mexican debt bonds might be a breather it holds little prospect of any significant improvement in the overall debt burden of Third World countries which now totals around $ 1300 billion dollars. There has been a net outflow from Third World countries in recent years.

Countertrade demands more negotiating/implementing executive time, thereby increasing the cost of deals. It creates additional legal work and tends to distort conventional international trade. The most compelling reason is that developing and socialist countries are presently unable to pay in cash for the imports they require, because a high proportion of their export income goes to pay foreign debt, interest and amortisation payments. World Bank has estimated that their indebtedness currently totals over US $ 1300 billion world-wide. Even developing countries like Brazil are finding it increasingly difficult to meet their interest payments. Many Latin American, African and some Asian commodity and oil producing countries have been forced to reschedule their debts at a time of highly depressed commodity prices and protectionist barriers affecting their exports of manufactures. The climate of aid and direct private investment has deteriorated and lately there has been a net outflow to OECD countries.

In Latin America and Africa, where the crisis has been most pronounced, unemployment and widespread poverty have sparked off serious social and political unrest. Venezuela, Ecuador, Argentina, Chile, Columbia and other countries in the region are experiencing symptomatic difficulties. Countertrade offers some escape from this haunting scenario. By exchanging resources—be they raw materials, semi-finished goods, manufactures or intermediate technology—for resources needed, countries have begun to meet their requirements without recourse to expending scarce foreign exchange. Brazil has completed countertrade arrangements worth several billion dollars with Mexico, Nigeria and Iraq, providing grains, frozen chickens, cars and machinery for the oil it lacks. Jamaica has bartered large quantities of bauxite for foodstuffs. Trinidad and Tobago have been negotiating arrangements whereby Japan would be required to purchase local oil equivalent in value to the cars and electronic goods Japan exports to these islands. China, Indonesia and Malaysia have led the way among Asian countertraders and the spectre is spreading to Thailand, the Philippines and even India and Pakistan. Around 100 countries are currently involved in barter/countertrade deals; 15 have gone so far as to publish regulations institutionalizing countertrade. Despite STABEX African Countries are in serious crisis.

Countertrade is basically a commercial practice involving linking of sales to purchases or purchases to sales. The term "countertrade" may be applied to the entire range of trade obligations between two or more contracting parties. Governments encourage or mandate countertrade in order to reduce their trade imbalance, foster the exports of certain industrial products targeted for growth, upgrade certain specified sectors through foreign investment and increase foreign exchange reserves. OECD governments purchasing nuclear equipment, aerospace and defence equipment from other developed nations have been known to impose tough countertrade requirements on the manufactures of nuclear reactors as also for purchases of defence and aerospace components.

Countertrade is becoming a fact of life in a growing number of countries. Companies find themselves obliged to enter into new types of contract negotiations, currency transactions, risk management and financing, in order to countertrade and remain competitive and in the mainstream in foreign markets.

Once companies take a closer look at countertrade, they begin to perceive some substantial benefits in getting involved in these types of deals. Companies can use their countertrade suppliers as reliable long-term sources of certain critical raw materials, component parts or finished goods. These supply sources may be essential to a company's operations and may also be not overly expensive because of relatively low labour costs. Undertaking long-term purchase contracts in a non-market economies or developing countries is one way to establish a company as a reliable trading partner, and thereby increase its visibility and its opportunities to gain major sales on a long-term basis. Counter-trading offers companies a means of adjusting their accounting records to take advantage of tax and tariff laws.

Rationale in Current International Economic Scenario

The debate continues whether countertrade is a reasonable response by hard-pressed nations or is a market-distorting practice that fosters economic inefficiencies; and whether countertrade is a cyclical phenomenon that will disappear when the world economy strengthens, or is here to stay because of widespread intractable poverty, hard-currency illiquidity and the undeniable short-term benefits that importing nations can obtain through "beggar thy neighbour" economic policies.

The present malaise in the world economy does not appear to be just a passing disorder which in time will correct itself. The decoupling of raw materials/minerals to evolving production technologies and the widespread use of synthetics and substitutes is a phenomenon of structural change. There has also been a decoupling of manufactures and employment owing to automation and robotisation. While existing production levels are being maintained in OECD countries, unemployment continues at very high levels. Following the delinking of the dollar and gold, the exchange fluctuations have increased enormously; while the global trade is around US $ 3000 billion, the daily capital movements amount to US $ 150 to $ 250 billion.

In 1987 the Central Banks of Japan, FRG, Switzerland and USA tried to stabilise the dollar. Despite their massive interventions the dollar continued to decline. The US domestic deficit continues to over around US $ 150 billion despite the $ 33 billion cut approved by the Congress. The US trade deficit has been running close to US $ 120 to US $ 130 billion annually. The sharp decline in the dollar has made some US exports more competitive but it will take a considerable time before the deficit is reduced to more manageable levels. Over the years the US will need to generate exports not only to cover the imports but also to meet the increasing interest and amortisation payments. Exchange stability for a reserve currency like the dollar in which much of the world trade is expressed is a *sine-qua-non* for return to free trade and greater transparency in international exchanges.

Estimates continue to vary concerning the number of countries imposing countertrade, the average countertrade requirements as a percentage of export sales to countertrading countries, and the proportions of world trade comprised by countertrade.

Most of the problems of quantification stem from failure of governments to record linked bilateral trade as a separate entry in their national accounts. Considerable countertrade business is handled by independent trading houses whose tendency is to keep details of trading volumes and trading partners as business secrets.

Estimates of the percentage of countertrade in international trade vary between 10 per cent and 25 per cent with higher proportions in some areas such as East-West trade. *The Economist* estimates that over 10 per cent of total world exports are paid for in kind rather than cash. Even the most conservative estimates by Western trading houses put the countertrade figure at 10 per cent of world exports. This means that, at the very least, US $ 300 billion dollars worth of exports are being paid for in products or services rather than in cash.

A recent US Department of Commerce study had reported that over 35 countries currently impose countertrade requirements. The list of countertrade countries is growing, as is the magnitude of countertrade mandates and is perceptively increasing in the current difficult international trading environment and low-developing scenarios of the nineties emerging.

Several Third World countries mandate counter-purchases. Some require foreign suppliers to purchase commodities, products or bauxite and non-traditional exports to establish markets and traditional export items to non-traditional markets to generate additionality and export diversification.

Some of the reasons why governments find it worthwhile to postulate countertrade are hard-currency illiquidity, and high levels of foreign debt; growing trade imbalances, worsening terms of trade for many less-developed and least developed and disadvantageously placed countries (LDCs); and the perception that importing governments can derive economic advantages by exercising leverage and strength of buying power over suppliers competing in an emerging buyer's market.

Over the last seven years the non-oil commodity and oil prices have remained highly depressed and in real terms are even below the levels reached in the depressed 1930s. There had been some improvement in metal prices particularly copper owing mainly to depressed supplies and the declining dollar. Even this modest recovery shows no signs of any sustained increase over the next couple of years. The demographic changes and near saturation of consumption standards in the OECD countries have brought down the share of LDCs in world trade from 1/3rd to almost 1/5th in the 1980s while the populations in Europe and Japan are ageing, the population of the young is growing in developing countries. The demographic picture in the USA is somewhat better owing to migration and higher proportion of young in the populace and population increase among Hispinacs & blocks.

Many of the poorer developing countries cannot import even essential goods unless they generate incremental foreign exchange through countertrade. The large foreign debts and hard-currency liquidity of many LDCs, coupled with declining prices for their primary commodities have crippled these countries' economic growth in the eighties. Countertrade is a response to both the liquidity shortage and the worsening terms of trade for LDC exports. The outlook for the 90s is for slower growth.

The LDC's are experiencing a growing need for market intelligence and sophisticated marketing channels. Countertrade is one way for them to find new customers.

The motivations for countertrade in the USSR, Eastern Europe and China are also related to seeking greater access to new Western markets and preserving hard currencies in economic exchanges with non-convertible currencies. In centrally-planned economies foreign commerce is managed and directed by governments, and countertrade is more integrated in their overall organization of the domestic economy and the conduct of foreign trade operations. In CMEA countries (CMEA – Council for Mutual Economic Assistance) foreign trade is viewed primarily as an equilibrating mechanism for meeting the excess demand generated, when the economic plans prescribed input levels which exceed the levels available in their domestic economies and for offloading any excess product that domestic markets cannot absorb. State Trading Agencies of non-market economy countries that engage in countertrade arrangements consider countertrade ideologically and operationally compatible with their domestic and foreign trade planning systems.

A related motivating force behind countertrade policies in centrally-planned economies is the desire to upgrade and modernise the manufacturing of selected domestic industries in the context of the selective liberalisation of their economies in recent years.

Importing East European governments often favour co-production and product buy-back arrangements, through which Western/Japanese technology is transferred to their industries. In addition to updated technology, East European governments may obtain access to Western/Japanese know-how and management techniques through participating in countertrade mandated co-production and product buy-back deals.

In China, countertrade is seen as an important tool of central economic planning. It is used to conserve foreign exchange and reduce balance of payments deficits. Chinese countertrade policies are aimed at encouraging investment in Chinese plant and equipment, and importing production technologies, know-how and technical training services. Countertrade offers the opportunity to introduce new or improved Chinese enterprises the opportunity to introduce new or improve Chinese products to fiercely competitive export markets.

Countertrade is still relatively new in China. The outlook for countertrade with non-market economy countries is that overall countertrade pressures are rising, the percentages of countertrade requirements are increasing, the goods offered are becoming somewhat less attractive and bilateral trade obligations are being imposed even on imports of priority goods. A relatively new phenomenon is the counter-purchasing of services, rather than products, in fulfillment of countertrade obligations–services such as consulting, travel and hotel accommodation, transport, construction facilities and industry symposia.

The best known Western countertrade technique is "offset", imposed by governments that purchase large value items such as defence equipments and aerospace transportation systems. Offset deals involve very large amounts of money and are fulfilled over long periods of time ranging from five to twenty years. Offset contracts span a wide range of economic activity, from investing in or purchasing from a selected industry or industries, to co-producing products, sub-contracting parts of large projects and transferring of technology and know-how.

Countries that impose offset requirements often do so more from policy decisions to benefit certain select/targeted industries. Offset deals are in vogue in Canada, Spain, Portugal, the Netherlands, France, Switzerland and Sweden. Austria, Greece, the Republic of Korea, Saudi Arabia and Israel are some of the countries that are negotiating major offset contracts.

The Western motivation for concluding a develop-for-import deal is to ensure that it will be paid for its exports to a cash-starved country. Japan has supplied investment capital to Brazil to develop an alumina-complex with the express condition that Brazil would allocate half the resultant output to Japan in payment of investment loans and credits. Develop-for-import arrangements are frequently implemented through a combination of policy decisions and export financing regulations. France has mandated buy-back arrangements for exports of any metal-processing units financed by soft government export loans. When the French Government provided export loans on easy terms to a French firm exporting aluminium refining machinery to India, the terms of the loan specifically provided for the French firm to receive alumina-shipments from India in partial payment for the equipment.

Variants of bilateral trade comprise—

1. Payment for a commercial transaction may be entirely in goods; it may be partly in goods and partly in cash; or entirely in cash, either financed separately from the reciprocal trade obligation or generated by the import, or, as the case may be, through export-proceeds.
2. Countertrade goods may be the output of plant and equipment that a country has purchased through a commitment to pay back in resultant products; the products used to pay for the plant and equipment can be related to it but not resultant from it; or they may be entirely unrelated to the original export sale.
3. Countertrade takes the form of direct investment, sub-contracting, co-production trading, or technology licensing.
4. In most forms of countertrade the two halves of the bilateral deal may be contractually separate, linked only by a protocol agreement.

Countertrade deals vary according to how the following features have been structured:

1. Penalties for non-performance of all forms of countertrade can range from a small percentage to virtually the full value of the transaction.
2. The fulfillment period can be as short as six months or can stretch out over two decades or longer.
3. Some countertrade contracts specify the exact products and suppliers, while others specify only the agro–industrial sector, the percentage of local content.
4. The value of the countertrade deal as a percentage of the original sale varies from a small percentage to well over 100 per cent in buy-back arrangements to cover interest and other charges.
5. Countertrade contracts may provide blanket permission to assign obligations to certain types of their parties.

In the real world, countertrade transactions usually include elements of more than one form of countertrade.

Barter

Barter is the exchange of goods between two or more parties under a single contract. There are no letters of credit *per se* in barter transactions. However, participants can obtain performance guarantees issued in matching terms by the parties–banks.

The United States Department of Agriculture implemented a barter programme from 1950 to 1973, in order to reduce stocks of agricultural commodities acquired through its programme of price supported by the US Commodities Credit Corporation (CCC). The CCC programme was discontinued in 1973. In 1982, the USDA signed an agreement with the Government of Jamaica to barter 9115 metric tonnes of dairy products for 400,000 tonnes of bauxite.

Counterpurchase

Counterpurchase deals tend to outnumber other forms of countertrade transactions. Each transaction is separately financed and is intended to proceed independently. Linking the two is an umbrella agreement, which outlines penalties for failure to carry out the counter-purchase contract or requires the counter-purchase to precede the sale.

The counter-purchase contract defines the parameters of the counter-traded goods. The countertrade obligation may be broadly defined to include any and all products manufactured locally or identified to include only certain specific products. Rockwell International entered into an offset agreement with the Dutch Government to purchase US $ 9.5 million worth of Dutch-made goods.

The typical duration of a counter-purchase agreement extends between six months and three years. A counter-purchase agreement normally allows the seller in the first contract to assign his counter-purchase obligation to a trading house, which will dispose off the goods for a commission or discount. These discounts range from under five per cent for disposal of easily-marketed goods to as much as 30 to 40 per cent for hard-to-market manufactured goods.

A new variation in the counter-purchase business is to buy local services as part of a countertrade obligation. Usually, services have to be used in-house by the committed company or its subsidiaries. The types of services usually offered in countertrade are transport, construction, printing, office and display space, research work, and creation of advertising. If a company is willing to pay for its trading partners' export servicing and marketing costs, this may be credited against its countertrade commitment. In another countertrade arrangement, credits which release the exporter from countertrade obligations, are sold by the importer for a consideration. This practice is known as reverse countertrade. This linking of import and export contracts requires the consent of the state-trading country. Such deals have found their application in East-West trade.

Product Buy–back

Product buy-back involves sale of plant, technology or equipment with a contractual commitment on the part of the seller to buy-back goods that are produced by, or derived from the equipment in the original sale. The duration of buy-back transactions is far longer than that of most counter-purchase deals, because of the magnitude of the projects and because of the time required to complete the projects before they come on stream to produce the contracted quantities for counter-delivery. The period of the buy-back obligation runs from three to four years. Lease buy-back deals are a variation of buy-back. The value of buy-back goods as a proportion of the original sale is typically greater than is the case in counter-purchasing; counter-deliveries in buy-back deals often total 100 per cent or more of the value of the original sale.

Compensation is organized by the means of two separate contracts linked by protocol. Separation of the two contracts is also important because the innumerable variables and unforeseen contingencies inherent in the establishment of full-scale facilities would otherwise place a large uncovered risk on the second buy-back contract. The protocol linking the contracts takes on additional importance. The main problem in implementing buy-back agreements is similar to that inherent in barter and counter-purchasing. Compensation trading may result in greatly distorting markets in specific products. The petrochemical industries of the Federal Republic of Germany, Britain, and France accepted large quantities of buy-back goods, particularly bulk plastics in fulfillment of compensation contracts.

Examples of buy-back agreements are common-place in East-West trade. The develop-for-import types of countertrade deal, exchanging investment and technology for supplies of critical raw materials, is basically similar to compensation deals. France, Federal Republic of Germany and Japan have turned to develop-for-import projects in LDCs to assure themselves of stable supplies of essential raw material imports.

Joint Ventures and Technology Transfer

Co-production or industrial cooperation, involves an agreement to transfer technology to a trading partner in exchange for obtaining large contracts for turnkey plants. The technology transfer takes the form of technology licensing, joint production or parts and components, joint ventures and sub-contracting portions of manufacturing to firms in the importing country.

The advantage of co-production over compensation deals is that the supplier has comparatively more control over manufacturing and marketing, because of participation in production and often has an equity interest in the production facilities. A joint venture requires a long-term presence and involves a risk on investments. Industrial cooperation can be a money-saver when it takes the form of sub-contracting the manufacturing of certain components to low-cost manufacturing facilities in the trading partner's country. A variation of this is production specialization.

In the developing countries, multi-national production-sharing deals have been made in the extraction and processing of mining products. An agreement to license technology to an importing country is sometimes made a condition, imposed by that country for awarding a contract to a manufacturer. These agreements are part of offset packages proposed by suppliers of military hardware to their potential clients. Sourcing of components against imports is increasing.

A variant of co-production and technology transfer is a tripartite transaction in which a Western/Japanese firm teams up with an East-European Chinese bilateral trade partner to bid on a project in an LDC The joint venture may obtain lower-cost supply sources, due to lower labour costs, the LDC payment becomes a source of hard-currency revenue for the East European country, with which it can pay for its purchases. From the East-European viewpoint, the contract represents incremental exports, and may result in transfer of technology and know-how. Such cooperative projects between Western and Eastern European and Chinese partners have been located mainly in Africa and the Middle East. China is interested in purchasing iron ore against supplies of coking coal.

Evidence Accounts and Switch Trading

An evidence account is an arrangement between an exporter and an importing country under which purchases by the exporter are automatically credited against its sales. The account is maintained—usually by the parties' banks—on which credits and debits are recorded in accounting units; the units are stated in terms of currency, but are not transferable into currency. The two parties agree to periods, usually one to three years, for the balancing of the accounts. The nature of the disagio is determined by the negotiability of the clearing currency. The switch deal need not be triangular. Evidence accounts hold certain advantages over separate countertrade arrangements. Balancing of payments occur over several transactions, each settled in cash, rather than for individual transactions. A broader range of goods is offered than in counter-purchase. The disadvantages of evidence accounts are considerable. Switch trading is practice when the party with a surplus credit in an evidence account transfers its purchase rights to a third party, usually a switch-trading house. Following World War II, switch transactions role rapidly. They are now on the upswing due to increased growth in bilateral agreements.

Switch transactions which amounted to US $ 300-400 million dollars annually, but have lately expanded to a current US $ 2.5-3.0 billion level. Large-scale barter, however, occurs in the petroleum trade and since the crude oil market is expected to continue somewhat fluctuating in the early 90s, at least in the near-term, large crude oil-barter deals will continue to be made, and might possibly increase. The OPEC reserve price of US $ 18 per barrel has been under pressure in the Rotterdam spot market with Iran-Iraq supplies and owing to reduced offtake the price has dropped to $ 15 - $ 16 dollars.

Counter-purchase is the most frequent form of countertrading. The Third World countries are particularly keen on counter-purchase. Indications point to counter-purchases entering into a rapid growth era. Compensation or buy-back deals have now stabilized after years of decline. China has also demonstrated increasing willingness to acquire Western/Japanese Technology through cooperative joint ventures which contain compensation components.

The most interesting development in this area of counter-trading is an incipient movement among developing Afro-Asian and Latin American/Caribbean countries to encourage compensation arrangements. Compensation arrangements also seem to be entering a modest-to-rapid growth period.

Offset transactions. on the upswing for a number of years, should continue to grow as an increasing number of OECD and developing countries recognize offset as a valid and effective means to upgrade their high-technology industries and have come to accept offset as a fact of international trade and are busy with each other to offer the most attractive offset terms to government procurement agencies.

Countertrade contracts tend to be concluded after a lengthy and difficult period of negotiations. The usual issues and risks that arise in international business dealings are compounded by problems of currency shortage, difficulties of handling unfamiliar products, and the reciprocal nature of the countertrade deal.

Key Issues

There are seven key issues–separation of contracts; the obligation to purchase; non-performance penalties; pricing; quality of goods; distribution; and transferability of the countertrade obligations. Countertrade transactions require three contracts: the umbrella contracts, under which the first party sells goods or services to the second party; the counter-purchase or buy-back contracts, under which the first party buys goods or services from the second party; and the protocol, which links these two contracts.

One of the most crucial reasons is the need for independent legal instruments in order to obtain financing and credit-risk guarantees from banks or other financial institutions. The use of two contracts also allows for different payment schedules for the import and export contracts. Dual contracts keep payments for the original sale unencumbered by the conditions of the obligation to accept counter-deliveries.

Where the obligations of the two parties under the two contracts are interdependent, the remedies under one contract for non-performance of the other should be specified.

In negotiating an export sales contract, the first party will normally try to get its trading partner to settle the contract for cash in hard/convertible currency and at the earliest possible date. Firms engaged in countertrade must be certain to include the financial cost in the price of the goods or services they are providing. In large commercial transactions, government credits often play a very significant role. Another issue related to the drafting of contracts is that of assigning or transferring the commercial and political risks that arise from each transaction. The contracts must define what kinds of events qualify as 'force majeure' and specify the adjustment in each party's obligation resulting therefrom.

Obligation to counter-purchase exists only as long as the principal sales agreement remains in force. The countertrade contract will commonly contain a provision defining the value of the reciprocal purchase, the time period during which the purchase has to be made and in transactions with non-market countries, the state trading organizations from which the goods must be purchased.

Negotiating Skills

Depending upon the exporter's bargaining position and negotiating skills, he may be able to secure agreement to best efforts promise.

However, as governments become more experienced and sophisticated in the ways of countertrade, this is becoming somewhat increasingly difficult. Exporters should anticipate that available countertrade goods are likely to be those that the foreign country has difficulty in exporting. The basic flaw in government countertrade policies is their inability to prevent traditional exports from being used to fulfill countertrade obligations. In many developing countries, the export potential of their domestic production has never been fully exploited; and there are usually products hard to locate that can be exported without much difficulty in sizeable quantities.

An exporter should try to avoid a commitment to buy a particular product at a specific price at a specific time. Rather, he should try to negotiate the right to purchase from a broad range of products spread over several years.

When negotiating the selection of countertrade goods a company is commonly supplied with a published countertrade list, listing suppliers and products. In CMEA countries, the Foreign Trade Organization (FTO) may provide a shorter, more accurate list of products offered for countertrading.

Options

A company's preference, among the countertrade goods offered, will depend on what customers it has identified, how large its operations are and what volume of goods it is able to offer.

(a) Raw material/commodities can be marketed through established channels at standardized prices, and pose relatively low risk.
(b) Products that can be used internally–components, intermediate goods, or simple tools that can be used by the company in its own operations.
(c) Goods related to the company's own product lines: These goods can be piggy-backed on to the company's own products and sold through its own or its suppliers' marketing channels.
(d) Manufactured products unrelated to a company's operations. These are generally the least preferred because they require the highest international marketing costs.

The range of countertrade products offered in return may be expanded to include products from other state trading organizations. The practice of one entity purchasing a company's product and another providing the countertrade goods is known as "countertrade linkage". In the absence of firm supply guarantees, a specific purchase obligation can be a liability for the first party, forcing him to either accept substandard or late deliveries or to pay a penalty for non-fulfillment.

A company should press for as lengthy a period as possible in which to purchase countertrade goods. Although the countertrade party may ask for a short time limit-say six to twelve months–for fulfillment, this can usually be extended through quiet negotiations to a period of two to three years. The contract should be reduced *pro-rata* as counter obligations are fulfilled. The exporter may wish to take counter-deliveries first, to obtain funds to deposit in an escrow account, which would be used to pay for his own exports. In some cases, involving construction of turnkey plants, the countertrade partner may wish the exporter to perform completely before the counter-trader is obliged to make any payment.

A crucial negotiating issue is the magnitude of the countertrade commitment, both in absolute terms and as a percentage of the value of the original exports. It is in the best interest of the exporter to keep the counter-purchase ratio as low as possible. In the East European countries and China they tend to range between 15 per cent and 50 per cent to 100 per cent in Indonesia. The counter-purchase ratio will depend upon three factors: the hard/convertible currency available for importation of the products involved; the importance of the imports to the countertrade country; and the details of the development economic plan.

The countertrade obligation can be measured in one of the three ways: in fixed quantities or value terms; as a percentage of the payment under the principal contract; and as a percentage of output. The total value of the countertrade goods is determined by applying a percentage of the total value of the principal sales contract. A clause should be included adjusting the counter-purchase obligation to reflect any adjustment in the amount of the principal contract. It is important to define the payments included in the base-ocean-surface freight, insurance, technical transfer (licence, royalty fees, etc.), technical assistance; in compensation deals, where a percentage is applied to the countertrade party's quantitative output of resultant goods.

A company negotiating countertrade will often press for a series of clauses dealing with the quality and timely availability of countertrade goods and of the effect on his own obligations in the event of the countertrade supplier's failure to perform. CMEA and developing countries are generally known for the relatively long period frequently required for fulfilling unanticipated orders for specific goods. Companies should negotiate provisions requiring purchase forecasts, procedure for deviations and clear obligations of the countertrade supplier to deliver goods within a specified time after notice of the company's intent is specified.

Mechanism

The umbrella agreement should state clearly how documenting of transactions are to take place. The documentation formats should satisfy the requirements of any bank guarantees given by the original exporter. Performance may be monitored in the countertrading country through the establishment of an evidence account. The procedures and conditions for recognizing credits in the evidence account should be clearly stipulated in the countertrade contract.

Penalties for non-performance by the countertrade supplier is stipulated in the countertrade contract—a reduction of the first party's obligations and/or specific remedies to compensate the first party. These remedies should be 'self-enforcing' and not depend upon the intervention of courts, arbitrators or other adjudicators.

If the first party is found guilty of non-performance, the countertrade country will normally impose a penalty on top of the countertrade obligations. The amount of the penalty normally ranges from 10 per cent to 20 per cent. The countertrade country will typically require a bank/performance guarantee for the amount of the penalty. The default penalty is more than just a form of liquidated damages–it is an alternative to the counter-purchase obligations, which may become commercially impossible for the exporter to satisfy. If small enough, the default penalty may become a preferred course of action of the exporter at the outset (e.g. the price of the export can be inflated to cover the penalty). The best advice for firms weighing this option is to ascertain at the outset whether buying out of an obligation is acceptable. Foreign trade organizations in certain non-market-economy countries have been known to demand specific performance, even after a penalty has been paid.

Force-Majeure

The counter-purchase agreement should contain precise definitions of *'force majeure'* events that result in permissible non-performance by either side. Such events include natural disasters, international and domestic export controls, planning problems affecting the countertrade supplier, dumping actions, countervailing duty impositions affecting the Western/Japanese party and anti-trust liabilities. In trying to define *'force majeure'* the negotiator should consider the extent to which the event in question renders performance physically impossible. The degree of control by either party which would preclude an event from constituting *'force majeure'* and the extent to which the event may have been foreseeable. The countertrade contract should also explain the rights and duties of the parties in the event of *'force majeure'*, including requirements of notice and proof, as well as rights of suspension or termination. A countertrade contract would not be complete without an explicit provision for the means of resolving disputes.

The arbitration clause in a countertrade deal should be drafted to include the place of arbitration, the governing rules, language of the proceedings and costs. Arbitration clauses can allow the selection of three arbitrators: one by each of the two parties and the third chosen jointly by the other two arbitrators. Arbitration provisions may designate an existing arbitrating body, such as the International Chamber of Commerce in Paris, the Stockholm Chamber of Commerce, or the Geneva Chamber of Commerce.

Bank guarantees should include details of required documenta-tion and required notice. The Bank Guarantee should allow a bank to reduce automatically the amount in the penalty fund as countertrade purchases are made and the necessary documentation presented to the Bank. Pricing provisions usually comprise pricing formulae rather than set prices. Pricing of standard traded goods, where the world market price can be ascertained with relative ease, consists of deliminating the price spread in a competitive range, subject to normal price fluctuations. When the goods are non-standard—the world market price is harder to come by—buyer should seek target prices as a starting point. Counter-purchases should recognize that the price spread may be large, and pricing may be erratic. One pricing formula that is used often is to define the price of as yet-unspecified counter-purchase goods as the "acceptable international price at the time of purchase".

One method by which Western/Japanese firms can try to reduce the price of countertrade is to determine whether there is a commission latent in the price offered by a state trading organisation.

In compensation agreements, the pricing formula often involves periodic review of re-negotiation of the product value, typically at intervals of three, six to nine months. If the buy-back products are primary commodities, whose prices can fluctuate widely, the price may be set as the value of the goods according to a mutually recognised index at the time of the order. An alternative in buy-back deals of this sort is to use a formula that calls for the review of the price if it rises above or falls below a certain value on a mutually recognized index for the goods. If buy-back products are semi-finished or finished goods, the pricing formula may call for periodic price adjustment to reflect market conditions, such as changes in raw material prices, changes in demand or changes in political conditions. When drafting contract provisions concerning quality standards and the right to inspect countertrade goods, particular attention needs to be paid to detail. All specifications regarding goods should be attached to the contract, thus becoming part of its terms and conditions.

Inspection Safeguards

The party should try to obtain the right to inspect goods with its own personnel or a recognised international inspection agency at the factory or warehouse of the countertrade supplier prior to shipment. An exporter should try to have the inspection performed by a third-party contractor of its choice or by a neutral surveyor agreed to by both parties. If a company fails to negotiate inspection prior to shipment, it should specify in the contract the maximum reasonable time for inspecting the goods at their destination and notifying the supplier of any defects. It might be appropriate to assign penalties for degrees of non-fulfillment. These penalties must be defined by reference to the most detailed index of specifications.

Many countertrade countries try to obtain geographic and commercial marketing restrictions on the re-sale of goods to avoid discounting of these goods in existing established markets. If the exporter is restricted to certain geographic markets, the firm should try to secure the exclusive right to distribute in those markets, to avoid being undercut by competing sellers.

The first party should try to insert a contract provision, either in the mainframe or in the section on its purchase obligations granting it the right to assign its obligation to a third party. The major determinants in any negotiation are the parties' needs to complete a transaction and their relative negotiating skill. In countertrade negotiations there are many other variables as well, including changing import requirements, the need of both parties to clear inventories, the availability of hard/convertible currency and the relationship of the importer to its government bureaucracy.

A chief determining factor is the priority of the import governed by the umbrella contract. Negotiating positions and practices tend to vary among countries. Research into the organizational structure of trade within a centrally planned economy including the study of the country's Five Year Plan, may shed light on the priority of one's export products and thus clarify the firm's bargaining position. If countertrade will become necessary, it is advisable to conduct the negotiations for the principal export contract simultaneously with those for the countertrade contract.

When negotiating the amount of the countertrade commitment, it is important to remember that trade organizations in centrally-planned economies operate under secret government directives.

In trade with CMEA countries, the type and degree of countertrade required is a function of the government planning process at the Ministry level. In developing countries, the degree of government involvement, in mandating countertrade and influencing contract terms, is not so clear. It is a good policy for a company to cultivate close relations with both countertrade suppliers and the appropriate trade ministries. Long-term arrangements also serve to enhance the reputation of the firm and increase its opportunities for future sales. It is vitally important that the countertrade contract, the principal export contract, and the bridging protocol agreement be drafted very clearly and unambiguously to avoid any later misgivings.

1. Protocol/umbrella agreement.
2. Primary sales agreement (the principal contract).
3. Secondary Sales agreement (the countertrade contract).

Contracts for compensation deals are similar to counter-purchase contracts in the form of having separate legal instruments bridged by a protocol. Compensation contracts contain additional provisions in the primary sales agreements, on such matters as performance of equipment/technology use, improvements upon and transfer of technology, roles played by employees, consultants and technical advisers, and overall operation of equipment and technology.

By its nature, countertrade decreases the financial burden of trade on a firm and/or country by providing it with a return on the money which it has spent on imports. Countertrade also decreases both the cash-flow burden and the hard-currency burden for countries where countertrade is practised. While countertrade represents a form of finance, it generally does not preclude the necessity for other forms of financing. Conventional financing methods are invariably used in conjunction with countertrade because of the delay between the export of goods and the receipt of proceeds from the disposal of imports. This delay is most critical for compensation agreements, where several years may elapse before the recipient of technology receives compensation from the firm providing the technology, in the form of payment for goods produced with the technology.

Latin American Debt

The bulk of the trillion-odd dollar debt amounting to over US $ 400 billion is owed by Latin American developing countries involving the multi-directional transfer of assets. Many companies–especially in Mexico and Brazil–are seeking to reduce or eliminate the level of receivables which are arising in this way. Certain banks have created what is commonly called the "Latin America Asset Transfer", describing the situation where banks have simultaneously passed along the discounts at which they acquired the Latin American receivables to the buyers of their own loans.

Such a transfer of assets enables the bank to shorten the maturity profile of its Latin American portfolio while maintaining the same risk and return. The asset-swap market is buffeted by constantly changing discount rates and the impermanency of local laws. Banks are also increasingly exploring equity swaps. Some loans are being converted into equity at discounted rates.

Some of the large US and British banks have lately been making provisions for non-recoverable debts and the Japanese have constituted an institution in Caymen Islands—a tax haven to cover some of the risks. Mexico is completing a deal whereby its bonds retirement would be guaranteed by the US in respect of principal but not in regard to interest. Such bonds are redeemable over a long period upto 20 years. This will help Mexico to reduce its indebtedness to commercial banks by nearly US $ 20 billion. Mexico has exchange reserves of over US $ 10 billion but other Latin American countries are not so fortunately placed in terms of large exchange reserves including Brazil, Argentina, and Venezuela. Mexico recently held an auction which attracted considerable bank interest.

There is no single technique or step that one can adopt to ensure the viability of a countertrade financial arrangement. For the more complex deals, a careful scrutinizing of the financial needs of all parties involved, or risks and how to minimize them, of cash flows and the timing of credit payments, cannot be replaced by any short-cuts. Countertrade involves the coordination of two or more transactions and parties, the financial package is complex as many contingencies have to be taken into consideration.

The decision to look into countertrade possibilities should be made based on the capabilities of the firm, its size, its export position and overall strategy in foreign markets and assets.

The availability of capital is an asset in situations where more funds may be needed to tide the exporter over until all countertrade obligations have been finalised. Products with a high import priority are more likely to have hard currency allocated for them. Whether training one's own personnel or hiring outside countertrade consultants, these costs need to be duly considered. Establishing a marketing plan before entering into countertrade deals reduces overall risks while identifying specific risks.

Research Identification

The firm should undertake research to identify in advance the types and quantities of countertrade goods for each particular country where countertrade constitutes a factor in exporting. It should take into account specific market factors, including commercial and political risk factors, patent trademarks and technology protection information as well as data on the import and investment policies, performance requirements, transfer of funds and settlement of disputes. The firm should unambiguously define the function of the countertrade in its foreign trade operations and determine if countertrade will be used as a marketing tool for furthering exports, or a profitable solution for new sources of supply.

A firm should attempt to absorb the counter-deliveries within its own production and marketing operations or try to absorb them within those of its suppliers and customers. Most firms which are presently involved in countertrade are fairly large since small and medium-sized firms find that they do not possess the financial and marketing resources necessary to handle countertrade.

Organisational Frame

The firm can produce goods required on its own either through the creation of a subsidiary unit or an in-house unit. The latter may be in the form of a countertrade coordinator, or a countertrade unit, comprising product, functional and country specialists. The firm may also need to use a trading house. Firms in the process of establishing in-house facilities for countertrade will generally retain the use of a trading house for some countertrade deals.

Countertrade units within a firm are costly to establish and, therefore, should only be set up by a firm with international, rather than regional, trade capabilities and a broad-based product line.

Some firms commence countertrade operations with a countertrade coordinator or staff consultant. As their volume of countertrade increases they find it best to move beyond this type of organization to the establishment of a countertrade unit or subsidiary.

Most units or subsidiaries are not designated as profit or cost centres at the outset. Cost centres are less risky and represent a more conservative solution for handling countertrade commit-ments. Cost centres also have important intangible values in promoting increasing trade and indirect sales for the firm. There are three main types of cost centres.

Countertrade Units

The direct countertrading organisation, the indirect countertrading organisation, and the countertrade purchasing organisation. Direc, countertrading units have been involved in several other forms of market entry such as direct exporting, joint venturing with a local partner or with a foreign firm via licensing, contract manufacturing, co-production, management contracting and direct foreign investment.

The indirect countertrading organisations have mostly developed in firms which receive oils, metals and/or food products/commodities in countertrade. The countertrade purchasing unit is a purchasing agency. A firm may want to transfer a cost centre into a profit centre. The nature and volume of the goods for countertrade, plus the margin of profit which the firm will make, depends on the skill of the the traders and prevailing market conditions. General Motors, Rockwell International, Sears Roebuck, Northrop Corporation, General Electric, and Control Data Corporation have trading subsidiaries which function as profit centres.

GE Trading Company

The GE Trading Company has offices in 30 countries and a staff of 200 and countertrade operations spread in 18 countries currently totalling US $ 100 million annually.

Sear Roebuck Trading Company

Sears Trading conducts countertrade in consumer goods and light industrial products for its own account and for other US companies.

General Motors Trading Company

General Motors is now marketing products such as metals, carpets, machine tools and farm products from Third World and Soviet block countries.

Rockwell International Trading Company

The trading company is responsible for the two-way trade obligations generated. Rockwell Trading has handled export sales of telecommunications, printing and automotive products in Europe, Australia, Canada, Africa and the Eastern block.

Commerce International, Inc.

Commerce International concentrates on exports of US high technology products, either for its own account or as a manager of exports for other companies. Commerce International provides the international support services such as export assessment, distributor, service options and limited market research to the manufacturer who wants to export directly.

Northrop Trading Company

Northrop is the aircraft industry's number one counter-trader. Northrop is also helping to set-up construction projects around the world to create outlets for its customers' exports.

Export Trading Company Act

In October, 1982, the Export Trading Company Act was signed into law in the US. ETCs should be instrumental in increasing countertrade deals for the US firms. The profit-centre trading subsidiary performs a range of functions outside the actual countertrade deals. These services include market identification, marketing research, marketing management, sales representation, distribution, financing, credit collection, customs documentation, importing-exporting and providing product service facilities.

Trading houses specializing in countertrade have developed in Western Europe to handle trade deals with Eastern Europe. With the induction of LDCs into countertrade, trading houses specialising in countertrade have also developed within the US and Japan. Trading houses provide advice on countertrade practices and procedures, recommendations on negotiations, and disposing of countertrade goods either as a broker or as a principal. Trading houses also provide other services such as: transportation (including warehousing and insurance); finance. The nine Japanese general trading companies (Sogo Sosha)– Mitsubishi, Mitsui, Sumitomo, C. Ioh, Marubeni, Nishow Iwai and others are able to fulfil all these functions as they have ample cash with which to finance countertrade transactions and a huge network of offices and marketing intelligence on a global scale. The Korean general trading Company's are also following suit like Hyundie, Samsung, Daewoo, Lucky, Gold Star and others.

When a firm employs a trading house to sell the countertrade products, it must pay a subsidy to the trading house. Subsidies required for countertrade goods in LDCs are generally much lower than for those from eastern Europe. It is important for firms to determine the required subsidy before concluding the countertrade contract, so that the cost of the subsidy may be included in the selling price of the Western/Japanese goods.

Bank's Role in Countertrade

Bank involvement is unavoidable because the medium required to make any countertrade transaction feasible is cash, which generally flows through a bank. Guarantees througn the Banking System can help bridge the gap between separate transactions within a countertrade deal. For Banks-involvement in countertrade represents an increased risk. Banks have gradually moved into the countertrade field, acting not only as financiers, but in some instances taking on all the functions of a trading house. This change in traditional banking practices is due to the growth of countertrade itself and the opportunities that banks have identified to exploit this growth.

The commercial banks drew on the strength of their relationships with corporate clients to identify countertrade transactions. Some banks initially introduce two bank clients who could then combine their sales and purchasing abilities to perform a countertrade transaction. Several banks have decided to establish specific countertrade units. This enables them to offer the services of structuring the deal, while avoiding the exposure of under-writing and purchasing risks.

Banks have been slow to realise that countertrade may be beneficial by alleviating the debt problem of many developing countries. Countertrade can also reduce lending risks and banks that are now providing credit for countertrade transactions may be seen to be providing credit backed by countertrade operations.

Some banks have run into trouble after setting-up specialised countertrade services. Countertrade is a difficult risk prone business— getting parties together and negotiating a price is heavily time-consuming. The poor success rate of negotiating countertrading transactions often makes for exasperating frustration. Probably one only in ten deals under negotiation ever reaches a successful conclusion.

Banks will not accept a countertrade transaction unless it involves a sizeable sum of money. Banks have been attempting to increase their share of countertrade deals:

— by acting as clearing houses for deals arranged by trading companies;
— matching buyers and sellers on their own and
— trading on their own account.

The second service brings banks closer to what has traditionally been the domain of traders and banks' exposure to risk which becomes much greater, as a result. Countertrade deals are arranged by Kleinwort Benson's subsidiary, Fendrake. If a buyer is not immediately found, Fendrake will hold the goods until one is found. Austria's Centro-Bank, is another bank operating in this way. French Sodiconex; 65 percent of it is owned by the major French Banks including Societe' General, Credit Lyonnais, Banque National de Paris, Indo-Suez, Union Europeanne, and Credit Agricole. Each of these Banks has its own countertrade units, but now they can offer pooled services through Sodicones.

Banks may offer a variety of services, and package them in different ways —

a) Evaluating the market potential of a country where providing creative financing could make the difference in concluding an international deal;
b) arranging a countertrade deal without other alternative financing;
c) arranging financial packages supplemental to countertrade;
d) providing back-up financing/referring clients to experienced countertrade sources;
e) recommending the most effective way to market a product or service to countries with countertrade requirements;
f) advising on financing, payment terms, letters of credit, and insurance protection;
g) providing back-up financing—referring clients to experienced countertrade sources;
h) determining the business/financial reputation of the trade partner and its leverage to perform;
i) drafting contracts, guarantees;
j) identifying the types of products which can be accepted in a countertrade arrangement and locating potential buyers for the merchandise;

k) preparing market studies and analysing specific industries of a particular country to determine the probability of success for selling to selected markets;
l) advising on the structuring of transactions and their documentation;
m) identifying buyers of specific products and establishing arrangements to satisfy the actual countertrade obligations at the lowest possible cost;
n) negotiating with foreign trade organisations of Eastern European countries and China, and with Central Bank and other government institutions to assure compliance with local regulations;
o) monitoring transactions and developing deal tracking systems;
p) monitoring and reporting profitability and performance;
q) arranging foreign exchange trades, which allow bank clients to accept payment in a foreign currency and exchange it for the desired hard currency.

The banks also offer retainer agreements. Under such an agreement, the bank will

1. provide and identify new export opportunities;
2. increase export potential through the exclusive offer of countertrade rights which may be obtained for the client;
3. provide on-going advice and pertinent country information;
4. insure the availability of at least a bank officer to work on the client's projects anywhere in the world; and
5. guarantee exclusivity.

Banks provide their services on a fee basis. Banks usually charge a fee of between 5 per cent to 10 per cent and will charge more for taking title to the goods.

The staff to furnish the export trading company comes mainly from the international and trade divisions of the bank. Citi Bank has created Global World Trade Services Division as a joint venture between its investment and institutional banking groups. Countertrade is looked upon as a means to solve problems which cannot be resolved through traditional trading means.

Wholly Owned, Staffed by non-Banker International Business

Bank of America has created Bank America World Trade Corporation and staffed it with traders rather than bankers. BAWT is expected to countertrade and to account for one-third of its income. BAWT aims to specialize in goods reflective of California's main areas of commerce;

forest products; agriculture; and high technology products. Crocker Pacific Trade Corporation formed by Crocker National Corporation, is similar in structure and outlook as BAWT. The company will attempt to maximize Crocker Bank's links with China. The expertise of Crocker Bank in engineering, particularly petroleum and mining, will undoubtedly aid the export trading company.

Security Pacific Trading Corporation has the most operational freedom of any bank, etc. Fourth model applies to First Chicago/Sears World Trade which is a joint venture between Sears World Trade and the First National Bank of Chicago. First Chicago also plans to engage in countertrade activities through joint ventures with Sears World Trade. The aim of this joint venture is to produce an international trading organization. A bank should determine which model is best suited to its structure and needs before making its selection.

One advantage which banks have over trading houses presently is the existence of their international network. They have a network of branches, offices and correspondent banks which give them access to commercial intelligence on countertrade practices and regulations in various countries. They have necessary contacts and data base which many trading houses do not have access to. The banks have made their services profitable by capitalizing on the spread between their costs and their earnings. As more banks and trading companies are becoming involved, the charges for these services are likely to become more competitive. In the short-term, banks can develop a form of insurance based on bank's credit assessment of the buyers.

After evaluating a buyer's creditworthiness and any possible political risks, a bank would be in a position to insure a particular countertrade against risk for a trading company or manufacturer. Chase Manhattan Bank has kept its countertrade activities within its own trade and export Finance Group. The European American Bank and the Bank of Boston are two of the major US banks involved in countertrade financing which have not established ETCs. The Bank of Boston created an International Trading Service Group. The Bank of Boston provides consulting services. It also provides a data resource base to address countertrade issues.

The Bank of Boston (BKB) has recently teamed up with General Foods Trading Company to launch a new concept aimed at multilateralizing countertrade obligations. New centres are coming up in Miami as also in London Vienna and Singapore.

Multilateralization is also being attempted in the offset area. The First National Bank of Chicago is considering offering International Industrial Development Certificates to serve as negotiable, transferable instruments evidencing compliance to offset obligations which would be honoured by the offset authorities in the host country.

Since in defence/military offsets, especially offsets involving NATO countries, the Project sale is normally financed and paid for; the foreign exchange from the underlying exports from the host country need not be held in an offshore escrow account. In less-established houses foreign exchange is generated by approved exports. Whether the benefits of countertrade involvement outweigh the costs still remains to be determined, so it is easy to appreciate the caution with which most banks have approached the facilitation of countertrade and the establishment of export trading companies. As regards the role of banks in countertrade, financial services and advice will continue without significant competition. Some banks will find that they are able go beyond this and provide other services to facilitate countertrade.

Country Experiences

After the debt crisis, depressed commodity prices and rising protectionist trends—both the number of countertrade deals and the interest in countertrade among Latin American/African and some Asian governments has grown. Latin American countries were at first unfamiliar with the techniques of countertrading and most deals were conducted with experienced countertrade partners in Eastern Europe. Ecuador maintains bilateral clearing accounts with GDR, Hungary, Poland, and Rumania. There is increasing interest in countertrading with the region's other trading partners in North America, Western Europe, and South-East Asia. Colombia, Ecuador and Mexico have formal guidelines postulating countertrade.

Ecuador

Ecuador has regulations that enable countertrade to take place; the government has laid out certain procedures and criteria that a countertrade transaction must adhere to, if it is to be approved. The conditions attached to countertrade deals are somewhat restrictive. Countertrade obligations for the foreign firm must be at least 100 per cent and range as high as 200 per cent. The countertrade transaction must begin with the Ecuadorian exports, and the import licence has to be issued thereafter within 180 days. The Ecuadorian export must open new markets and many traditional products are prohibited from being exported in a countertrade arrangement.

In 1984, the Government toughened its criteria used to define non-traditional exports. The Ecuadorian Government's attitude towards countertrade is presently quite cautious.

Mexico

Mexico's countertrade situation is rather complex. There are no standard procedures in putting through a countertrade deal together. The multinationals in Mexico, in the automotive indus-try, have fairly explicit local content and export performance requirements which they must satisfy in order to remain eligible for import licences. Countertrade is mandated since these regulations link exports to imports. The Mexican Government also has several government-to-government arrangements with East-European countries and Canada. But countertrade for the non-multinationals in Mexico remains a very elusive practice.

Columbia

Columbia enacted countertrade laws that are part enabling and part mandating. The regulations have listed 30 products including air-conditioners, cash registers, cinnamon, chain saws, cumin, computers, electronic calculators, gin, jeeps, microfilm, photographic equipment, movie equipment, tractors, typewriters, vodka, whisky and wine, which can only be imported under countertrade though exceptions to such exclusions are at times allowed. Countertrade exports must be "non-traditional" and "incremental". The government agency charged with approving countertrade transactions has been slow to grant approvals and a huge backlog of countertrade proposals has accumulated lately.

The majority of the remaining Latin American countries are interested in studying countertrade.

Brazil

Brazil is one of the bigger, if not biggest counter-traders in South America. Brazilian companies in the private sector have non-fairly solid access to the Central Bank's foreign exchange. Most countertrade is done by government authorities and parastatal policies with Petrobras, the most active of the government counter-traders.

Petrobras purchases crude oil from countries, its purchases will be counter-balanced by imports from Brazil. Petrobras' trading subsidiary, Interbras, thus has an inside track when it exports Brazilian products. Petrobras' oil imports and Interbras' exports are separate and independent transactions. There is no formal linkage; linkage is, however, well-understood.

The Brazilian Government also has several bilateral payment agreements with East-European countries. The Brazilian Govern-ment has agreements with Banque Francaise du Commerce Exterior. Such agreements are extremely useful in that they lower the risk and remove many potential obstacles to a successful conclusion of a switch deal.

Latin America's heightened interest in countertrade is exemplified by meetings in Caracas of the Andean Pact countries to formally discuss countertrade. The Andean Pact signatories, including Peru, Columbia, Venezuela, Ecuador and Bolivia, met to discuss the use of countertrade to help restore regional trade. Brazil demands 100 per cent local content in its auto industry. Mexico and Argentina require 85 per cent and 95 per cent respectively. Argentina is the only country which prohibits barter trade.

Three types of countertrade are practised in Latin America. Counter-purchase is used by Latin American countries to obtain necessary supplies in exchange for their surplus commodities and agricultural products. Uruguay counter-traded meat for US $ 20 million dollars of telecommunications equipment purchased from Italy. Columbia counter-traded coffee for trolley buses from the Soviet Union and Rumania. Counter-purchase is undoubtedly the most popular form of countertrade when it is done in conjunction with an advance purchase.

The second type of countertrade frequently practised is compensation between Marubeni and the Peruvian company, Mineroperu, to develop a copper mine. In return for a US $ 35 million Japanese loan, Marubeni takes 70 per cent of the annual mining output.

The third type of countertrade in Latin America is barter. Brazil has exchanged cement, textiles and foodstuffs for crude oil from Qatar. The total value of the deal was US $ 2.5 billion.

Crude oil is a potential countertrade commodity in several countries like Venezuela where oil constitutes 95 per cent of the country's export earnings and in Peru and in Brazil. A French firm, Elf-Aguitane signed a contract to build a refinery in France to process Venezuelan crude and receive payment in crude oil. Ecuador refuses to countertrade oil. Among the Caribbean countries, Jamaica is the leading counter-trader. In Jamaica countertrade is predominantly a public sector activity. The future of countertrade in Latin America rests with the private sector to negotiate and execute deals. The parastatals are also important in determining the volume of countertrade and in Brazil.

Asia–Pacific

In Asia, Indonesia set the precedent for countertrade. The Indonesian Government instituted a countertrade policy in 1982. Foreign companies which are awarded government purchase tender contracts in excess of 500 million rupiah by the Indonesian Government or state-run enterprises must import an equivalent value of Indonesian commodities. It became evident in 1983-84 that there just was not enough marketable products to satisfy the rapidly growing countertrade obligations of foreign suppliers. Indonesia has learned to be flexible in applying and enforcing its countertrade regulations. It increased its non-oil exports of garments and plywoods.

Exporters in Malaysia, the Philippines, China, S. Korea and Japan, were pressurised to countertrade in order to maintain established trade patterns. These countries were induced to con-sider adopting countertrade policies themselves. Malaysia outlined guidelines for potential foreign exporters, the initiation of countertrade proposals with Malaysian importers such as the exchange of 30,000 tonnes of Malaysian Palm Oil against 35,000 tonnes of Thai rice. The Philippines traded rice at a discount for Indonesian crude petroleum. Both countries strongly encouraged foreign bidders to include countertrade proposals in their bids for government tenders. Neither Malaysia's nor the Philippines policies mandate countertrade *de jure*, they have the same effect *de facto*.

South Korea and Japan have also been forced to countertrade because of trade with South-East Asia. By using such develop–for–import strategies, South Korea and Japan are not only winning contracts by complying with Importer's requests for countertrade but are insuring supplies of necessary materials. The Republic of Korea, China, India and Bangladesh have been included to countertrade with cash-starved developing countries or centrally-planned economies. South Korea has established a Development Countertrade Promotion Committee in its Department of Commerce. In 1982, South Korea amended its Foreign Trade Management Regulations to include "Exports and Imports by Countertrade".

China and India's countertrade experience stems primarily from government–to–government agreements. China has clearing agreements with 23 countries as well as a 13-year trade agreement with Japan. The majority of countertrade is in the form of compensation agreements done largely through Hong Kong with the US, Japanese and West Europeans.

In India countertrade deals have been entered into by public sector organisations—Minerals and Metals Trading Corporation and the State Trading Corporation against purchases of fertilisers, palm oil and inward contract payments due from some of the oil producers. A countertrade cell has been constituted in the Ministry of Commerce. Though there is no declared official policy in deference to GATT and IMP, countertrade deals are actively encouraged by parastatal bodies and for large aerospace and defence supply contracts.

In Asia and the Pacific Basin, three countries consistently request offset for military and civilian government procurements. Australia mandates offsets of 30 per cent of the contract value when the contract is worth US $ 1 million or more. New Zealand does not mandate offset, but the government suggests that offset provisions on contracts exceeding NZ $ 2 million will be given more serious consideration. The Republic of Korea requires offset provisions on bids for defence contracts.

Africa

Minerals and agricultural commodities account for over four-fifths of Africa's exports. They have largely insisted on offering poorly marketable goods in countertrade arrangements, such as low-quality manufactures. With respect to countertrade, the lack of coordination among industries, and between industries and the state, makes it difficult to tie the foreign exchange earned by the sale of one export to the foreign exchange needed for another import.

Due to the debt crisis in Africa, countertrade may prove to be a necessary recourse for financing future trade. There exists bilateral-payments between Somalia and the USSR; typical are the sale of the US manufactured tractors in exchange for cotton from Sudan and phosphates from Uganda in exchange for spices and technical assistance from India. Substantial opportunity for switch transactions exists due to bilateral payments agreements among African nations, among East Africa and those among the 14-member nations of the West-Africa Clearing House.

One U.S. can manufacturer in Zaire relied on countertrade from 1981 until 1983 to earn foreign currency with which to import essential manufacturing inputs. Western exporters have demonstrated interest in counter-trading Nigeria's oil. As long as the world demand for oil remains soft, Nigeria and the other West African oil exporting countries may remain receptive to countertrade arrangements. Most African governments have not established parastatal mechanism to handle countertrade-proposals.

Iran, Iraq, Libya, Algeria and Jordan have resorted to countertrade Saudi Arabia and Qatar barter oil occasionally. Abu Dhabi, Egypt, Kuwait and Oman do not normally countertrade oil. Iran negotiated an oil-for-textiles deal with Spain worth US $ 100 million over a six month period. Saudi Arabia ordered 10 Boeing 747–300 jetliners in a US $1 billion oil-for-planes agreement. Jordan sold phosphates/Potash in countertrade deals against road construction contracts with India.

The governments in Iran, Iraq and Libya have issued directives to their respective state-run oil enterprises to counter–purchase imports with crude oil and oil products. The oil surplus will mean a growing tendency among the oil-producing countries to use oil as a means of exchange. Mandated policies in the Middle East have been issued by the

Governments of Israel and Saudi Arabia. Israel Central Authority for
Reciprocal Purchases requires foreign suppliers to the public sector to
counter-purchase products equivalent to 25 per cent of the contract Israel
has traded agro-chemicals for coffee from Costa Rica. Israel delivered
potash to Poland, Poland shipped sugar to Brazil and Brazil sent coffee
to Israel. Israel has also instituted military offset requirements. Offsets
must be a minimum of 25 per cent of the contract. Saudi Arabian
Government has established mandatory offset requirements. 30 per cent
of a contract must be sub-contracted to Saudi contractors.

East-West

Sophisticated counter-trading developed in Europe in mid-forties and
early 1950s. A typical estimate for the percentage of countertrade
transactions for East European countries engaged in countertrade
arrangements to facilitate financing of imports by earning hard currency
for the East European importers, are compatible with the domestic and
foreign trade planning systems and provide channels through which the
East European countries obtain access to Western markets and and
upgrade their manufacturing capabilities.

Countertrade arrangements with East European countries normally
take the form of counter-purchase compensation. Switch transactions
have also been consummated. The US medi-cines and European-made
components for Rank-Zerox Photocopying machines manufactured in
India have been shipped to the Soviet Union through the Indo-USSR
clearing agreement and the US Fertilizers have been exported to
Pakistan through the Rumanian-Pakistani agreement.

The Soviets engage in large-scale compensation agreements with
long-term pay-offs. This facilitates planning while placing Soviet trade
on a more stable basis. The only East European country which legally
mandates counter-purchase is Rumania where 100 per cent counter-
purchase is mandated by law.

The percentage can be negotiated depending upon the priority of the
import. Linkages of countertrade services is relatively simple in
countries where all foreign trade transactions are supervised by the
Minister of Foreign Trade as in Czechoslovakia, Hungary and the
USSR. Reforms are on the anvil.

Australia has an administrative directive which requires counter-
purchase for automobile imports, parts and accessories and counter-
purchase is required of all foreign vendors selling Australian goods
valued at more than US $ 52,500.

Offset

Some countries market defence/aerospace offset arrangements for other nations' procurements. The Federal Republic of Germany and France "sell" offset to make their military packages more attractive to potential buyers. Countries most strongly soliciting offset arrangements for military purchases are Austria, Greece, Portugal and Spain. Neither Austria nor Spain have official policies, but both have engaged in large defence offset procurements.

Massey Ferguson, the Canadian Agri-business Company has bartered about two per cent of its gross sales, and plans to boost that figure to 25 per cent. General Electric, Dow Chemical, Coca-Cola, General Motors, Rockwell International, Sears, Cargill established countertrade units with the primary objective of maintaining a competitive edge against global competition. An information and market-intelligence service of the US firms involved in countertrade is being set-up through domestic and Foreign Commercial Service. As per the 1983 legislation, private banks allow them to deal in countertrade on their own account.

Canada is one of the world's leading purchaser of military offset procurements. Lockheed has offset agreements with Canada and Australia, the Netherlands, Belgium and Italy. Rockwell International is working on 20 individual offset programmes in 10 different countries.

Insurance

There is now an increasing demand for credit insurance of countertrade arrangements. A dozen or more private insurers presently provide coverage on countertrade transactions, the insurance market for countertrade is not yet fully developed. Countertrade is full of potential pitfalls.

Insurance policies providing coverage for countertrade transactions are usually divided into two sections—pre-and post-shipment. The pre-shipment portion is similar in coverage for any other exports. The following are considered eligible for insurance coverage:

1. "Compensatory" transactions involving local investments–including joint ventures;
2. currency transfers;
3. escrow accounts held in the suppliers' country;
4. US Product failure warrantees;
5. port-quarantine preventing delivery or shipment;
6. unconditional letters of credit;

7. confiscation of products prior to title transfer while located in a
    foreign country;
8. blocked currencies: future non-transfer of hard currency.

Lloyds is facing increasing competition. American International
Group, Cigma Group, Chubb, Alexander and Alexander Services,
Panfinancial are operating in the area. Commercial underwriting is
flexible. Lloyds' indemnity is usually 90 per cent of the amount
insured. Each enquiry will be appraised on its merits by the underwriter
and importantly according to the demonstrated skills and presentations
by the broker.

US Insurance Companies provide various forms of credit insurance
cover. The premiums vary depending on a number of factors. To take
full advantage of an insurance company's expertise, it is best to obtain
their services at an early stage of structuring a countertrade contract.
Premium costs can be as high as 12 per cent of the contract value, or as
low as 0.125 per cent.

The risks coverable by private-market insurance policies are
primarily political, but also include purely commercial events such as
insolvency, loss of profit or extra costs incurred in handling the
products.

Indemnity

Is normally for 90 per cent of the amount covered. *Private market*–pure
barter cover.

Obtaining insurance may be a requirement of obtaining financing,
in addition to a means of transferring or spreading commercial risk.
Some of the countries that require countertrade obligations on the
original export are Nicaragua, Uganda and Afghanistan.

Specialist credit insurance brokers can offer practical guidance on
how to prepare a countertrade bid: negotiating disposal arrangements,
scanning contract conditions and countertrade conditions to identify the
remaining risks; advising on risks and those which require insurance
and drafting and placing the appropriate insurance for the identified risks
with export credit guarantee departments and their equivalents and/or the
Lloyds' coverage.

There is no legal regime and no set of rules, applying specifically
to transactions involving private companies. GATT does not apply to
private countertrade transactions nor to offset arrangements for
government purchases of military hardware and possibly not to
voluntary inter-governmental arrangements such as bilateral cooperation
agreements.

Countertrade is essentially a phenomenon of the current crisis in the international economy, trade and debt environment. The type of government conduct that could give rise to possible complaints under GATT include: national laws and regulations requiring countertrade, import and export regulations, licensing linkages and international directives to state trading firms. Countertrade requirements that a foreign exporter purchase local goods a condition for his export act as a *de facto* restriction on access to the countertrade country's markets. Countertrade requirements can be seen as imposing obligations beyond tariff schedules. Countertrade by its nature discriminates on the basis of the foreign party's willingness and capacity to undertake countertrade obligations and counterrrade obligations are arguably mandated. There is no body of international rules or principals related specifically to countertrade. U.N. Commission on Int. Trade Law has lately formulated legal framework and guidelines.

Companies must be sure to comply with a host of national laws, regulations and policies of the government of their home countries, host countries/trading partners, and any third country to which they export countertrade goods.

The most important relationship is that of set-off under which one party claiming failure of performance by the other party might be entitled to withhold amounts due to the other party under a separate and unrelated contract.

In the context of GATT –many industrialized country governments disfavour the trade-distorting and market-distorting aspects of countertrade. Regulations governing manufacturing in and purchasing from countertrade countries include: local-content rules; minimum export requirements and buy local rules. The coercive element of countertrade is very difficult to conclusively prove.

Predatory pricing—of countertrade imports or any other imports—that displaces domestic suppliers and thereby restrains trade, is frowned upon. The lack of transparency in countertrade transactions makes comparison extraordinarily difficult to determine. Companies that purchase countertrade goods for resale in the US or other Western countries and Japan should carefully evaluate their potential exposure to the dumping laws. As with anti-dumping provision, countervailing duties, provisions are difficult to apply to countertrade cases.

The principal considerations in selecting countertrade goods will be price, quality and marketability. Purchasers of countertrade goods should also consider whether such products, if they are destined for the US may be the recipient of countervailable subsidies whether the country producing the goods is one for which a material injury determination is needed in the US; and if so, the likelihood that a claim of material injury will be filed, and investigations of Trigger Price Mechanism, dumping and surveillance may be instituted.

When disputes–such as claims of non-performance or faulty performance-arise between the parties to a countertrade contract, the usual method to resolve them is by neutral arbitration.

Most disputes arising in countertrade transactions are similar to those in other international business deals, claims of non–performance or faulty performance, different interpretations of contractual obligations, different ideas about what constitutes *force majeure* and claims of material changes in markets or economic circumstances that should affect a party's obligations under a contract. Publicly-available case material on disputes among parties to countertrade agreements is somewhat scarce. The award language should indicate enforceability in any jurisdiction where the party has assets or is personally present.

Countertrade Practices

There is persistence and continuing extension of these countertrade practices independently of the economic reasons for their recent proliferation in the context of the current worldwide economic recession and the liquidity crisis experienced by a number of countries. In the developing countries countertrade transactions are mainly handled by state agencies, while in OECD countries these transactions are generally negotiated and carried out by private enterprise, with no government intervention. It is perfectly true that the alternative options are for economic or potential reasons, more difficult to implement in the short/medium term.

Trading practices based on barter or variants thereof have always existed. They tend to increase when increasing economic difficulties disrupt international trade channels and in the East European state-trading countries—where the propensity to bilateralism has continued to be a major factor in foreign trade relations. From the 50s and 60s, the East European countries have expanded their countertrade transactions with various developing countries. While countertrade is fairly well-documented where East–West trade is concerned, very little information is available on the state of the art in other areas. These occur in specific sectors: "industrial compensation", also referred to as "trade offset" in respect of sales of aeronautical or military equipment and the barters of food for strategic raw materials. A co-relation seems to exist between countertrade and commercial transactions of public sector bodies. The dissuasive factors play a smaller if not non-existent role in most developing countries. These countries' trade policies are, in the majority of cases more complex, more changeable, less transparent and less subject to multilateral regulations. State intervention in foreign trade tends to be more common and more active. The governments exercise close control over the factors liable to influence their macro-economic equilibrium and the developing countries wariness of international markets which they suspect are often manipulated by cartels.

Countertrade transactions find favourable terrain in the context of the exchange-starved developing countries. The number of countries concerned has increased appreciably over the past few years. By 1986-87 it has risen to 100 if those countries are added whose countertrade requirements relate solely to contracts for military/defence/aerospace supplies. The expansion of developing country requests for compensation would thus seem to have gained momentum around the mid-1970s and in eighties have gathered considerable force and continuing in 1990.

Developing Centrally Planned Countries Showing Interest in Countertrade

Africa: Algeria, Angola, Congo, Egypt, Ghana, Ivory Coast, Kenya, Liberia, Libya, Morocco, Nigeria, Senegal, Sudan, Tanzania, Tunisia, Zaire, Zambia, Zimbabwa, Algeria, Angola, Congo, Egypt, Chana, Ivory Coast, Kenya, Liberia, Libya, Morocco, Nigeria, Senegal, Sudan, Tanzania, Tunisia, Zaire, Zambia, Zimbabwe.

Latin America: Argentina, Brazil, Columbia, Costs Rica, Cuba, Ecuador, Dominican Republic, Guatemala, Guyana, Jamaica, Mexico, Peru, Trinidad, Uruguay, Venezuela.

Asia: Bangladesh, Burma, India, Indonesia, Iran, Iraq, Jordan, Malaysia, Pakistan, Philippines, Qatar, Saudi Arabia, South Korea, South Yemen, Thailand, Vietnam, China and Israel.

Europe: Malta, Yugoslavia. and East European Countries/ U.S.S.R.

Countertrade takes a wide variety of forms. Countertrade transactions usually combine several elements: a variable and negotiable percentage of the countertrade transaction, staggered transactions, partial or total financial settlement, elective third party participation, resale conditions for the products involved and so on. Each transaction often presents unique features. The many variants of countertrade are usually divided into two main categories:

1. Commercial compensation transactions and
2. Industrial compensation transactions.

International trade statistics do not identify goods traded under compensation arrangements. It is hence nearly impossible to make an inventory of these commercial transactions and to determine their precise characteristics.

In order for a commercial trade transaction to take the form of compensation, the trading partners should in principle arrange that both their respective requirements and transaction values will coincide. Trade through the medium of countertrade transactions involves procedures that are more complex, more risky and ultimately more costly than those entailed by two entirely separate transactions financed in the conventional way. With East Euro-pean countries several developing countries concluded their first countertrade transactions during the fifties, sixties and the seventies, the transactions were probably not on the whole so very disadvantageous for the countries concerned.

Some diversification took place at a time when the demand for their traditional export products slumped or stagnated in developed countries. Also some non-traditional items were at first introduced as their quality and specification requirements were not so exacting as in the highly sophisticated OECD markets. On the other hand there was some switch trading and import of machinery items not very technologically advanced at high prices.

In 1982, the Soviet Union maintained clearing arrangements with Afghanistan, Egypt, India, Iran, Pakistan and Syria. Even so instances of switch trading surfaced not so specifically with USSR but other East European countries.

The motivations of the developing countries that favour countertrade are based on less dogmatic concerns. Most of the developing countries seem somewhat hesitant in giving an official status to their countertrade demands. Compensation is a mode of trading which might be better suited to the economic situation of developing countries.

Countertrade might be seen as a trading mechanism for countries with little or limited economic weight to seeking greater reciprocity from other traditional metropolitan trading partners. The developing countries appear to enter into counter-trade transactions in an ad hoc manner. Yugoslavia and Indonesia have established an official policy incorporating general regulations on countertrade. A few other developing countries have laid down regulations which—while not making compensation mandatory—provide for it in certain circumstances. Many other developing countries are reputed to be in favour of compensation and to have issued government departments with directives to this effect.

Governments in many developing countries tend rather to confine it to a limited number of firms or agencies so as to be able to monitor these transactions more closely, making sure, in particular, that countertrade promotes additional exports and does not reduce traditional trade flows. Developing countries seem to confine countertrade to transactions under direct government control. Developing countries may be allowing a parallel trading system to evolve, one which could provide same kind of marginal alternative when current exports do not progress as planned, or when the difficulty of penetrating certain markets acts as an incentive for trying to bring more direct pressure as planned, or when the difficulty of penetrating certain markets acts as an incentive for trying to bring more direct pressure on potential customers or to use their buying strength in a highly competitive international framework as globalisation proceeds apace.

Countertrade as a Consequences of the Liquidity Crisis Triggered by External Macro-economic Imbalances

In the case of Brazil and Mexico, external imbalances began to worsen in 1979-80 and became more manifest in 1982 in Mexican debt crisis. The coincidence is even more apparent in Indonesia and Malaysia. For both countries, current account imbalances became more marked as of 1981-82 and accentuated in 1983-86.

A very large number of developing countries are currently having to contend with comparable economic difficulties—external imbalances, growing debt service burdens, a drop in demand for their exports and fall in primary product prices. Given their shortage of convertible currency resources, these countries are obliged to make structural adjustments through a steep cutback in their imports. Import licences are allocated according to national priorities set by the authorities. These measures generate disruptions of greater or lesser severity depending on the degree of rigidity of the system for rationing means of payment and the adaptability of the domestic economy.

In such circumstances countertrade may be perceived as a way of imparting flexibility to a somewhat inflexible system, by marginally increasing import possibilities beyond the limits set by the authorities in accordance with the availability of convertible currency reserves. In an emerging situation where regulations are frequently changing and the outlook for the future is uncertain, transactions tend to disregard the fact that compensation is economically irrational in the longer term. In such a perspective, the short-term prevails over the medium and long-term.

The liquidity crisis is sometimes so acute in certain developing countries that they are rendered incapable of meeting their payments deadlines for industrial or civil engineering projects that were planned on the basis of over-optimistic projections of their export earnings. Several oil-producing countries (Iraq, Kuwait, Libya, Qatar (have recently offered to pay creditor countries–both developing and developed—in the form of oil). Poland has settled part of the arrears on its debt to Brazil in goods–oil, coal and sulphur. Depletion of their convertible currency reserves has led many developing countries to administer stricter controls over financial transfers. Many Western firms are now finding them-selves with blocked assets and claims in developing countries. One way of unfreezing these sums is to transform them, through a countertrade procedure, into goods exported and sold for the creditor's benefit.

Had these liquidity crisis been a temporary phenomenon which the current adjustments and debt rescheduling arrangements were able to solve in the space of a few years, resort to countertrade might also have been temporary. The outlook, however, remains different as observers believe, the imbalances that many developing countries are having to contend with, are the reflection of structural phenomena. The scarcity of convertible currencies remains chronic and countertrade, despite its high cost, would continue to attract followers in the foreseeable future.

Countertrade as a Means of Circumventing the Trading Problems Caused by Inconvertible and/or Overvalued National Currencies

In many developing countries, the national currency is either non-convertible or is maintained at an exchange rate which does not correspond to its real market value. Countertrade transactions may be a means of correcting the distortions introduced by an unsuitable exchange rate in that they allow for a selective devaluation, on a case-by-case basis. The non-convertibility of the national currency is conducive to the adoption of bilateral trading and financial arrangements which make it possible to refrain from drawing on convertible currency reserves. The clearing system is more flexible than countertrade since it allows across-the-board adjustment of trade balances on a deferred basis instead of requiring that balance to be achieved on each transaction. It sets the point of equilibrium at the level of the weaker partner. If an across-the-board clearing arrangement is not possible, compensation could serve as a partial clearing system.

Countertrade as a Means of Increasing and Regularising Commercial Trade Flows

Developing countries–and chiefly those largely dependent on earning-monocrop or bicrop–from sales of primary products–complain bitterly of the instability of the markets to which they export. LDC's perceive countertrade transactions, which enable them to exchange their primary products for essential imports, as a means of imparting greater stability/flexibility to their trade. Developing countries are interested not so much in compensation itself as in medium and long-term sales contracts to provide stable and guaranteed outlets.

Countertrade transactions with developing countries based on buy-back are not very common, except for Yugoslavia and a handful of the more industrialised developing countries in their trade with the East European countries. The few select cases involving OECD countries concern transactions which are aimed at exploiting mineral/natural resources in the developing countries. Here the aim of countertrade is not only to secure stable outlets for producing countries but also to counter–balance and guarantee the heavy investment with long amortization periods required to operate mines. Countertrade may also be used with the objective of reducing trade deficit vis-a-vis a given trading partner.

The general aim common to most of these operations is to export a product which is difficult to sell for cyclical or structural reasons. Compensation has been used on a number of occasions to support primary products that were coming up against a saturating market. One of the advantages ascribed to countertrade transactions is that they enable the seller to lower his prices in a less transparent manner without officially contravening producer agreements (international commodity agreements or producer cartels) or setting off a reaction on international commodity exchanges.

The United States imports chiefly ores and metals in countertrade arrangements with developing countries, particularly bauxite and iron ore. Countertrade may also be used to run down stocks of agriculture products or to adjust the level of strategic stocks without affecting international prices. The initiative for this type of transaction has sometimes come from the Western firms who wish to retain overseas markets in the emerging difficult international economic environment.

Another developing country objective may be to foster exports of non-traditional products. Many of the countries concerned tend to be producers of primary products and are anxious to diversify their exports and which are at an early stage of industrialisation. Their manufactured products are little known internationally. Owing to lack of brand images, packaging or differentiated manufactures, these countries generally present their suppliers with a list of products from which to effect purchases. They attempt to make these offsetting sales additional to their normal exports of the same products. Other developing countries seek to channel countertrade transactions towards sectors whose exports they wish to promote. A third objective is to disguise the offer of goods on preferential terms whether this be in the sale part of the transaction, the purchase part, or both. Exports at dumping prices are probably easier to conceal in the framework of countertrade transactions when a third party is responsible for marketing the products and when these sales channels are more complicated.

Countertrade as Component of Developing Policy

Cyclical movements in primary product prices have also had an influence. Malaysia had earlier not encountered serious problems in balancing its overall payments, though its current account position began to deteriorate in 1980 and became more pronounced in 1981-86. In the case of Malaysia, its interest in countertrade transactions would seem to have coincided with the disappointments of an over-ambitious industrialisation policy. Countertrade can be perceived as a means of saving on resources which may alternatively be assigned to major public industrial projects. Likewise in Indonesia, it is government procurement that is subject to the compensation requirements. The measure was introduced at a time when a series of major investment projects had to be postponed/deferred because of financing problems due to a fall in budget receipts in the wake of depressed oil and commodity prices and reduced crude volume exports. This was accentuated by the steep fall in raw material prices.

The underlying objective of some countertrade proposals is that of transfer of technology. This is frequently the case in the East European countries and China. It does not seem that the developing countries are using compensation for this purpose. There is a big difference between the East European countries and most developing countries in that the latter accept direct investment. Developing countries often impose conditions for these investments which may relate to technology transfer, the dissemination of patents or manufacturing processes, the increase use of local inputs and the export of a part of output.

Motives Ascribable to Western Partners of the Developing Countries

The most frequent reasons is the introduction by developing countries of import control measures which have the effect of impeding normal trade flows or making them more uncertain, in particular when foreign currency or licences are allocated on an irregular or discretionary basis. Exclusion from a market, even if temporary, can have very harmful consequences for many exporting firms. A way out for them is to transfer production to the countries that restrict imports, provided the market is of sufficient size and inputs can be obtained locally and to enable some of the factories relying on imported components and packaging, machinery or spare parts to operate continuously; to maintain market shares and the presence of brand names in countries that have interrupted normal imports, to develop new markets for its products and to create a favourable business climate for itself in the country in question. Western/Japanese firms also propose compensation when financial settlements are blocked owing to the tightening of exchange controls in the partner country.

The initiative may also come from Western trading companies which attempt to make up for the "dis-organisation" of countertrade in the developing countries. The administrative procedures involved in finalising countertrade transactions are habitually lengthy and complex, particularly where no official regulations exist in the matter. Developing countries in Africa are just begin-ning to display interest in compensation arrangements. Western trading companies and some US banks using a new piece of American legilsation (Export Trading Company Act 1982) which enables them to engage in commercial transactions, have offered to advise a number of developing countries on how to organize countertrade transactions. It would seem that compensation has become a factor in competition among Western firms to win foreign markets. Negotiations with a view to obtaining major capital contracts have become extremely difficult with the increasing scarcity of such contracts, growing financing problems and the demands of customers who are conscious of the strength of their positions. Efforts usually centre around the financing of the projects. Organising countertrade transactions is both delicate and risky. It is sometimes difficult to revert to the normal pattern of trade and financial settlement once countertrade arrangements have been set up with a partner country.

In the short-term, in the context of the macro-economic constraints that characterize economic transactions in most developing countries where distortions are often present in prices, markets and particularly exchange rates, countertrade may be viewed as a practical means of introducing flexibility into an otherwise rigid economic system. Countertrade operations may provide the possibility for carrying out trade in a situation where the price system no longer allows realistic appraisal of the goods in question and consequently where the assignment of a shadow price is necessary, whether this be in terms of a new price specified in the countertrade arrangement or in terms of allocation through physical quantities of goods. Countertrade in this situation operates as a selective devaluation for exports. Countertrade operations produce a selective devaluation which operates case by case in function of the agreed transactions.

For private firms the move to engage in countertrade transactions under conditions of instability in financial markets may prove to be the least expensive way of hedging against instability as well as overcoming price distortions. Countertrade may allow firms to continue trading in situations where the economic policies in force may be such that rigid requirements to conserve or ration foreign currency holdings would have otherwise blocked the possibilities of exports. For those firms in developing countries which sell products such as crude petroleum or other commodities under obligations of international price control, countertrade transactions may allow the firms to sell at a concealed discount.

Latent High Cost of Countertrade

Even though countertrade transactions may be a practical solution to continue trading in specific individual situations, they represent an inefficient way of doing so and their disadvantages will become apparent if these procedures become more generalised. The difficulties inherent in matching the needs of sellers and buyers–which must eventually resell–for totally unrelated products results in the aggregate in economic rigidities and heightened costs. These costs are made up of transaction costs which come from the search/identification involved in matching buyers, sellers and products, and the time and effort required for the negotiating of such arrangements. Also relevant are costs derived from restricted supply which comes from the inability to choose the cheapest seller as the two transactions—import and export—must be simultaneously attempted. The'supplementary costs of countertrading a developing country would have to incur if it tried instead to follow traditional multilateral trading practices.

During the period of macro-economic difficulties and implementation of authority programmes, it may be tempting for developing countries to view countertrade operations as a means of conserving foreign exchange, either to fulfill requirements specified in loan agreements regarding minimum levels of reserve holding, or to conserve scarce foreign reserves for essential imports. The developing country avoids having to spend the foreign exchange through the countertrade transaction, it does not obtain any foreign exchange from the world either. Engaging in countertrade transactions is a way for government to defer taking action with regard to existing economic distortions. Unilateral requirements of countertrade, which are not the subject of prior negotiation, have the effect of changing the trade balance with partner countries. It is often generally the case when these measures are applied in a non-discriminatory manner. This is generally the case when the countertrade is imposed by an official regulation and is mandatory for certain transactions. Any gain in flexibility may be offset by the lack of transparency surrounding the mandatory procedure.

In the long-term, countertrade transactions appear to supply less obvious benefits for developing countries. Increased countertrade transactions in the area of commodities might well serve to disrupt existing trade patterns in commodity markets. Where the unloading of countertrade products rivals existing commodity agreements, this will tend to bring downward pressure to bear on prices and push producers to non-compliance with output quotas. The short-term benefits of lower commodity prices on world markets brought about by the increased flux of countertrade products might, therefore, in the long-run turn out to be disadvantageous through the destabilisation of attempts by commodity producers and consumers to smooth out highly volatile markets.

In the area of manufactures, market disruption through the sale of countertrade products might be less obvious. However, problems arise with respect to countertrade activities in this area in a longer term context. One is the control of the marketing of these products and the other the problem of their disposal in certain situations. As manufactured products—distinct from commodities–can be differentiated, the channels and type of marketing involved to influence consumer preferences and packaging, labelling, advertising—are often of crucial importance for their export. Developing countries have traditionally been weaker in the international markets and have had less experience in these activities. In the medium and long-term this would definitely be to the disadvantage of the developing countries, as they would lose control over the marketing and distribution aspects of their output and fail to develop sufficient expertise in this areas.

The other problem with countertrade and manufactures is of disposal of these products. Due to the difficulties in selling to consumer in developed countries, lower quality manufactured goods are sometimes channeled towards third world markets, at eventual additional costs to

consumers in the latter countries. Upto the present, however, most of
the goods offered by developing countries for countertrade transactions
have been raw materials or semi–processed goods. Import demand being
fairly inelastic in the export of these goods, countertrade operations can
only displace competitors, possibly by undercutting them in third
markets.

i) Bilateralism in trade relations has the effect of reducing trade
    to the level of the country with the lowest export capacities;
ii) Insistence upon a systematic balancing of trade at the micro-
    economic level will have even more pronounced limiting
    effect than an equilibrium set at the macro-economic level—
    through a clearing system. Trade policies which have insisted
    upon a balancing of trade either at the regional level–
    Yugoslavia–or at the sectoral level–Indonesia–have so far
    produced limited results.

Through countertrade operations, Western/Japanese firms have in
certain cases become more involved in developing country products,
whether this has been through an increase in joint ventures, production
cooperation and/or on the marketing side.

a) The opportunity to engage in countertrade transactions raises the
    problem of monitoring these transactions.
b) The short-term advantages which can be drawn by developing
    countries through placing the marketing of their products with
    third partners will most likely be perceived in the long run to be
    counter-productive. Cut price sales are pushed in markets where
    parallel sales are carried out; after sales service offered is poor and
    often not readily available; finally, a distorted sale or product
    image may come to be associated with the country/product in
    question.
c) Supply constraints on the side of the developing countries may
    well be major drawback to the expansion of countertrade as these
    countries find difficulty in providing the type, quality and volume
    of products that Western/ Japanese firms would be willing to
    take.
d) In the long run, countertrade goods, like any others, will have to
    face the protectionist barriers that exist in certain developed
    markets. Disguised attempts at dumping which countertrade may
    offer by allowing to propose a discounted price may appear
    attractive in the short-run. Repeated attempts of this kind would
    certainly be subject to anti-dumping and surveillance/trigger price
    investigations.

Faced with the choice in the long run of trading in a more restricted economic environment of rigidity and heightened transaction costs or having access to the multilateral clearing system for international payments, those developing countries with convertible currencies or the possibility of returning to convertibility have an obvious advantage in maintaining or reforming an exchange rate system which allows them to facilitate trade transactions and to accumulate a universally recognised store of value whose use is not restricted. Engaging in countertrade is a complex activity and great expertise and a strong network of trade connections are needed to move countertrade goods efficiently and rapidly.

i)   Developing countries' countertrade transactions almost always fall within the category of commercial compensation.

ii)   Trade diversion due to countertrade operations has not yet become very highly important.

iii)   A relationship between the degree of state participation in foreign trade and the frequency of requests for countertrade can be observed in the developing-country context. Developing countries wish for an increase in their exports which will enable them to obtain more hard currency earnings and improve their competitive position.

iv)   The increasing interest of this group of countries for these practices appears to coincide with the aggravation of their external disequilibria. The list of countries which are reputed to request countertrade, represents fairly well that of heavily indebted developing countries which are attempting to re-establish their external balance through a reduction of their imports and a parallel expansion of their exports. The attraction of compensation is augmented by the existence of stocks of products that are difficult to dispose off because of lack of competitiveness or inelastic demand.

v)   Developing countries have not attempted to integrate countertrade into their trade policy —

— A move to bilateralism through countertrade limits the volume of trade to the level of the partner who can do the least.

— Selecting a supplier by taking as a decisive criterion the fact that he agrees to compensation is not necessarily the optimal producer.

— Countertrade will not bring about an increase in demand for the primary products which are mainly the object of these transactions in the North-South context: its effect would rather be that of lowering prices and compromising efforts at market regulation through commodity agreements.

— Engaging in countertrade transactions will not allow developing countries to conserve foreign exchange unless their deliveries of countertrade goods are "additional" to normal patterns of sales, which is in any case doubtful and extremely difficult to convincingly demonstrate.

— As concerns manufactured/differentiated products, countertrade will not allow developing countries to generate demand if the market appeal of their goods is rather unsatisfactory.

vi) It is somewhat doubtful that the system will allow developing countries to secure additional and long-term outlets for their products. Countertrade cannot bypass protectionist import barriers. Countertrade introduces rigidities and distortions into trade by inhibiting competition. It is a regressive factor in that it delays adaptation of production to changing markets.

vii) Requests for countertrade do not emanate exclusively from the developing countries. Western/Japanese firms suggest these procedures to countries which close their borders to their exports.

viii) In a situation of strong competition between Western/Japanese firms for the procurement of equipment contracts in developing countries, countertrade may be seen as an additional element which may sway the choice between different firms offering similar technical and financial conditions.

ix) The inconveniences caused by countertrade requirements is disproportionate in comparison with the volume of trade involved.

Switch/Countertrade and Cooperation with the People's Republic of China

In the early and mid-sixties, switch transactions were quite common, but since then they have become somewhat less important. Switch transactions in the past were often resorted to after counterpurchase or compensation proved to be not feasible because no appropriate merchandise was available.

The Volume of Countertrade with China

Countertrade had not developed to the extent that it is being used in Eastern Europe–probably because the Chinese were somewhat uncertain about the actual working and intricacies earlier. They have lately set up a separate fullfledged countertrade unit in the Ministry of International Economic Relations and Trade. Shortage of foreign exchange would logically be an incentive for China to seek out countertrade possibilities. A large number of countertrade deals have been put through Hong Kong with Japan, the USA, West-European and some developing countries.

Planning down the volume of countertrade deals currently under way between China and foreign partners is complicated by Chinese reticence to divulge precise data and by the problem of definition.

"For utilization of foreign funds in the form of compensation trade, China had reached agreement in 1980 with foreign businessmen for about 350 medium and small compensation trade items. The technical equipment imported totalled more than US $ 400 million. In addition, the technical equipment imported for three big items totalled more than US $ 7 million".

Countertrade possibly amounted to between US $ 150 million and US $ 200 million in 1980 and somewhat more in 1981 and has grown substantially in recent years. The volume has risen substantially in the eighties. Large offset deals have been entered into with the US and Japan. Large countertrade deals have been negotiated through Hong Kong. The share of countertrade in total trade has risen sharply over the past few years as China's economic growth has been spectacular in the last three years (1986-87). China's economy slowed down following June 1989 developments and in wake of austerity measures in 1989-90.

Pressure to Enter into Countertrade Commitments

In one area, Western firms have experienced considerable pressure to engage in countertrade is product buy-back. Product buy-back involves not only the same Ministry, FTC or other trade units, but actually the same factory. Moreover, product buy-back may be arranged at grassroots, its benefits to the unit involved are easily recognised, and the required permissions are, therefore, not too difficult to get. Offset deals have also become important in China and some US firms have accumulated large blocked balances. China emerged as a major buyer of aircraft.

The Outlook for Countertrade with China

Chinese leaders maintain that they are in favour of countertrade arrangements that help them acquire Western and Japanese capital goods and know-how without having recourse to hard currency payments. The PRC Ministries, FTCs, Central and Provincial Units and even factories are clearly coming under increasing pressure to improve export performance. This pressure to export can be expected to heighten further. From the Chinese point of view, one of the easiest means of raising exports is to force Western and Japanese manufactures into countertrade transactions.

The Western and Japanese suppliers will have to dispose off the Chinese goods taken in countertrade and these Chinese goods may well gain a market foothold that can be exploited directly after the fulfillment of the Western/Japanese countertrade obligations. Countertrade fits neatly into the Chinese basic principle of bilateralism for balanced trade on a country-by-country basis. The final destination of Chinese countertrade goods may not be the home of the Western/Japanese party committed to taking PRC goods. China has emerged as a large exporter of textiles, silks, leather products, consumer goods, carpets and light engineering manufactures.

The Chinese will consider it convenient for themselves to have the PRC purchase and sale in one contract. Chinese officials claim that product buy-back deals will instead predominate, possibly with some counter-purchase. The outlook is for increasing Chinese pressure for countertrade arrangements with Western/Japanese suppliers. Chances are the readjustment period will have been completed by 1987-88 and that countertrade will rise by then. Countertrade is now a fact of life. Chinese officials have repeatedly stressed Chinese interest in such practices.

Negotiating Guidelines

Although some countertrade deals may be put together by the Western/Japanese suppliers, it may be assumed that most are insisted upon by the Chinese. At some point in the process of negotiating a sale to China, the PRC party will indicate that countertrade–and this means virtually always product buy-back—will be necessary if the deal is to go through.

The Chinese interest lies in the technical aspects of the product. Sophisticated and advanced engineering technology has put the Western/Japanese sellers into a strong position, provided the product is also in a category that has been singled out for priority treatment. Increase will have to cover the cost of disposing off the countertrade goods. The stress is on drafting the contract, and based on payment practices in Eastern Europe.

Although in relations with China, it is not–yet usual that the Western/Japanese company can choose from a list of products available for fulfillment of counter-purchase obligations.

Fulfilling Countertrade Commitments

Counterpurchase and buy-back commitments should always be separated from the sales contracts and higher export promotion credits and risk insurance. Some companies in Japan also wisely separate the two contracts because of official discouragement of countertrade deals. By having two separate contracts, they can rightly claim that the two deals are independent—one covers the sale of equipment, the other the purchase of goods from China.

The countertrade commitment should be formulated as a specific figure in absolute terms. Probably the most important point in entering into a purchasing commitment is the price of the goods being taken in the trade exchange. If the exact product is known and the price can be set then and there, few problems are likely to emerge in negotiations and implementations.

In the purchase commitments, setting the fulfillment time period is another crucial point. Considerable time may be needed to find adequate counter-purchase goods to obtain documentation and shipping in China, to arrange interim financing and if necessary to find buyers for the goods taken in this way. Most counterpurchase and buy-back agreements include penalty provisions for non-fulfillment.

Buying PRC products for use within the company, i.e., to meet in-house requirements, the crucial question in any countertrade deal is, of course, what type of goods are received in payment. The usual offer is for products produced with the very equipment China is buying–i.e., the countertrade is strictly product buy-back.

Possibly the least painful method of settling the Chinese countertrade demands is to take back merchandise that can be used within the company, i.e., companies can go over their list of regular supply purchase and attempt to find items that might as well as be sourced in China.

Buying Related Products for Resale

In dealing with China, the problem is the same as with trying to find products to be used in-house.

Setting-up an Internal Countertrade Unit

Some larger firms that have consistently been faced with countertrade demands they had to meet, they resorted to creating an internal countertrade unit—or a separate trading company—charged with disposing off such goods. The large Japanese trading houses are, of course, ideally suited to act as trading arms for the manufacturing companies within their groups, and for other manufacturers whom they represent as well with their global network and top class commercial market intelligence feedback.

Using Trading Houses to Dispose off Countertrade Goods

A prerequisite for commissioning a trading house with the disposal of buy-back products is the inclusion of a transfer clause in the buy-back contract. The services of trading houses will be most useful if the Western/Japanese company has no experience with buy-back; the buy-back volume is too large to be handled by the company itself; the buy-back goods cannot be used in-house by the company; the buy-back goods cannot easily be disposed off to outside end-users; the Western/Japanese company is not willing to set-up its own organisation to handle its buy-back commitments; and if interim financing of the buy-back settlement is required.

Examples of Firms Engaging in Countertrade Philip Morris Inc.

Although the arrangement of Philip Morris Inc (PM) with China has some elements of a co-production deal, it must be classified as a product buy-back—hence a countertrade contract. Basically, Philip Morris supplied China with cigarette making machinery and equipment, and payment is being spread over a period of several years in the form of cigarettes.

The elements of co-production that are included and make the case a borderline one include the following:

a) Philip Morris also undertook training for the Chinese workers.
b) The cigarettes Philip Morris received in payment are its own L & M brand.
c) Philip Morris also supplies all the materials used in the manufacture of L&M cigarettes in China—i.e., filter tips, processed tobacco, cigarette-paper, etc.
d) Although Philip Morris gets paid for its machinery and training in the form of cigarettes, it also pays a processing fee (which it calls a conversion fee) for the manufacture in China of its L&M cigarettes.

Another interesting factor is that the L & M cigarettes made in China for Philip Morris do not leave the country—they are intended for sale inside China and are sold through foreign-exchange outlets in

Guangdong province as well as nation-wide through friendship stores which caters to visitors from abroad; their sale in China amounts to the same as if they were exported. Since these cigarettes can only be bought with foreign exchange certificates, they are not marketed to the average Chinese citizen. Yet, despite Government efforts to prevent it, some local Chinese have access to foreign exchange certificates, probably through visiting relatives from abroad.

Philip Morris–through its Hong Kong regional headquarters — Philip Morris Asia Inc–first approached the Food Bureau of the Ministry of Light Industry in Peking. This Central authority subsequently referred Philip Morris to the provincial Bureau of Light Industry of Guangdong and also put the company in touch with the Guangzhou No. 2 Cigarette Factory.

Later, the Guangzhou Provincial Branch of the Economic Planning Commission participated in these negotiations, and a contract was signed in April 1980 between the Guangzhou Bureau of Light Industry and Guangzhou No. 2 Cigarette Factory on one side, and Philip Morris on the other. Under its terms, Philip Morris supplied the factory with machinery worth around US $ 500,000 dollars and sent six technical experts to instal the equipment and train the workers. After the training programme of about three months was completed, Philip Morris has maintained only four technicians on site. The first shipment of L&M cigarettes–made with Philip Morris equipment and materials–was received in November, 1980, i.e., barely seven months after signing of the contract.

The conversion fee paid by Philip Morris to the factory for making the L & M is US $ 1.20 per one thousand cigarettes. It is somewhat unclear whether—

(a) an additional undisclosed sum is also set aside as payment for the equipment over a period of time or

(b) whether the conversion fee is applied towards payment of Philip Morris inputs into the Chinese factory.

It has been estimated that the Chinese factory will have to produce 460 million cigarettes until Philip Morris inputs are retired in full. Since the processing fee for that volume of cigarettes is US $ 552,000, the second possibility seems the more likely arrangement. If so, the sum of US $ 552,000 dollars is probably for training and related Philip Morris services. Alternatively, the value of the machinery supplies may have been somewhat in excess of US $ 500,000. Depending on current and future rates of production, it will probably take five years to reach the cumulative total of $ 460 million dollars.

In the Chinese plant, Philip Morris has no say in management, and the firm does not handle the distribution of its L&M cigarettes directly. Rather, Philip Morris sells the Chinese made US cigarettes to the respective Chinese foreign trade corporation (Native Produce and Animal By-products Import-export Corporation) at a price determined in 1981 of US $ 9.38 per one thousand (or US $ 1.876 per carton) for subsequent sale in foreign exchange outlets, where L & Ms retailed for Rmb 8 per carton. By comparison, imported cigarettes like Marlboro carried a retail price tag of Rmb 10.50 per carton.

It appears that all those involved are so far satisfied with the agreement and how it has worked out. The Chinese factory acquired equipment without any cash outlay–that it uses partly for the making of L & Ms, but also to manufacture its own filter cigarette brands when the machines are not in use for L & M production. The Chinese Government benefits from its import duty on foreign cigarettes, which also applies to the locally made L & Ms because all materials are imported, and the Chinese state trading organisations profit from their distribution margins–all in foreign exchange. Philip Morris, on the other hand, sold to China machinery and know-how and gets paid in products that it judges to be top quality and that apparently are in healthy demand in the foreign exchange retail outlets, and has at least a reasonable chance to be in the running if and when the domestic market opens up for foreign brand cigarettes. In view of the tremendous market potential–an estimated Chinese consumption of some 750 billion cigarettes per year, plus about 1.2 billion imported ones–such a possibility would be interesting to any manufacturer. That the local market is already somehow being reached was evident from the results of some promotional lucky draws that were initially held (together with some TV, Radio and Newspaper advertising) in Guangdong : All winners, who sent in empty L&M packs, turned out to be local Chinese.

By and large, Philip Morris deal with China has been satisfactory and the US company is helping the Guangzhou No. 2 Cigarette Factory with design and layout of a new primary processing facility for steaming, cutting, cleaning and blending tobacco. The possibility of using some Chinese packaging materials for the L&M cigarettes is also being explored.

Handels–and Industrieausruestungs GmbH

This company is a trading firm created by Daimler Benz of West Germany for the specific purpose–at least originally of disposing off merchandise taken in trade from non-market economies and developing countries around the world. Generally known as Industriehandel, its abbreviated name, the company has also engaged in counter-purchases from China, but with the important proviso that such buying from China was not a contractual condition for selling Mercedes-Benz products to China.

What Industriehandal did—and does,—is voluntary countertrade, or what may be called goodwill buying.

The company finds, however, that China's readjustment has hamstrung not just large volume buying but even the practice of counter-purchases. While Daimler-Benz sells its passenger cars usually for cash only, it tries to balance its sales of trucks and other utility vehicles with purchases of an equivalent value. For some time, sales of such vehicles to China have dwindled to annually between 20 and 50 units valued around some DM 2 million.

Industriehandel is not obligated to buy for an equal amount from China—it merely does its best to do so in an effort to demonstrate the parent company's goodwill. The merchandise bought from China consists of virtually all kinds, but primarily skins and furs, Chinese carpets, art objects, silk, silk flowers, porcelain and various kinds of handicraft items. Some of these goods have subsequently been traded with healthy profits, among them carpets.

Buying from China has been important at a time when Daimler-Benz was seriously negotiating with China for the supply of a large truck plant worth several billion Deutschemarks. In expectation of such huge business volumes, Industriehandel engaged in heavy anticipatory buying from China. The obviously informal agreement with China was that all these purchases would be evidenced in an Industriehandel account, later to be applied to any counter-purchase agreement that might result from the implementations of the truck factory sale. The way things turned out, however, as part of the re-adjustment, the truck plant project was temporarily put in cold storage by the Chinese alongwith a number of other huge investment plans, affecting mainly West German and Japanese suppliers.

Daimler-Benz through its trading company practiced counter-purchasing from China before such buying was actually required. Since the goods thus bought could be disposed off at a profit, the company has no reason to regret its premature action. The highly important aspect of the arrangement, however, is that it is the only known example of at least the possibility of China agreeing to purchases by a foreign supplier of almost any kind of Chinese products, to be credited to subsequent Chinese buying from that supplier.

The Chinese have conceivably found ways and means of involving several Ministries or Foreign Trade Organisations in countertrade instead of insisting that only one unit deal with the foreign supplier.

Mitsui & Co.

Mitsui of Japan put together a product buy-back deal that demonstrates that, with ingenuity, the sale of Japanese textile machinery can be coupled with getting a readily saleable product.

The deal is with Dongsheng Cashmere Sweater Mill in Inner Mongolia, which will be upgraded into a facility for the production of cashmere products for export. Mitsui sold machinery and equipment manufactured by Unitika of Japan in its third such deal in the textile field. In 1979, a men's suit factory started in Shanghai with equipment supplied by Mitsui, and in February 1982 a cotton underwear plant started operations in Shandong province with machinery sold by Mitsui.

Under the latest contract, Mitsui sold the Dongsheng Mill modern Unitika equipment and know-how worth approximately US 13 million dollars. The contract, signed with the Inner Mongolian Regional Textile Industrial Co., provides for the Chinese to make a down payment of 20 per cent in cash, with subsequent payments every six months until the balance is paid in full. However, a second contract was signed simultaneously, providing for the purchase by Mitsui of products from the mill. Mitsui says that the two contracts—one for the sale of the machinery, and the other for the buy-back of woollen sweaters—are independent of each other and, therefore, do not violate MITI "Administrative Guidance" that officially discourages countertrade deals.

Clearly, the Dongsheng mill expects to repay Mitsui from the money it earns from the sale of its output to Mitusui from the money it earns from the sale of its output to Mitsui. The latter is reluctant to disclose the current unit price it is paying for the sweaters, mainly because it fluctuates depending on international market conditions. The original contracts were signed in May 1979, expansion work at the Mill—located in the Yih Ju League of the Ordos Highlands of Inner Mongolia—began in August 1979, the new equipment went into trial operation in April 1981 and the plant began formal production in October 1981. The plant which was originally established in 1971, had problems with low yield of processed wool per tonne of raw wool, consuming some 1200 tonnes of raw cashmere wool for every 300 tonnes of finished wool each year. With the equipment supplied by

Mitsui, this yield was expected to improve substantially.

According to its buy-back contract, Mitsui will purchase some 100 tonnes annually of the mill's output, which is expected to reach 510 tonnes of cashmere plus 300,000 sweaters annually–which would make it the world's largest cashmere wool production facility.

The idea of Mitsui's putting together the product counter-purchase deal came from the company's Hong Kong branch. Later, when Mitsui chose Unitika as supplier of the needed equipment, implementation was shifted to Mitsui's Osaka Brand. Mitsui sent delegations to China on several occasions. With the support of the Inner Mongolian Government, the Japanese company was able to clinch the deal in the fourth round of negotiations.

Construction by Chinese contractors proceeded smoothly thereafter, as new facilities for wool washing, carding, dying, spinning, and finishing were installed alongwith air-conditioning and waste water treatment equipment. Unitika trained Chinese engineers, and Mitsui also sent several advisers for the construction and at installation stages. In late 1981, Mitsui sent a team of instructors for the downstream portion of the operation because the Japanese judged the Mongolian knitting techniques and sweater designs were getting outdated.

In March, 1982, another plant was upgraded with equipment supplied by Mitsui and started operations in Jinan in Shandong Province. Mitsui is being paid in the form of the plant's output of cotton underwear and pajamas, which in turn will be marketed in Japan by Gunze. The output of the facility will be three million cotton underwear garments in the first three years of operations and of five million units thereafter.

Under a similar deal signed earlier, the Shanghai No.12 Factory started operations turning out 100,000 men's suits annually from end-1970 on, after having been upgraded with US $ 300,000 worth of modern equipment supplied by Mitsui. Most of the suits are shipped to Japan for marketing there by Mitsui.

As long as the output of plants supplied with equipment by Mitsui is in demand, the Japanese trading company obviously is pleased with such arrangements. Although the countertrade deals thus concluded are product buy-backs, Mitsui apparently is careful to separate the sale of machinery and equipment from the purchase of production resulting from such sales. It merely enters into a separate contract covering the subsequent buying of a plant's output–or part of it–after modernization.

Chapter 3

COUNTERTRADE IN CHINA & INDIA

China

Almost all joint ventures in China constitute production sharing countertrade arrangements, the main alternative to countertrade arrangements would be for the Chinese to take title of the entire output of a venture and pay the Western/Japanese side a share of the profits.

Although Beijing officials consider joint ventures the best way to maximise the import of high technology and Western/Japanese management know-how, they are not very common-place. Many joint ventures are now operational. Chinese attitude towards joint ventures is undergoing another transition. The average joint venture decreased in value from about $3 million in 1980 to just $1 million in 1981-82. Priority was being given in 1982-86 to joint ventures involving industrial projects such as development of energy resources. Recently a joint venture has been entered into with General Motors of the USA for the manufacture of cars/trucks. Two earlier European joint ventures did not sufficiently organise production of indigenous components.

If China is to keep pace with its overall modernization effort, the development of its indigenous energy resources is of paramount importance. China's ambitious plans are to double its coal output to 1.2 billion tons by the end of the century, and the stepped-up development of infrastructure, particularly rail lines and port facilities. The most lucrative contracts for investment have been in design engineering and consulting services, extraction equipment and technology and thermal generating technology and equipment.

Offshore oil production is the biggest, most lucrative area in joint ventures. China plans to develop offshore fields in the South China Sea, Yellow Sea, Tonkin Gulf, and, eventually, East China Sea. The China National Offshore Oil Corporation finalised its model contract, which contains compensation provisions to help speed up the development of its 150,000 sq. kms. (58,000 sq. miles) off China coast. China's six offshore basins may contain as much as 50 billion to 70 billion barrels of recoverable reserves, of which the South China Sea may account for as much as 15 to 30 billion barrels.

Once commercial production begins, 50 per cent of the crude oil obtained will be used to recover exploration, development, and operating outlays.

The number of joint ventures could increase in view of the supplementary legislation dealing with the ambiguities of the joint venture law that had been enacted.

Joint ventures are also granted preferential treatment in respect of taxes, equipment and other materials. Foreign participants in joint ventures need to import, raise investment abroad with cash of their registered capital, for running of enterprises which can be applied for exemption of import duties and unified tax. Raw materials required for the manufacture of exported goods are exempted from export duties and the unified tax.

Investment in Special Economic Zones (SEZs) is given preferential treatment. Production equipment, raw materials and other items can be imported duty free with tax rates set at 15 per cent with special exemptions or reductions available under certain conditions. Beijing has extended to all the provinces some of the autonomy enjoyed by the Special Economic Zones (SEZs) in Guangdong and Fujian in order to better attract foreign investment. Both Guangdong and Fujian were given the authority to conclude compensation trade contracts upto US $ 5 million without prior approval of Central Government organs.

The regulations set up a Provincial Administrative Committee to plan the development of the SEZs and to review and approve individual investment projects, including those involving countertrade.

Municipal or provincial governments look upon counter–trade as a means to earn foreign currency allocations. Countertrade can also supplement government assistance provided to manufacturing plants slated for upgrading or can increase the number of plants being refurbished such as AMF did in supplying machinery and technology for tennis ball manufacturing. Those negotiations involving countertrade may begin at the local levels, but are usually concluded in Beijing. Foreign parties must negotiate highly detailed contracts which clarify as many ambiguities as possible and specify standards of quality. The Chinese usually refuse to grant exclusive marketing rights but are eager to have their products marketed abroad. China will allow a foreign firm to play an active role in ensuring quality control. Nike, the athletic shoe manufacturer, concluded a compensation agreement in which it took total responsibility over quality control, by-passing third party inspection by the highly regarded China National Import and

Export Commodities Inspection Corporation. Compliance with quality control standards is especially important. The Chinese involved in the purchasing process are likely to be extremely well-versed in all relevant technological details.

Problems of an economic nature have prevented the desired investment in compensation, processing, and joint-ventures. Among the key problems encountered include their being somewhat unaccustomed to the marketing concepts of supply and demand and risk-benefits. The Chinese sometimes fail to understand the full complexities of countertrade. They tend to view it as a way to shift risk factors to the exporter who is expected to provide capital equipment and technology for the plants modernization and to ensure needed outlet markets.

Inadequate means of resolving inter-agency disputes prolong negotiations and hinder countertrade agreements from being reached.

China created MOFERT, (the Ministry of Foreign Economic Relations and Trade). MOFERT will also supervise the China Council for the Promotion of International Trade (CCPIT) and provide guidance to the China International Trust and Investment Corporation. The CITIC was set up to channel foreign funds into Chinese projects (via joint ventures, countertrade agreements, and wholly-owned foreign operations) that promise to earn a profit. The Foreign Trade and Aid Affairs Division within MOFERT's Treaties and Law Department has drafted an omnibus foreign trade law covering compensation and countertrade. Within the Finance Investment Administration the Compensation Trade Division is the Chinese Organization specifically responsible for compensation and countertrade. Normally a maximum of only 30 per cent of compensation trade output for domestic sales is allowed.

The Chinese are determined to have the final say over joint ventures operations on Chinese soil, as evidenced by their reservation of the right to appoint venture chairmen. The most viable Chinese exports for countertrade products include petrochemicals, grinding machines, carpets, machine parts, textiles, apparel and other consumer goods. Another novel form is the practice of build, operate and transfer. Large power generation plants have been set up in Canton by Hongkong based enterprises and the transfer after successful operations is through the purchase of manufactures/equipment resulting from the setting up of plants based on critical power supplies at economical rates.

An increasing number of countertrade deals have been designed to obtain Western/Japanese industrial products, which are then exchanged with the USSR under bilateral trading arrangements, and for which some developing countries receive arms and essential raw materials, besides some manufactures.

India

In 1970-71, India entered into special trading arrangements–akin to countertrade—with some of the leading West European countries, the UK, the USA and Japanese Corporations to promote the export of non-traditional exports to sophisticated markets. The counter-purchases were to be made against global tenders and other things being equal preference was accorded to these firms who were instrumental in generating these exports. In 1973, in the wake of the global boom in commodities and the small trade surplus registered for the first time in post-independence era, the special trading arrangements were dispensed with. Earlier a few selected links/parallel deals had been entered into in the sixties but their volume/operations were not substantial.

Since early 1983, India has encouraged state trading through Minerals and Metals Trading Corporation and the State Trading Corporation to develop its business in West European/Japanese/US/Canadian firms through countertrade. The export promotion Councils (EPCs) autonomous bodies that serve firms in a wide range of industrial sectors initiate and organize countertrade deals on behalf of their members. Since February 1987, countertrade is being made mandatory for large public sector purchases. Lately an apex trading Co. has been set up.

The government "100 per cent export-oriented policy" adopted four years ago, increasingly promotes any buy-back deals by Indian importers of capital equipment. Indian companies importing industrial machinery must export 75-90 per cent processing if they are to avoid import duties (160-190 per cent of the purchase price). These companies oblige the suppliers of the machinery to take back a large portion of the output; the suppliers then resell it.

Rank–Xerox shipped a large number of photocopying machines to India in return for components and other industrial manufactures. The photocopies were exported to the USSR.

Felix Foods of Switzerland signed a US $ 3 million contract with the Indian subsidiary of a Swedish company for the supply of potato granules of the grade specified by USSR. Felix was paid with tomato paste.

Countertrade deals not linked to the USSR include the supply of 100 Sulzer weaving looms by Andre & Sie Trading Co. in Lausanne in exchange for oil cakes used as cattle feed.

The EPCs account for the majority of all countertrade and offer the widest range of countertrade products available in India currently. These EPCs include cashews, chemical and allied products, coffee board, cotton textiles, gems and jewellery, handloom products, leather goods, marine products, plastics and linoleum; and silk and rayon textiles. Projects and Equipment Corporation, a subsidiary of State Trading Corporation, frequently offers large consignments of industrial equipment in countertrade for foreign machinery.

The Ministries of Industry, Commerce and Finance obtain the details of all proposed countertrade deals in which private firms are involved.

India has had long standing bilateral trade and clearing/payments agreements with the USSR, the GDR, Czechoslovakia, Poland, North Korea, Rumania and Bulgaria since 1953–56. Under these agreements, specified categories of industrial equipment and commodities are imported and paid for with rupees, which are credited to the account of the exporting country. These rupees are then used to finance Indian exports. Hungary and Bulgaria moved out of rupee payment agreements.

Certain items such as photographic films, newsprint, ball bearings, machine tools, tractors and parts, laboratory chemicals, tools and printing machinery, Kerosene, crude petroleum and fertilizers are allowable as imports under the rupee payment system and can be imported by approved agents for inventory and local resale. Newsprint, electronic instruments, agricultural machinery and precision tools are imported through government owned state trading companies for resale to actual users.

Several Indian firms have chartered fishing vessels from Japan, the Republic of Korea and Taiwan province of China in collaboration with firms from Singapore. The Indian chartering group purchases one vessel every 18 months with its share of the proceeds of the fish sales. When all the vessels have been pur-chased, the group will handle the entire marketing operations.

Indian Countertrade Highlights

1. Minerals and Metals Trading Corporation exported earth moving equipments and wheat for a total value of US $ 8.13 million dollars to Jordan against import of Rock Phosphate.
2. Kudremukh iron ore concentrates worth US $ 4.9 million were exported to Yugoslavia against import of steel billets and structurals.

3. Wheat exports valued at US $ 10.53 million dollars were made to Democratic People's Republic of Korea (DPRK) against import of zinc. Some quantities of wheat were also exported to Jordan against import of potash/ phosphates.

4. Electrical and electronic items, transport items, chemicals etc. worth US $ 2.8 million were exported to Zimbabwe (against ESCROW account) against import of asbestos.

5. Soyameal worth US $ 6.3 million were exported to Bulgaria against import of urea.

6. Items like coffee, mushrooms, cut emeralds, walnuts, cashew, etc. valued at US $ 3.619 million dollars were exported against import of asbestos from Canada.

7. Rice bran worth US $ 1 million dollars were exported against import of urea from Indonesia.

8. Rice and cashew worth US $ 1.8 million were exported against import of urea from Saudi Arabia.

9. Coffee, shrimps worth US $ 1.5 million were exported against import of DAP from the USA.

10. Readymade garments valued approximately at US $ 1 million were exported against steel billets from Hong Kong.

The guidelines formulated for entering into countertrade deals are designed to promote and argument export of Indian goods, services and projects and to maximise foreign exchange earnings through optimum utilization of the purchase leverage enjoyed by MMTC/STC and other government companies and importing departments.

Conversely, to facilitate imports by MMTC and other government companies and departments, of goods and capital equipment essential for the nation's economic growth, at minimum cost in terms of outgo of foreign exchange, financing, etc. by resorting to countertrade in various forms.

Strategic Policies

In pursuing the above objectives, MMTC/STC will follow a policy of giving preference to the parties quoting at the lowest price, on countertrade terms without any price preference, so as to ensure that incremental earnings from linked exports are not unduly eroded by higher cost of imports.

Whether or not countertrade should be insisted upon for an import item at a particular time and, if so, to what degree will be determined from time to time, keeping in a view *inter alia* the availability and extent of purchase leverage based on the above paramount principle.

Reciprocity to achieve more balanced trade flows vis-a-vis producers, countries and traders will be an important determinant of MMTC's/STC's trade relations with them in quantitative and qualitative items.

Consistent with these policy guidelines and depending on the degree of response and reciprocity, MMTC/STC may change sourcing of supplies from traditional suppliers to new ones, from producers to traders and from one country to the other subject, however, to adequate and stable supplies being ensured at most internationally competitive prices.

MMTC/STC may resort to negotiate purchases on a larger scale than at present wherever imperatives of countertrade so warrant, subject always to import prices being demonstrably most competitive internationally.

On the export front, consistent with the paramount objective of generation and maximisation of incremental exports, preference will be given to the following kinds of exports:—

Tentative List of Countertrade Export Items

i)   Value-added, manufactured, non-traditional items, for example, plant, equipment, machinery, vehicles, light engineering products, consumer durables, computer software, etc.

ii) Items with exportable surpluses, but hard to sell, for example, manganese ore, low grade bauxite, barytes, other mines/mineral, mica, wheat, rice, etc.

iii) Products identified as thrust items by the Ministry of Commerce, for example, packed blended tea, processed fruits and vegetables, packed foods, leather goods, basic chemicals, handloom and handicrafts, gems and jewellery, etc.

iv) Selected items identified by MMTC/STC for direct exports, for example, cut and polished diamonds, jewellery, soyabean meals and certain engineering and chemical products, besides brassware.

v)   Export products with high potential for remittances of foreign exchange to India.

vi) New products and penetration of new markets.

vii) Items with potential for sustained bulk exports.

viii) Products of small scale industries.

Export of primary commodities not satisfying the above criteria, traditional and easy to sell items will normally be discouraged.

With a view to facilitating fulfillment of MMTC's/STC's target of earning through exports of at least 50 per cent of the foreign exchange involved in its own imports from hard currency areas, apart from a similar target in the case of imports of other government organisations entrusted to MMTC/ STC priority in countertrade exports will be accorded to contracts with domestic suppliers in a way that foreign exchange earnings are realised in MMTC's/ STC's account.

At the time of negotiating purchases, depending on the leverage available, efforts will be made to secure maximum possible reciprocal obligation in one or more of the following forms of countertrade in descending order of priority:—

(a) Barter.
(b) ESCROW account.
(c) Clearing account providing for credit to be liquidated by exports.
(d) Evidence account with companies having countertrade agreements with MMTC/STC.
(e) Counter-purchase backed by suitable guarantees.

In the case of import of plant, machinery and capital equipments, possibilities of buy-back, offset, compensation and a forfeit, would be attempted to minimise outgo of foreign exchange.

Import Departments should keep constantly in view the possibilities of switch deals to facilitate routing of goods, originating in hard currency areas through rupee payment countries, to effect savings of foreign exchange. Both in the case of imports and exports in deciding shipping terms, priority to use of Indian bottoms as well as possibilities of Swap may always be kept in view to reduce outgo of foreign exchange.

In cases other than Barter, ESCROW account and Clearing managements, a Performance Guarantee of 3 per cent of the value of imports in the prescribed form covering both the import and export legs will be taken to secure the obligation of the suppliers.

In the event of failure of the supplier to fulfil the countertrade obligation within the period as stipulated above, the Performance Guarantee Bond will be liable to be encashed; however, in special cases where failure is due to reasons and circumstances accepted as reasonable and justified, extension for a further period upto six months subject to the defaulting party furnishing an additional Performance Guarantee Bond of 2 per cent of the value of export, over and above the original Performance Guarantee Bond of 3 per cent which has also to be revalidated for the extended period. There will be no extension granted beyond the period so extended and in case of failure to fulfil the obligation wholly, the Performance Guarantee Bond of 3 per cent and the additional 2 per cent will both be invoked. These policies and guidelines relating to countertrade have been effective from January 1, 1987.

List B—   Items which will qualify for countertrade credit at the rate of only 50 per cent of their export value

1. Coffee within quota restrictions
2. Bulk tea, to new markets
3. Naptha
4. Sea goods including shrimps and other marine catch in bulk form
5. Raw cotton
6. Cashew
7. Spices

List C—   Items which will qualify for counter–trade credit at the rate of 100 per cent of their export value

1. Engineering goods;
2. Chemicals and allied products;
3. Leather and sports goods;
4. Foods, agriculture and forest products except frozen shrimps, cashew;
5. Textiles, except readymade garments under quota restriction;

6. Gems and Jewellery;
7. Handicrafts;
   (Items under the above categories would be restricted to items specified and defined in Appendix 16 of Import Export Policy Volume–I 1985-88 of the Ministry of Commerce, Government of India.)
8. Iron ore concentrates and pellets.

List D—   Items which will qualify for countertrade credit at the rate of 150 per cent of their export value.

1. Engineering capital goods;
2. electronic components;
3. computer software;
4. projects and services (export value limited to actual net foreign exchange inflow);

5. tourism package;
6. third country shipping freight;
7. products from MMTC's own developed captive sources of supply;
8. direct exports, where MMTC would at its own risk and responsibility buy, stock and sell; and
9. Mica and mica products through Mica Trading Corporation–a subsidiary of MMTC.

The nucleus of a small countertrade cell has been set up in the Ministry of Commerce. There are, however, no set guidelines issued by the Ministries of Finance/Commerce. However, countertrade is specifically encouraged *de-facto* by the public sector orgnisations and in case of substantial purchases, countertrade is normally insisted upon. The Public Sector Corporation, however, needs to develop specialised negotiating skills and to formulate monitoring mechanisms to ensure additionalities of exports destination-wise. The Economic Ministries/ Banks also need to develop specialists in countertrading and there may also be need to associate large private sector organisations in the negotiations and implementations of countertrade deals. There is increasing interest in this sector in view of the large imports of palm oil, soyabean oil, pulses, oilseeds, fertilisers, crude petroleum and aircraft currently in the face of shortages, trade deficits and very difficult foreign exchange situation and large interest amortisation payments.

Chapter 4

COUNTERTRADE–DEVELOPING COUNTRY PRACTICES

Countries requesting countertrade have few alternatives; it is, on the other hand, true that the alternative options are, for economic or political reasons, more difficult to implement in the short-term. For the East European state trading countries and China—the propensity to bilateralism has continued to be a major factor in foreign trade relations. From the 1950s or 1960s the East European countries have expanded their countertrade transactions with various developing countries. From the mid-1970s, the East European countries have also strongly increased their requirements for compensation vis-a-vis the OECD countries.

Countertrade is fairly well-documented where East-West trade is concerned, there are bilateral transactions between OECD countries that contain certain features of countertrade. These occur in specific sectors "industrial compensation" also termed as "trade offsets" in respect of sales of aeronautical or military defence equipment, whereby the buyer country is entitled, in exchange, to assemble part of the equipment locally, or to deliver to the supplier local products and services which may or may not be directly linked to the equipment purchased. The barter of food dairy pro-ducts for strategic raw materials was a practice followed by the United States on various occasions under a special regulation (PL 480).

A correlation seems to exist between countertrade and commercial transactions of public sector bodies. These countries' trade policies are in the majority of cases more complex, more changeable, less subject to multilateral regulations than those of developed countries. State intervention in foreign trade tends to be more common and far more active. Countertrade transactions, therefore, find favourable terrain in the context of the developing and non-market economy countries. The number of countries concerned has increased appreciably over the past few years.

By 1963 it had risen to 67, with countries from all geographical areas represented, and possibly to 100 if those countries (mainly OECD Members) are added whose countertrade requirements relate solely to contracts for military/defense and aerospace supplies. The expansion of developing-country requests for compensation would thus seem to have gained momentum since around the mid-1970s and recently to have gathered considerable clout. About 50 developing countries appear to satisfy this broad criteria in Afro-Asia, Latin America/Caribbean and Oceania.

Countertrade takes a wide variety of forms. To match the value of the goods or services exchanged on each side, countertrade transactions usually combine several elements: a variable and negotiable percentage of the countertrade transactions, staggered deliveries, partial or total financial settlement, elective third party participation, resale conditions for the products involved, etc.

In virtually all cases there are commercial compensation transactions. International trade statistics do not ventilate goods traded under compensation arrangements. It is hence nearly impossible to make an inventory of these commercial transactions and to ascertain their precise characteristics.

Estimates of Quantities

The amount of countertrade transactions in the total trade of industrial areas account for an assumed 10 per cent of world trade. A reasonable figure would be 15 per cent of this trade with the East European countries, an assessment borne out by the various studies of East-West countertrade at $ 15.6 billion on the basis of latest world trade figures published by GATT and IMF. It is unlikely that countertrade accounts for as high a per-centage of trade between the industrial areas and the developing countries though it is growing and likely to increase in 90s.

Western oil imports are paid for mostly in foreign currency. A plausible assumption is that trade in both directions represents three per cent at around $ 6.0 billion. The proportion of countertrade transactions with the other developing countries (non-oil exporters) is probably higher possibly of the order of 8 per cent as most of the trade is with the OECD area (some $ 16.6 billion). A figure of two per cent of trade between industrialised countries ascribed to them ($ 15.7 billion), 10 per cent of intra-developing country trade takes place as their trade with the East European countries ($ 14.2 billion). Trade among the East European countries usually takes place under bilateral clearing arrangements. Bilateral clearing and payments trade between countries belonging to other geographical areas is estimated at a total of $ 50 billion to $ 100 billion. The value of world trade to be excluded is thus about $ 200 billion to $ 300 billion of a total world trade of $ 2800 billion to $ 3000 billion. Lately a number of countertrade deals have been concluded by Pepsi-Cola in USSR, China and the opening of Mc Donald fast food joints, Fiat and West German conglomerates.

Some developing countries are more deeply involved in countertrade than others, either traditionally or because they trade more extensively with the East European countries. World trade in the form of countertrade, the absolute amounts involved have apparently tended to increase fairly rapidly in the last few years.

It is with Eastern countries that several developing countries concluded their first countertrade transactions during the fifties, sixties and seventies. In 1982 the Soviet Union maintained clearing arrangements with Afghanistan, Egypt, India, Iran, Pakistan and Syria. Countertrade transactions have recently shown some increase in the contest of East-South trade.

Developing countries maintain fairly strict controls over such transactions, which are subject to a licensing system involving submission to an administrative body whose task is to check that various criteria are respected. Other developing countries seem to confine countertrade to transactions under direct government control. Several Latin American countries are reported to have agreed, alongside other trade integration measures, to encourage bilateral compensation agreements.

Temporal correlation can be observed between the worsening of liquidity crises in Third World countries and the emergence of proposals of commercial compensation.

The Philippines

The worsening of the Philippines foreign payments position became much more pronounced in 1983-1986 and thereafter and it was towards the end of 1983-85 that information surfaced indicating that the Philippines were seeking to develop compensation with the East European countries and the Republic of Korea.

A very large number of developing countries are currently having to contend with comparable economic difficulties—external imbalances, growing debt service burdens, a drop in demand for their exports and in primary product prices. These countries are obliged to adjust through a steep cutback in their imports.

In a situation where regulations are frequently changing and the outlook for the future is uncertain, transactors tend to disregard the fact that compensation is economically irrational in the longer-term.

Depletion of their convertible currency reserves has led many developing countries to put stricter controls over financial transfers. Many Western firms now find themselves with blocked assets and claims in China and several developing countries. One way of unfreezing these sums is to be transform them, through a countertrade procedure, into goods exported and sold for the creditors benefit.

Compensation has been used on a number of occasions to export primary products that were coming up against a saturated market. By obliging foreign trading partners to take up a consignment of these products, whether for their own use or for resale to a third party, the producing country obtains a greater market share to the detriment of other producers. One of the advantages of countertrade transactions is that it enables the seller to lower his prices without officially contravening producer agreements (international commodity agreements or producer cartels) or setting off a reaction on international commodity exchanges.

Requests for compensation have been prompted by other considerations, possibly bound up with longer-term aims.

The most frequent reason is the introduction by developing countries of import control measures when foreign currency or licences are allocated on an irregular or discretionary basis. A way out is to transfer production to the countries that restrict imports, provided the market is of sufficient size and inputs can be obtained locally.

Western firms also propose compensation when financial settlements are blocked owing to the tightening of exchange countries in the partner country. Sometimes they suggest that an account be opened in a third country in which would be recorded the value of the transactions of both the firms and the debtor country.

Voluntarily engaging in countertrade operations for individual traders may be the second-best solution in a situation characterized by the presence of such distortions as overvalued currencies and foreign exchange rationing. The additional trade which takes place in a second-best situation can be viewed as improving domestic economic welfare.

For private firms the move to engage in countertrade transactions under conditions of instability in financial markets may prove to be the least expensive way of hedging against instability as well as overcoming price distortions. Countertrade may allow firms to continue trading in situations where the economic policies in force may be such that rigid requirements to conserve or ration foreign currency holdings would have otherwise blocked the possibilities of sales.

During periods of macro-economic difficulties and implementation of austerity programmes, developing countries tend to view countertrade operations as a means of conserving foreign exchange, either to fulfill requirements specified in loan agreements regarding minimum levels of reserve holdings, or to conserve scarce foreign reserves for essential imports.

Countertrade transactions may be seen in this context as representing sales "additional" to those which would normally occur, and would thus be a way of continuing to trade without worsening the balance of trade.

Private enterprises are obliged to operate within the context of a given macro-economic framework, with its corresponding set of economic policies and distortions.

Countertrade is not a rational economic choice, especially in a longer-term perspective. The unilateral requirements of counter-trade, which are not the subject of prior negotiation, have the effect of changing the trade balance with partner countries. When countertrade is an option, subject to rules that are unclear, the way in which it is applied is left to the appreciation of the bureaucracy. Any gain in flexibility may be offset by the lack of transparency surrounding the authorisation procedure, which may well conceal discriminatory practices.

In the long-term, countertrade transactions appear to supply less obvious benefits for developing countries, although the realisation of the disadvantages associated with this type of trade might only come after an extended period of time. Increased countertrade transactions in the area of commodities might well serve to disrupt existing trade patterns in commodity markets. The short-term benefits of lower commodity prices on world markets brought about by the increased flux of countertrade products might therefore, in the long-term turn out to be disadvantageous through the destabilisation of attempts by commodity producers and consumers to smooth out highly volatile markets.

Where countertrade products are of low quality and/or outdated style, marketing skills may have their limits. Lower quality manufactured goods are often channelled toward Third World markets, at eventual additional costs to consumers in the countries.

Countertrade transactions by developing countries have tended to be restricted to short-term. Through countertrade operations, Western/Japanese firms have in certain cases become more involved in developing country products, whether this has been through an increase in joint ventures, production cooperation and/or on the marketing side.

Giving national firms the opportunity to engage in countertrade transactions raises the problems of monitoring these transactions to determine additionalities both product and destination-wise.

The short-term advantages which can be drawn by developing countries through placing the marketing of their products with third partners will most likely be perceived in the long run to be counterproductive. Supply constraints on the side of the developing countries may well be a major drawback to the expansion of countertrade as these countries find difficulty providing the type, quality and volume of product the Western/ Japanese firms would be willing to take. In the long run, countertrade goods, will have to face the protectionist barriers that exist in certain markets. Disguised attempts at dumping which countertrade may offer by allowing to propose a discounted price may appear only attractive in the short-run.

Faced with a choice in the long run of trading in more restricted economic environment of rigidity and heightened transactions costs or having access to the multi-lateral clearing system for international payments, those developing countries with converti-ble currencies or the possibility of returning to convertibility have obvious advantage in maintaining or reforming an exchange rate system which allows them to facilitate trade transactions and to accumulate a universally recognised store of value whose use is not restricted.

Negotiating Experience/Commercial Intelligence Needs

Great expertise and a strong network of trade connections are needed to move countertrade goods efficiently and rapidly. The more complex the procedures, the higher will be the associated risks and the cost of the transaction. Developing countries will likely find themselves on the lower end of the scale in the division of costs and benefits involved in any countertrade transaction as their negotiating power and ability to strike a favourable deal will be weaker.

In a situation of strong competition between Western/Japanese firms for the procurement of equipment contracts in developing countries, countertrade may be seen as an additional element which may offer the choice between different firms offering similar technical and financial conditions. There is, therefore, a danger that countertrade be made an integral part of sales to developing countries, either through a genuine desire on the part of the buyer to sell his products, or through the use of countertrade as a bargaining ploy to obtain concessions on other elements of the contract.

Chapter 5

INTERNATIONAL WORKSHOP AT KUALA LUMPUR IN MARCH 1986 ON COUNTERTRADE

Developing countries' position has been constantly weakened by their debt interest/amortisation repayment obligations, which forces them to become net capital exporters, thereby depriving them of the scarce capital needed for their own economic growth and development. The developed countries would be equally concerned by this enormous debt burden and open their markets to the exports of the developing countries, but unfortunately, protectionist tendencies have been spreading in recent years. This situation had caused many developing countries to turn to countertrade, not as a substitute but rather as a complement to conventional forms of trade.

This system of trade covers more trade between nations than before and it was likely to increase in trade coverage and greater country participation.

The real issues of countertrade are centered around price transparency, transaction compensation, legal contracts involving terms and conditions, financing, monitoring, countertrading skills and expertise, coordination of countertrade activities.

In many developing countries practising countertrade, no clear and consistent policy formulation exists or has been formulated either in the form of legislation or guidelines concerning this form of trade. Responsibilities for policy implementation are divided among several ministries, parastatal agencies and the Central Bank, often causing uncertainty and delay in the clearance of countertrade proposals. There are difficulties of ensuring that countertrade exports do not cut into traditional markets and that they serve to diversify the country's basket and expand existing export lines.

The control of the ultimate destination of countertrade exports could be ensured by mandating their C & F contracts or by stipulating the production of discharge of customs clearance certificates. The objective of product diversification could be assisted by differentiated countertrade requirements, depending on the competitiveness of the export goods involved.

Despite the fact that countertrade has increasingly assumed a North-South direction in the 1980s, most developing countries have not yet developed specialised skills on a par with the massive growth of such expertise in the developed countries, where both trading houses as well as banks have accumulated considerable expertise, commercial intelligence and information in this field, partly based on long experience in East-West countertrade. Developing countries which have large trading houses—generally state controlled—are in a better position to meet the challenges of countertrade if professionally manned.

Some countries may decide to create a consortium of trading houses to establish a non-profit trading house along the Swedish SUKAB model, which has now become parastatal, or by encouraging one or a number of commercial banks to establish specialised subsidiaries or branches following the lead of commercial banks to establish specialised subsidiaries in the industrialized countries in order to take advantage of their existing network of contacts, giving them access to the knowledge of a vast range of emerging countertrade opportunities.

In view of the unequal experience of procurement agencies importing under countertrade compared to foreign suppliers making countertrade offers, the danger exists that the underlying opportunity cost (shadow) price relationship of a countertrade transaction might be less favourable than a corresponding cash transaction, resulting in an undesirable deterioration of the developing country's terms of trade on that account. Price surveillance function might be given to the coordinating body.

The recent experience has shown that countertrade of developing countries has had particularly strong North-South bias as contrasted to a very small South-South component. The ultimate purchasers of countertrade goods are very often located in other developing countries unknown to the exporting country that demands countertrade. The reasons for this are partly attitudinal, institutional and partly of an informational nature and lack of infrastructural presence.

Countertrade requirements could be softened with regard to suppliers from other developing countries, following the example already practised by Yugoslavia and Argentina. Countertrade could become an element of the global system of trade preferences (GSTP).

Countertrade in its pure trading sense was not a useful tool for development and might in fact prove counter-productive by infringing upon existing cash markets and/or raising import prices without any real export gain. Countries in such a situation might require long-term investment commitments in joint venture exportable industries and a long-term market support and corresponding commitments. Sufficient attention needs to be paid to the problems of risk management and pricing, including shadow prices and public accountability under countertrade situations. Countertrade is an innovation in international trade flows.

Chapter 6

COMPENSATORY TRADE AS AN INTERNATIONAL ISSUE

Presently, when shrinking export markets, industrial overcapacity and contraction of international credit are straining the world's trading system, nations are groping to find innovative means to sustain previously achieved trade levels and to redress deteriorating economic conditions.

The inadequacy of financial transfers to compensate for diminishing market transfer privileges has driven many developing countries and an increasing number of developed countries to impose conditions that link imports of foreign goods with exports of domestic products on conditions that are tied to commitments to maximise the domestic content of the transactions.

Compensatory arrangements mostly involving exchanges of products, have found application periodically during times of prolonged worldwide economic sluggishness. Compensatory arrangements have the option of making full use of the international network of commercial and financial linkages established in the last four decades, in order to multi-lateralize through the inclusion of additional parties located in diverse countries in what essentially started as a bilateral commitment. Compensatory arrangements may require creative marketing and financing approaches that conform to the particular nature of the products traded.

Not every compensatory transaction involves complex arrangements, Many such arrangements are still implemented on a bilateral basis. Many developing countries considering the adop-tion of compensatory practices are doing so with circumspection. Trading parties attempt to conclude transactions with little or no outside guidance or assistance. Inexperience and over-estimation of ability to perform renders many of the contracted arrangements uneconomical.

The importing governments attitude is to shift all risks associated with the marketing of counter-delivered goods to the exporter. For the importing countries, government involvement entails administrative directives or resolutions intended to create guidelines for compensatory transactions. Compensatory strategies become part of the planning process of both importers and exporters. For the importing countries, government involvement entails active assistance to compensatory arrangements by facilitating, for example, the sourcing of counter-deliveries from diverse industrial section of the country.

"Compensatory arrangements" refer to a whole range of business arrangements whereby the exporter commits himself contractually to cause or actually generate desired benefits such as revenues for the importer. A main goal of compensatory arrangements is to reduce or eliminate, over a stipulated period of time, the net outflow of foreign exchange for importers. Other arrangements, specifying conditions for reciprocity in the commerce of two nations, may aim at balancing the trade levels of the two countries.

Compensatory arrangements involve the linked trade obligations of two commercial enterprises in two countries involving exchanges of products, technology, and services, as stipulated in their import and export contracts.

Compensatory agreements are designed to minimize trade and payment imbalances. Such agreements foster bilateralism and tend to introduce rigidities and distortions in the global economy. Once introduced, these are hard to eradicate, given the inertia inherent in government actions and the increasing domino-like interdepen-dence of nations. In the long run such agreements are likely to result in shifts in industrial-production capacity and in sourcing from developed to developing countries, and are likely to perpetuate shortcomings in the marketing skills of the latter countries.

The onset of the global economic slowdown coincided with the occurrence of the worldwide energy crisis of the mid-1970s. The crisis signalled an end to the era of cheap energy, which had contributed so much to international industrial growth. During the late 1970s, oil-importing nations financed their deficits through debt. Developing countries in particular were encouraged by the willingness of private banks to finance borrowings against future earnings forecast on past performances. Interest on foreign debt constituted the single biggest drag on the finances of an increasing number of developing nations currently in Latin-America, Africa and some Asian countries. Adjustment processes are under way in Brazil and Mexico.

The debt-repayment crunch is forcing nations to allocate an inordinate portion of their foreign exchange earnings to debt payments rather than imports. One-third of total external debt and about half of the commercial bank debt fell due in 1982. The servicing of debt by the world's debtor countries would require an annual export surplus of well over $ 130 billion. The spectre of default and the problem of repeated debt reschedulings are now straining the world's financial resources to cope with anticipated and unexpected crisis.

The lending to developing countries by private banks, which carry the bulk of the approximately $ 1300 billion, debt these nations now own (compared with the $ 100 billion owned in 1973) is slowing sharply. The slowdown is further jeopardizing the developing nations ability to service interest payments and to sustain economic growth.The increasingly difficult task of securing the needed bridge-loan financing to service debt, coupled with apprehensions that their countries future has been mortaged to pay foreign bankers, could also tempt some major debtor countries to impose moratoriums on repayments or to impose unilateral debt-rescheduling terms. Peru and lately Brazil moved in this direction though there has been softening of late in these countries and in the context of the new Mexican debt plan.

Past policies of import substitution based on capital-intensive heavy industrialisation are being shelved in favour of smaller scale public works projects which are low in foreign exchange cost and are labour-intensive. Economic retrenchment is resulting in imports being slashed, industrial production being crippled, and standards of living being reduced in Africa and America.

Many foreign-exchange-poor developing countries are pressing for compensatory arrangements to carve export markets for their manufactures against protectionistic pressures in sluggish markets, as a hedge against volatile prices for their commodity exports and assuasion for private investment of foreign resources in local industries. Compensatory arrangements may well provide one of the means for fulfilling the latter goals and is being looked upon by these nations as a desirable tool of trade for as long as their credit and exports remain constrained. Given the feeble recovery pace projected for the world's economies over the next two years, well below the growth experienced in the aftermath of previous recessions, and because of the high debt-service burden carried by the Third World, the prospects for global credit relaxation and strong trade expansion for developing nations' exports appear rather bleak in the near term in 1990 and 1991.

As trade frictions, sectoral trade restrictions, and protectionistic pressures have intensified worldwide, the developed countries are increasingly treating international commerce as an extension of national economic policies and are preferring to deal with problems of trade competition through bilateral accommodations. Countertrade is increasingly promoted by exporters as a means to circumvent payment restrictions on foreign exchange imposed by developing countries.

Global economic rebound appears to be slowing and uneven. Whether the hoped for recovery will become durable hinges on the capacity of the industrialized countries to sustain a synchronised and coordinated pace of growth devoid of protectionism — an arduous task in view of continuing high unemployment and mounting budget and trade deficits. The uncertainties and tenuous balance of factors required for stable recovery of the interwoven economies of the world nations make it doubtful that the current crisis will be short-lived or that some nations will be able to resist seeking short-term redress cures to payments or trade imbalances through the vocation of reciprocal trade privileges and bilateral arrangements. The crisis is compounded by violent exchange rate fluctuations.

Economic initiatives in domestic markets, such as financial discipline, may not suffice to restore strength to a country's economy. There is a dire necessity to take into consideration the Third World needs and aspirations for continued economic growth through trade. The need for financial credit has not abated. The current debt load accumulated by the developing countries poses a formidable challenge to the world's financial institutions and precludes purely financial remedies in restoring strength to international trade.

As compensatory arrangements proliferate, the success of that fraction which proves to be viable will require creative financing and marketing approaches. It may involve piecing together sources of financing, supplies and services in different developing and developed countries. Thus, the type of compensatory arrangements encouraged and facilitated by Third World governments will be those tied to extended counter-delivery arrangements or to those involving long-term cooperation or investment agreements.

Compensatory arrangements may become a requirement in those industrial sectors which relay on imports of semi-finished goods and components from industrialising countries and which lack export markets in the West/Japan for their outputs. They may provide the needed alternative for the undertaking of industrial projects for which foreign exchange cannot be made available. As compensatory arrangements proliferate, they are increasingly becoming an accepted option in the planning process of both Western/Japanese exporters and developing countries. Given the inertia implicit to government actions, the limited prospects for economic recovery for many developing countries, and the accommodating attitudes of Western/Japanese exporters competing for shrinking markets, it is likely that compensatory arrangements will affect international trade flows for many foreseeable years to come.

Military or civil aviation offset programs will continue to be a major portion of compensatory trade flows because of their high dollar value. Compensatory arrangements involving counter-purchases of agricultural commodities probably will not show any significant growth as their consumption is declining in the face of synthetics and substitutes. The largest potential growth lies with those related to extractive and capital projects and in the light-industry goods area where considerable production over-capacity currently exists in several developing/newly industrialising countries and in agro-processing and value added products.

In the changed international trade environment since the mid-1970s, bilateral arrangements comprising textiles, leather, steel, automobiles, ships and consumer electronics are once again proliferating in world trade, even gaining a measure of legitimacy through their unchallenged acceptance. Protectionism and bilateralism are again creeping into world trade under newer forms.

The proliferation of compensatory arrangements in international trade is creating a dilemma for the US government, torn between its long-standing policy objectives of multilateralism and its programmatic desire to expand foreign trade. The US government seems content not to interfere with the private sectors' market decisions to involve itself with such arrangements except when national security considerations are at stake.

Support of compensatory arrangements by the industrialized countries of the USA, Canada, Western Europe, Japan and Australia has been facilitated by these countries export policies. Compensatory arrangements are undertaken under government-negotiated bilateral "economic agreements" which provide for exchange of natural, technological and capital resources.

In the Federal Republic of Germany, compensatory trade assistance to German firms is provided by the Internationals Zentrum fur 'East-West Cooperation'. The Centre was established in 1976 as a private institution by the Central Association of German Chambers of Industry and Commerce, the Confederation of German Industry, the Berlin Chamber of Industry and Commerce, and the Berlin Marketing Council and will get impetus with monetary union with G.D.R. and changes in East Europe.

In Austria, the Liaison Office of Foreign Trade (Evidenzbure), originally created in 1968 as a non-profit organization to promote its members' East-West trade, is increasingly becoming engaged in the compensatory arrangements among its member-ship. Evidenzbure operates under the auspices of the Austrian Federal Chamber of Commerce, the Ministry of Trade, and the Austrian Association of Industrialists on behalf of its dues—paying Austrian and foreign membership, and it tends to concentrate on the product ranges of counter-deliveries that can be absorbed by its members or other Austrian firms.

The French service for compensatory arrangements was formed in late 1977, with support of the Ministry of Foreign Trade, by four national trade and industry groups and five banks, with the specific purpose of developing a national capacity for dealing with worldwide compensatory trade organised by French exporters. Known under the acronym of ACECO (Association Pourla Compensation des Exchanges Commerciauz), this semi-official, non-profit body serves in an advisory capacity to French public authorities and private firms. ACECO cannot become involved in the implementation of compensatory arrangements contracted under government-to-government agreements which have been a rather common, although not prevalent, practice in the trade among developing countries. Mounting foreign debt, shortage of capital, and socio-economic pressures resulting from annual population growth are forcing developing countries to walk a razor's edge tightrope.

Multinationals are among the best-suited exporters with the staying power and resources necessary to weather the current economic predicament in Third World markets. Foreign companies' perceptions of long-term risks will be influenced by the ability of developing countries to act with despatch and to overcome bureaucratic and attitudinal bottlenecks which dis-courage foreign involvement in Third World economies.

Compensatory arrangements consist of continuously evolving techniques whose forms of implementation are designed, sometimes creatively, to match specific needs and contingencies of the contracting parties. Compensatory trade refers to any contractual commitment imposed as a condition of purchase, by the importer on the exporter, with the intention of creating *quid pro quo* benefits for the former. Compensatory arrangements can be transacted under contract between two commercial enterprises, either on their own initiative or in accordance with official, directive, or they may be conducted under government-to-government bilateral agreements.

When compensatory arrangements result in exchanges of goods and services between two parties in different countries the transactions are known as countertrade or barter, respectively. Barter agreements are increasingly rare in international trade. Commodity traders may swap deliveries of equivalent products to each other's clients around the world in order to save on transportation costs.

Bangladesh

Barter arrangements are also found in the trade between countries under government-to-government agreements, Bangladesh has barter agreements with Pakistan, North Korea, Czechoslovakia, Poland, Rumania, Bulgaria, and the People's Republic of China. Bangladesh exports agricultural commodities, textiles, hides, paper products and other goods to these countries in return for industrial equipment and machinery, chemicals, fertilizers, metals and medicines.

Barter trade exchanges have been a growing industry in the United States and Canada. There are about 300 organisations in the two countries, which serve collectively about 100,000 members, mostly small businesses and professionals. A barter exchange serves as a clearing house for the sale and purchase on either a full barter basis or a part-cash, part-barter basis, of goods and services belonging to its membership.

Bartered goods and services include business services, air travel, hotel accommodations, advertising, insurance, medical care, office space, and unsold inventories of new materials, equipment, machinery and consumer products. Major US corporations also conduct barter/link operations among business units within their own company, as well as with other companies. When reciprocal and contingent exchanges of goods and services are specified by contract and each flow of deliveries is valued and settled in monetary units, the compensatory arrangement is known as countertrade.

Countertrade transactions may be settled under a single contract or under two parallel contracts setting out conditions for imports and exports as well as their linkage. Countertrade contracts specify the percentage of the import value to be offset by counter-deliveries. This countertrade can be a fraction of equal to or more than the value of the imports. Direct compensation (or buyback), whereby the counter-deliveries are resultant from and related to the original export is becoming increasingly commonplace. Indirect compensation (or counter–purchase), occurs wherein the counter-deliveries are not derived from or related to the original export.

Reverse countertrade denotes whereby anticipatory purchases by an exporter are contractually qualified for credit to be offset against his subsequent sales. Such credits can be made transferable to third parties.

Direct compensation arrangements may involve capital projects erected with Western/Japanese supplied technology, capital and equipment, for which the Western/Japanese countertrade obliges himself to market a portion of the projects output. Fulfillment of direct compensation obligations generally takes place over 5 to 10 years, with the cumulative value of Western/Japanese purchases spread over the lifetime of the contract often exceeding the value of the original export contract.

In some developing countries direct compensation arrange-ments involve production-sharing ventures in the extraction and processing of mineral ores, with output shared among the investors. Counter-deliveries under an indirect compensation arrangements may involve manufactured or semi-manufactured goods, raw materials, machinery, or other items which are not related to the primary export for which they constitute repayment.

In the Soviet-bloc countries, indirect compensation arrange-ments with Western firms date back at least to the late 1960s. Such deals usually involve counter deliveries of foodstuffs, chemicals, industrial products and machinery.

Reserve Countertrade

In the Soviet Union or other Eastern Europe economies the counter deliveries may be supplied by the state foreign trade organisations which negotiated the import contract or by other such organisations. The latter procedure is known as countertrade linkage or reverse countertrade. Such deals have found application in East-West trade involving deliveries of Romanian machines tools to European and American importers who marketed the associated credits to other Western firms wishing to export and avoid countertrade obligations.

Evidence Accounts

Indirect compensation transactions may sometimes occur under a trade arrangement known as an evidence account. Evidence accounts are umbrella trade agreements between a exporter and a government entity in a developing country, which are designed to facilitate trade flows when countertrade is an essential requirement and when the existing trade turnover between the two parties is significant and expected to increase.

Individual trade transactions do not need to be offset by counter-deliveries, but cumulative payment turnovers at the end of the specified period have to balance according to the agreements' terms.

Each import or export transaction is settled by cash. Trade flows are monitored, and financial settlements occur through the developing country's bank dealing with foreign trade and a bank specified by the signatory to the agreement. Evidence accounts hold certain advantages over compensatory agreements.

Disadvantages associated with evidence accounts are also numerous. These can be attributed to the costs of monitoring individual transactions, by the difficulties in assembling matching appropriate exporter and importer mixes on either side whose trading interests match. There is a general lack of incentives of participating firms to exceed the annual trade levels set by the agreement terms. Trade under evidence accounts has been practised in the Soviet-bloc countries and in China.

Bilateral Clearing and Switch

Another form of bilateral compensatory trade is the clearing arrangement by which two governments formally agree to exchange a number of products over a specified period of time. The agreement specified the type and volume of products and may additionally list goods or commodities which each side has the option to export to the other for a total agreed value. Conditions regarding the goods' quality, prices and transportation are agreed upon in individual supply contracts, with exporters in an account—at a designated domestic bank—in a clearing currency that can be used only to buy goods in the importers country.

The value of the goods traded under the agreement is denominated in clearing accounting units. The agreement requires that all trade exchanges stop beyond a maximum specified trade imbalance, or swing, which usually is set at about 30 per cent of the yearly trade volume agreed upon. Exchanges of goods are not resumed until additional exports from the country with the trade deficit decrease the imbalance below the level of swing allowed by the bilateral agreement. Such an imbalance, until removed, re-presents an interest-free credit to one country by the country with the trade surplus. Trade imbalances at the end of the specified date are converted into cash by switching the rights to the trade imbalance to interested third parties at discounted prices.

Switch

The limitations inherent in clearing agreement led to the practice of switching to third parties. Switch trade is based on the multilateral use of bilateral clearing currencies.

The prices of goods transferred to third parties are substantially discounted from the nominal values assigned to them in the clearing agreement. Trading houses that specialize in switch dealing are instrumental in concluding these complex transactions. Bilateral trade agreements, often tied to Western/Japanese credit lines, are intended to preserve or enhance the countries share of each others market in one or more economic sectors or to support the development of a major industrial project in the developing country.

Domestic content requirements are government mandated regulations calling on foreign companies to perform locally a specified portion of the work contracted on a project or product. Domestic content programs may be designed to protect a specified industrial sector from foreign imports, or may apply to government procurement contracts as administrative regulations, as is more common. Several countries have established domestic content requirements for foreign procurements.

Regulations are enforced under the Australian Offsets Program, a civilian program relating to non-military procurements, and the Australian Industry Participation Programme which governs military purchases. All New Zealand Government tenders exceeding NZ $ 2 million in value have been included in the last years as an optional requirement to purchase for export local goods or if feasible, to contract for domestic manufacture a portion of the project or of any other product.

In Israel, administrative regulations require that where procurements above $ 100,000 through government financial assistance are made, clearance from the Israeli Industrial Cooperation Authority is to be sought. Generally, the offset requirement is for at least 25 per cent of the contract and is negotiable on a case-by-case basis.

Because of exchange restriction imposed by developing countries and the general unwillingness of many Western banks to discount these countries receivables which are owned by Western exporters, the *defacto* value of any soft currency payments translates into hard currency only to the degree that it is possible to obtain goods and services in the developing country and market them in hard currency countries.

Soft currency derived from partial payments for Western/ Japanese exports also has been used on several occasions for defraying local costs incurred by Western/Japanese exporters in Yugoslavia and Latin America.

The procuring of equipment and services in developing countries, in cooperation with a Western/Japanese company's subsidiary or other local firms, is an alternative for Western/ Japanese contractors which could minimize hard-currency outlays for major capital projects contracted in third markets.

Sóviet-bloc countries, which have been involved in several such third-country cooperation projects with western firms, have also in past provided the services of construction crews to Western engineering firms as compensation for plan construction by the Western firms in Eastern Europe.

Offsets

Compensatory transactions involving military, trade, defence and certain civil procurements, such as sales of commercial aircraft, are known as off-sets. These arrangements usually combine domestic content, co-production, and technology transfer requirements with long-term counter-purchase requirements. Under offset agreements, suppliers such as aircraft and ammunitions makers accumulate credits for efforts that facilitate earnings or savings of foreign exchange for their customers, by means that range from counter-purchases to tourism promotion.

Governments of developed and developing countries alike have been using offset requirements as a tool for industrial development, with benefits often accruing to industrial development, with other than those in which the procurements took place. Offsets enhance the customer's employment and export levels~and may result in improvements in the productivity and technical sophistication of the domestic industry.

The characteristics of individual offset arrangements bid under competing export proposals vary considerably from contract to contract and from transaction to transaction.

Proposed offset packages may include commercial compensations to alleviate the customer's trade and payment imbalances, may involve direct or indirect investment in depressed industries or regions, or may provide technology transfers intended to benefit designated industrial sectors in the customer's country.

Co-Production/Sub-Contractings

Co-production is inclusive of assembly, processing and the manufacture of components or equipment in the buyer's country, based upon transfer of technical information and know-how by the supplier. Overseas production is subject to government-to-government license and involves advanced manufacturing technology, metal and composite material processing techniques and fibre optics systems.

Technology transfer, involving production of components and equipment in the buyer's country, under direct contractual arrangement between the supplier and the purchasing government or manufacturer.

Sub-contracting for compatible components manufactured in the buyer's country. Its main intent is to defray procurement costs and to benefit depressed industrial sectors or production facilities in the buyer's country.

Investment, involving funding of the operations of a joint company established between the supplier and one or more commercial entities in the buyer's country.

Countertrade, co-production and subcontract production have in the past accounted for the major portion of offset contract values, with technology transfer and foreign investment normally representing less than 10 per cent of the value. Co-production programs are probably the oldest form of offset, dating back to the early 1960s when such arrangements were entered into to assist the sale of DC–9 aircraft.

Governments play major roles in negotiating or facilitating most offset arrangements. The common roles played by a government in offset transactions are as supplier or facilitator under foreign military sales agreements and as active negotiator or approver of export licenses for co-production arrangements. Governments may act also as purchasers of products and services from the country exported to. Commitments assumed under offset arrangements can divert business from firms in the supplier's country and foster the emergence of competitors in the buyers country.

Co–production arrangements may also result in increased manufacturing costs, while offset requirements which exceed sales values by an average of 20 per cent, will result in heavy burdens for the supplier. The multiplicity of sources allows the buyer to impose acceptance of large offset commitments on competing suppliers.

Aircraft production and trade is a unique economic sector which in different countries relies on various degrees of government backing. What sets the commercial aircraft production sector apart from the military one, even though the same manufacturer may be in both businesses, is the more difficult path to profitability and the higher risks assumed by the commercial sector.

The credit squeeze facing airlines, alongwith pressure on commercial aircraft manufacturers to quickly recoup through sales, their multi-million dollar investments for development and manufacturing is forcing the industry to accept offset as a necessary alternative to sales losses and as a competitive edge in marketing.

Offset

The amount of offset required by purchasing countries has varied from approximately 30 per cent to over 100 per cent. Fulfillment of offset obligations may also vary according to the transaction at hand, spanning from one to ten years. Aircraft offset agreements have often been on a best-effort basis.

Offset programs in the aircraft industry are being used both as sales incentives and as marketing tools and have become an integral element of marketing strategy. Because co–production arrangements are usually limited by the supplier's government technology-transfer policies and by the purchasing country's industrial and technological base, countertrade requirements are becoming increasingly important, albeit nowadays difficult to implement, the element of offset packages. Countertrade-related export-development initiatives by aircraft suppliers on behalf of their customers are designed to open doors to new markets for the latter through market and product research, through identification of foreign trade partners and business opportunities and by bringing together prospective buyers and sellers. Growing in importance as part of offsets alongside with countertrade is the development of tourism programs which are designed to benefit customer countries through the earning of foreign exchange.

Given that economic sluggishness and credit constraints are expected to persist in many world markets, especially those of the third world, innovative approaches to financing aircraft exports will be required in order to allow sales to explore likely market potentials.

International competition among the world's manufacturers of commercial airplanes, while intensifying, is shifting emphasis from protection of domestic markets against foreign imports to share financial risks and for securing foreign subcontractors. Refinements in offset programs could facilitate trade opportunities and allow more countries to purchase aircraft. The credit squeeze affecting growing numbers of prospective clients is forcing some general aviation and helicopter manufacturers to shift the sourcing of export finance from commercial banks to merchant banks and private financial syndicates, and increasingly to consider compensatory transactions whereby repayment occurs through disposal of counter-delivered goods.

Military and large transport aircraft sales also increasingly rely on offset for financing exports to both industrialized and developing countries. Offsets will continue to represent a major portion of the world's countertrade flows. Obligations assumed under offset programs are altering the working of the market place by causing shifts in product sourcing and manufacturing capacity, and by bringing down market shares over prolonged periods of time.

Offset-related investments may involve real estate develop-ments or the customizing of existing manufacturing capacity to the specific requirements of an export market. The fulfillment of future offset obligations will require increased sophistication and the services of parties in different professional fields.

Some developing countries with large populations may see fit to emphasize as offsets, programs resulting in domestic employment and social development, in addition to the need to generate foreign exchange.

Commodity Exchanges/Countertrade

As part of countertrade arrangements, commodity transactions offer both advantages and disadvantages. Except for government -to-government arrangements, where prices of the traded goods are adjusted to offset each other, the issue of any price adjustments may become difficult to settle whenever both legs of a countertrade transaction involve only commodity flows whose prices are pegged to those in the world market.

Government sponsored exchanges involving commodities under barter or protocol arrangements are most common in trade between developing countries. Settlements of these transactions usually involve small amounts of cash flows with no interest charges and often benefit from price discounts on the traded commodities.

The US Department of Agriculture conducted a barter program from 1950 to 1970. In the second stage, from 1963 to 1973, the program was used primarily to procure foreign supplies and services used in projects sponsored abroad by the Agency for International Development and by the Department of Defence.

Under the Department of Agriculture barter program, American exporters acquired agricultural products held by the Commodity Credit Corporation at world market prices, held by them for buyers in countries eligible under the programme. The proceeds of the exports were then used to import into the United States raw materials to be transferred to the strategic stockpile. 60 strategic materials valued in excess of $ 1.2 billion were transferred to the strategic stockpiles. Between 1963 and 1973 off-shore procurements of supplies and services accounted for another $ 4.8 billion.

France, Federal Republic of Germany and Japan have also instituted compensatory arrangements type programs to assure stable supplies of essential raw materials for their countries. The latter arrangements often do not involve discounts on commodity prices. The amount of countertrade as a percentage of annual turnover trade of commodity trading houses, has been somewhat small. Commodity over-supply and price volatility have contri-buted to the decline in earnings for many developing nations in 1980s. A slight recovery in terms of depreciated dollars is becoming evident lately but there are renewed signs of falling commodity prices.

Indonesia

The reasons behind the adoption of countertrade measures by the Indonesian Government were multiple and compelling in the early 1980s. The country's non-oil and natural gas exports were dropping by 10 per cent in 1980 and 25 per cent in 1981-82; the oil glut was affecting Indonesia's main earner of foreign exchange; imports and government expenditures were on the increase and the country was facing a balance of payments which by 1981-82 had swung from surplus to deficit and remained so in 1983-84.

All Indonesian Government procurements in excess of 500 million rupiah with the exception of procurements financed by the World Bank, the Asian Development Bank, and the Islamic Development Bank, as well as the domestic procurement portion of foreign contracts, professional services, and joint venture projects must be fully offset by exports of Indonesian products other than petroleum and natural gas. Eligible Indonesian products and exporters are to be identified periodically. International prices prevailing at the time of delivery of Indonesian goods will apply.

Counterpurchases by foreign buyers must be above normal trade levels previously established by them in order to satisfy the countertrade requirement (additionality requirement).

Counter-purchases must be exported to the country of origin of the procurement, unless otherwise allowed by the Indonesian government and the related contracts must be completed three months prior to the completion of the Indonesian procurement.

Indonesia neglected the fact that the Soviet-bloc countertrade included manufactures and machinery, while Indonesia offered as countertrade mainly primary commodities, already subject to in-ternational controls such as quotas and other protectionist safeguard measures. Fewer contracts than expected were signed in the first 12 months. Less severe guidelines for countertrade would have permitted counter-purchases of non-traditional, semi-finished and manufactures as well as traditional export goods and would have provided

Western/Japanese exporters with alternatives to counter-purchase obligations tied to investments in joint marketing and other ventures benefiting the Indonesian economy; and would have created incentives for Indonesian exporters to encourage them to investigate and get involved with countertrade arrangements. Indonesian exports of garments and plywood have increased in the last three years.

Compensatory Arrangements

Compensatory arrangement rationale spans economic and political arguments and reflects the personal perception of benefits and liabilities of the parties involved. Generally, they are undertaken whenever one or both trading parties lack sufficient foreign exchange reserves to pay for imports of goods and services intended for economic development, or they do not wish to use scarce foreign exchange reserves for trading.

Compensatory arrangements offer importers a viable mode to gain access to foreign sources of raw materials, technology transfers, industrial manufacturing processes and capital investment. Trading parties will engage in such arrangements only if, in their assessment, the expected benefits out-weigh the transactions' liabilities. The major motivation for exporters to engage in countertrade is an option that could preserve market shares or increase trade levels in the face of credit constraints, foreign exchange restrictions and import limitations.

For Western/Japanese firms contemplating future expansion of their production capacity, compensation arrangements may also offer the opportunity to acquire a temporary supply source from the developing country unit, the Western/Japanese firm decides to undertake expansion of its own production. These practices in-crease the costs of trade and distort its patterns, and emphasize short-term or temporary needs over the orderly, long-term development of selective export positions.

Unfettered, competitive markets are the most efficient allocators of resources. However, today's globally interdependent economic *malaise* and the narrowing of the communications gap and widening of the resource gap between the industrialized and the developing worlds, together with the explosive short-fused social challenges created by current unemployment levels, are fostering pressures which may not afford the time to wait for self-induced market readjustments.

Faced with protectionstic attitudes in the West against their industrial exports, the Soviet bloc countries have also increased their penalty clause levels above the 10 to 15 per cent postulated in past years, in order to prevent Western/Japanese companies from building the penalty fee into their export prices and then opting to pay if non-performing.

Other countries favour the use of countertrade as a financing tool, especially for construction projections such as industrial plants. Buy-back arrangements requiring annual counter-deliveries of plant output in the range of 20 to 30 per cent would recover for the importer the entire cost of the foreign-supplied plant in a few years.

The nature of most indirect-compensation transactions is to promote marketing of the importer's goods. The plant output could benefit from comparative advantages which may be collected in the cost of the goods offered as compensation.

In non-market economies, profit is viewed mainly as a return on sales or capital investment, rather than a blend which includes returns on such committed resources as management, technical services and marketing. The differing ways of doing business, following the contract signing, that have the potential to affect the costs of compensatory arrangements assumed by a company and such problems could result from:

Shortcomings with the counter-delivered products resulting from design models that do not conform to Western/Japanese style and tastes, costs incurred by the Western/Japanese importer prior to marketing because of the need to repackage or refurbish the products; poor quality-control standards used in the manufacture of the products, unavailability of spares and components; non-competitive pricing and unreliable delivery schedules; and any inability to provide after-sales service to customers.

Also bureaucratic impediments in developing countries, import permits and other reviews; limitations on the spectrum of goods made available as counter-deliveries; and limitations on linking of Western/Japanese exports to counter-purchase from more than one manufacturer in the developing country.

The volume of direct-compensation transactions which is related to the erection of new plant facilities in developing countries is levelling off because of current constraints in credit and markets. The trend is to finance expansion or modernizations of existing production facilities through the sale of products processed in these facilities. Direct compensation trade on a limited scale entailing the processing and assembly of light industry manufactures such as textiles, garments, leather goods, and appliances is on the increase in China's areas bordering Hong Kong and Macao as well as in other provinces and municipalities with access to ports, overland shipping facilities and strong traditional ties to overseas Chinese communities.

Products such as raw materials or certain commodities that can be sold without difficulty in hard-currency markets may be made available for counter-purchase in Soviet bloc countries only when necessary to ensure high-priority Western/Japanese imports and they are quickly used up.

Although the use of countertrade is expected to further increase during coming years as an integral part of many developing countries' economic planning, these countries' planners recognize that certain countertrade transactions are not in the best interests of the development of trade with the industrialized countries. The most successful type of compensatory trade involved is direct-compensation transactions. These span from erection of new production capacities, extraction and processing of mineral resources, of processing of materials or assembly of finished goods making use of existing plant capacity.

The most difficult compensatory arrangements to conclude are those involving Western/Japanese exporters with narrow fields of specialisation and single-type products. Successful completion of compensatory arrangements depends on several qualitative factors:

(i)   the degree of flexibility and acquaintance with compensatory practices by both trading parties;

(ii)   the understanding of the parties' reciprocal limitations in making or requiring concessions, and the matching of their commercial objectives;

(iii) the transactions' priority for the importer as reflected in the allocation of at least some foreign exchange for the importers;

(iv)   the uniqueness of the exporter's equipment and technology, as well as the attractiveness of his commercial terms;

(v)   the risk assessment of compensatory arrangements under evaluation in relation to the benefits derived by the exporter;

(vi)   the existence of a coordinating bureaucratic structure within the importing country which can facilitate linkage of counter-deliveries within and across industrial sectors;

(vii) the existence of government-sponsored incentives in the importing country which benefit counter-traders;

and long-term strategic planning for market development which involves current understanding of the evolving political, social, and regional influences as well as of risk factors in the targeted export markets, rather than market planning based only on demographic factors and annual economic indicators.

Development of programmes and strategies that will include options providing for sourcing of materials and labour in markets targeted for a company's exports, rather than including only exports of finished goods and turnkey projects. Acceptance of compensatory arrangements as one of the available tools—alongwith others such as pricing and investment—for preserving or enhancing the exporter's market share.

The more far-sighted companies are redirecting their efforts under pressure from the rapidly changing market environment-to development import strategies at the business unit level, that of the product line or related product lines. They are also expanding the role of management from that of implementer of marketing goals formulated by entrepreneurs, expected to devise opportunistic and creative approaches to the problems encountered in their areas of individual responsibility.

The success of a company's operations in the competitive trade environment will depend on adding to the responsibilities of management personnel who have been most burdened in the past with day-to-day operating problems and have not dedicated much time to the assessment of emerging trends in export markets or to the formulation of hedging operations.

At corporate levels, management may have to exchange growth for the emerging challenges of opportunistic business development. Such strategies may involve diversification of the company's resources and markets and integrate the activities of all the company's business units for the fulfillment of occasional tasks such as those related to countertrade requirements.

Countertrade represents only one of the options available to the exporter for market entry or preservation of market shares, along with such other alternatives as leasing and investment. The use of compensatory arrangements may be specified in the marketing plans aimed at a target market or project. In today's changing trade climate of limited opportunities and rising risks, the importance of securing access to diversified sources of current intelligence and of acquiring the ability to assess the information within the context of a marketing plan cannot be over-emphasised.

Countertrade Requires

the selection of a target market,
the identification of market objectives,
the choice of market-entry modes,
and the monitoring of market performance and the adjustments to achieve desired results.

It is necessary to identify sources of outside assistance for countertrade, for example, consultants, banks, trading houses, other specialized brokers, company clients and sub-contractors receptive to sharing compensatory obligations and suggest in-house organizational and logistical steps designed to facilitate handling of compensatory arrangements.

Companies which expect to encounter, or are already confronted with compensatory demands in their export markets face alternative options; avoiding these markets altogether; negotiating price discounts and other concessions in lieu of assuming compensatory obligations, it is important to invest time in advance preparation aimed at identifying the applicable strategies, the needs, and the policies of the importer as well as to invest time in devising varied fallback options or counter-proposals to be advanced as substitutes for compensatory obligations. Some developing countries view technology transfer as an asset only in so far as it is embodied as an integral part of equipment or production plants.

In China, technology transfer represents only about 2 to 3 per cent of the total cost charged. If the developing country is strapped for foreign exchange, it may be reluctant to allocate additional funds for the acquisition of process know-how, start up services, and training, even though this decision could delay for a considerable time use of the newly acquired technology.

If the exporter is prepared to accept compensatory arrange-ments, he will have to quote a price that makes allowance for any costs he expects to incur, such as those involving the marketing of any counter-deliveries he receives in payment.

If an exporter is faced with countertrade demands and has not already consulted with trading houses or other experts and has not already secured a commitment for the disposal of the counter-deliveries, the price quotation will have to reflect a best-estimate guess concerning all marketing expenses he is likely to incur, inclusive of transportation costs. Shipment of counter-deliveries to developing countries which could be targeted as potential markets for these goods may involve high costs if the destinations are not adequately serviced by the transportation network.

An exporter confronted at the last minute with a request for counter-trade may face difficult decisions. Exporters who choose to engage in compensatory arrangements may consider a range of options in developing their negotiation strategies such as:

price discounts,
extension of repayment terms,
extension of performance guarantees,
expansion of training programs for the customer's personnel,

increase in other export-related support services,
guaranteed fixed prices over a specified period for all or part of the spares to be supplied under the terms of the contract,
and transfer of part or all of the compensatory obligations against a subsidy to a third party,
accept partial payment in local currencies, even when these are non-convertible or cannot be transferred abroad:

(a) the currencies are transferable to third parties within the importer's country,

(b) the currencies cannot be used to defray the exporter's own costs in the importer's country,

accept partial payment in services made available by the customer's country domestically or abroad, such as those of construction and engineering crews to be used by the exporter in third countries;
assist in identifying business opportunities or create sales for the customer in foreign markets;
sub-contract, license, or invest in other projects in the customer's country as part of the compensatory arrangements;
negotiate lower compensation commitments in return for guarantees to the customer to cooperate with him in marketing in third markets.

The option of reinvestment for any partial payments received in non-convertible currencies will hinge on the developing countries' policies affecting foreign ownership of domestic assets such as real estate, stock and equity.

When assuming counter-purchase commitments, exporters should be aware that many of the products offered as counter-deliveries may be unavailable because of prior commitments or limited production. Exporters should first select goods that can be absorbed within their own company or those of their clients or sub-contractors. Such procedure is preferred by the country where the counter-deliveries are sourced. Some companies have found it advantageous to engage in anticipatory purchases in order to create goodwill and eventual credits for future exports devoid of countertrade obligations.

Risks and Coverage

Risks associated with countertrade are scarcely understood. Current coverage of compensatory arrangements is spotty among insurance companies and is an extension of existing risk policies. Insurance companies often prefer to insure a transaction on deferred payment terms rather than to guarantee countertrade performance. Project risk liability—which should be normally shouldered party by government organisations of developing countries—is shifting back to the exporter, his bank and his insurance company because of the deterioration of the credit worthiness of many foreign countries.

Possible hedges against countertrade risk assumed by an exporter are:

(i) a viable, construed and priced commercial transaction,

(ii) a written contract which deals with identified exposures that the exporter has to assume and,

(iii) an insurance policy covers insurable risk. More risk categories for an exporter include:

political risks resulting from adverse actions by recognised governments involving;

seizure of assets,

interference with contractual performance,

import or export license cancellation,

currency inconvertibility

war and civil strife damage,

casualty risks resulting from legal liability claims against the exporter, because of his actions;

property risks involving direct damage to assets as well as time-dependent exposures; and

pure business risks resulting in losses for exporter.

Except for pure business risks, all other forms of risk described above are insurable. Manufacturing scheduled to fulfill counter-purchase commitments has lower priority in the Soviet-bloc countries' production planning than that for exports, when countertrade involves sales of Western/Japanese machinery, and equipment becomes the exporters' collateral and a basis of repayment through the delivery of processed goods.

Another potential cause of business interruption is the way centrally planned economies control allocation and pricing of materials or feedstocks destined to production. It may be necessary to include in countertrade contracts a clause specifying the option of the Western/Japanese party to source production materials whenever it may be more cost-effective. The Western/ Japanese party may reserve the right to source the finished products elsewhere whenever the counter-deliveries are not competitively priced.

Centrally-planned Economics Experience

Planned production and marketing goals in centrally planned economies often conflict with the Western/Japanese company's aims of maintaining flexibility in production and marketing conditions. The exporter involved in a long-term export involving a long-term countertrade contract should make efforts to assure himself of the following:

Allocation of local resources and materials to the project and their pricing structure;

availability of adequate local utility resources;

accuracy of domestic-demand dates or estimates, and the production plant's commitments, if any, to fulfill such demands;

applicable official regulatory policies and current environmental concerns with the plant's methods of operations;

the adequacy of transport from the plant to foreign locations;

the managerial and labour skills of the plant's personnel, and local customs for personnel rotation and retention.

The record of equipment malfunctioning and provisions for repairs and for procuring spares in the host country, particularly for the plant under contract; the record in meeting prescribed production levels and delivery schedules in the host country's industrial sector, or in the plant under contract. The degree to which outside subcontracting is necessary for the manufacture of the finished product to be exported to the Western/Japanese party.

The drafting of countertrade contract usually requires protracted negotiations involving co-production or sub-contracting and will require the structuring of contracts which will conform to the particular conditions and requirements of the project under consideration and which, in most respects, do not differ from similar contracts used in Western countries or Japan. Significant economic reforms are under way in the USSR and East European countries and need to be assessed in the fast changing economic scenario.

Structure

In structuring a direct or indirect-compensation arrangement, except for barter transactions, it is a preferred practice to keep the export contract separate from the related imported contract. Two separate contracts allow the flexibility of separate financing and guarantees and insulate the obligations of the two transactions from each other.

The conditions of the two parallel countries—if not the details of the countertrade commitment—are negotiated at the same time. The obligations of the exporter are spelled out in a document called a "framed contract", "protocol" or "letter of undertaking", this binding document serves as the basis for guidance and referral for subsequent

contracts signed by the exporter—or third parties designated by him—
with appropriate organizations in the importer's country, in fulfillment
of countertrade obligations agreed to in the umbrella contract:

Identification of responsible parties and/or a third party designee to
whom the countertrade commitment can be transferred;
cross-reference to the original Western/Japanese export contract;
the value of the countertrade obligation expressed as percentage of
the Western/Japanese export contract;
deadlines of the countertrade commitment and
range of products available for counter-delivery and the suppliers of
industrial sectors from which they are available, or the right to link
counter-purchases to any goods available in the importer's country;
quality and pricing requirements concerning the counter-deliveries,
offered at "internationally" competitive prices;
conditions relating to transportation and delivery, right of the party
or his designees to market the countertraded goods in third markets
of choice without restrictions by the supplier of the goods who may
want to protect his own marketing outlets abroad;
right to choose a neutral surveyor, selected by both parties, to pass
a binding judgement on the quality of the countertraded goods in
case the concerned Western/Japanese purchaser finds them
unacceptable;
provision that payment of the penalty for non-fulfillment of the
countertrade obligation automatically releases the Western/ Japanese
party from all further countertrade obligations associated therewith;
provisions for separation of the obligations relating to penalties for
non-performance by the Western/Japanese party from the payment
obligations of the importer;
adjustments in the Western/Japanese party's countertrade obligations
resulting from his claims of force-majeure, and seat of the
arbitration court and the governing law in case of legal conflicts.

In China, legal formalities are less established. The traditional and
preferred mechanisms for solving disputes are conciliation and as a last
resort arbitration. Contracts, including countertrade ones, have been
kept simple and brief although this practice is now changing as China
acquires more experience.

No penalty provisions affecting the Chinese party are usually
included in the contracts covering counter-delivery commitments.
Adhoc mechanism for solving disputes is through "mutual" or
"friendly" negotiations. Chinese negotiators may also oppose clauses
in the countertrade contract relating to quality control inspections. The

careful drafting of contracts is imperative because of the lack of a developed commercial body of law in China.

Imports related to countertrade arrangements have not been a significant factor in the United States market. The spread of countertrade practices from the non-market economies of the centrally planned countries to those of the Third World and even to some industrialized countries, has increased the complexity of consistent application of the US trade laws, not only because of the apparent lack of transparency that exports from different economic systems might exhibit, but also because of political considerations and the US government's foreign policy preferences.

The methods of financing do not differ significantly from those which support other, more conventional types of exports. These methods include government-supported credit programs, back-to-back credit lines and suppliers or buyers credits, specially when a revenue stream depends on delayed availability of counter-deliveries. Financing policies vary among industrialized countries, with the official export credit agencies of Western/Japanese competitors following more liberal policies than those of the United States.

Government-supported export credit agencies represent the most important source for financing large compensation projects such as turnkey plants, sales of civil aircraft or major ventures such as the 3000-mile natural gas pipeline construction from Siberia to Western Europe. Owing to the large value and long-term aspects involving credit extension upto 20 years and exposures for hundreds of millions of dollars-only government credit programs may be available to provide the necessary financing and assume the risks for such long maturity periods.

Major government agencies in the industrialized countries provide export support to domestic suppliers through direct loans, guarantees, interest rate subsidies, and insurance programs that provide coverage against one or more risks such as inflation, currency exchange fluctuations or arbitrary action on bid and performance bonds. They operate under guidelines established by the International Arrangement on Officially Supported Export Credit among OECD governments. The guidelines are periodically adjusted. They do not apply to the financing of aircraft and nuclear power plants and defense equipment.

The main characteristics of export credit finance, as government credit is upto 85 per cent of eligible value, the interest rate is fixed and below commercial rates, repayment is in equal, consecutive, semiannual instalments and extends over a period which is normally longer (typically 10 to 20 years for capital projects) than that of a commercial loan.

Although foreign policy considerations play a role in the extension of credit by government financial agencies, these banks have a responsibility to adhere to sound financial practices.

When the project involves a countertrade transaction the banks will have to evaluate the impact of resulting counter-deliveries on the lender's domestic markets, the importance of the transaction in the context of the lending country's foreign relations with the importer's country, the banks own policies on credit extension to such transactions and the credit worthiness of the guarantees and resources provided by the borrower. Lenders also analyze the currency exchange risks pertaining to the financed projects, to avoid problems related to debt servicing in a strong currency and revenue earning in a weak currency. This is particularly significant in the context of the highly fluctuating exchange rates in recent years. Daily exchange transactions run into $ 250 billion.

Commercial bank financing represents the main source for medium-term financing. Loans normally bear a floating rate of in-terest linked to the London Interbank Offered Rate or the US prime rate plus a fixed margin of spread over LIBOR or prime rate.

Commercial bank financing offers a more flexible alternative than institutional loans, its drawdown grace period, and interest rate terms can be tailored to specific projects and the loan is not tied to procurement in the country providing the financing. Interest rate is higher than the of institutional loans and is floating, thus complicating the transaction's economic planning.

Western banks have financed countertrade transactions by assuming title to the counter-delivered goods as collateral, until these goods were marketed for cash. A major US commercial bank has helped finance a textile plant expansion in China, which was collateralised. The cash derived form the cloth sales were de-posited in a trust account held by the US bank. Forfaiting-the-recourse financing procedure is known as forfaiting buyers credit.

Forfaiting was developed as a medium-term refinancing of suppliers' credits, using the technique of non-recourse financing. Forfaiting denotes the purchase of trade bills and promissory notes by a financial institution without recourse to the seller. The discount relates to the cost of refinancing and includes a margin to cover the risks assumed. Other factors included in the cost are the commitment commission and a "days-to-grace" fee to compensate for the loss of interest due to transfer and payment delays.

Forfaiting is normally done at fixed interest rates for forfaitable claims and carries a promise to pay, representing an unconditional, irrevocable, and freely transferable guarantee of payment of a bank— usually the bank transacting foreign trade in a developing or Soviet bloc country or a government agency.

A countertrade transaction consisting of separate but linked export and import contracts could finance the export leg of the transaction through forfaiting as long as the related trade bills or promissory notes represent an unconditional, unencumbered and irrevocable guarantee of payment of a bank acceptable to the forfaiter.

Whether lease financing is beneficial to a specific project, especially when it entails countertrade depends on a complex set of economic criteria involving financial, legal, tax, accounting and acceptable-risk which are peculiar to individual transactions and have to be evaluated accordingly.

Companies facing the prospect of compensatory obligations are confronted with requirements that many exporting firms, specially the small, medium-sized, product-specialized ones, are not equipped to handle. A company should assess risks that in the likelihood of countertrade will represent a persistent occurrence during coming years in the firm's traditional export markets, and whether the company should bear the loss of countertrade related opportunities that these markets offer.

The benefit of concluding spot sales which would not occur without acceptance of compensatory demands, against the risk and difficulty of evaluating costs associated with compensatory arrangements has to be weighed against the importance of gaining or maintaining a long-term competitive presence in the targeted export markets, against the time, money and effort expended in organising for countertrade and the subsequent commitment to the obligations assumed by such an undertaking. The challenge or necessity to adapt and move with trends in export markets against the efforts needed to readjust the thinking of corporate managements needs to be evaluated.

A few chemical companies and commodity trading firms are known to have profited from both the export and the import contracts of countertrade obligations. Certain other major producers of consumer goods have undertaken countertrade obligations, alongwith promotional activities to penetrate the markets with products which rate low in priority in the developing country's imports.

Exporters, especially the small, medium-sized, and specialized firms, generally rely on prompt repayments for their exports. The initial step is to assess the firm's resources which could represent potential assets in such arrangements, especially for countertrade. Assets include: capital availability, type of goods and services exported, trained or trainable personnel to be assigned to manage countertrade transactions, operation plans and the firms capacity to discharge its own countertrade commitments.

Capital Requirements

Capital availability plays an important role in countertrade arrangements, especially when receipt of proceeds from the disposal of counter-deliveries occurs only after the Western/ Japanese goods have been exported. During the intervening period, the Western/Japanese exporter may have to shoulder costs associated with the credit extended to the importer as well as costs that could occur as a consequence of late deliveries of counter-traded goods or be related to quality deficiencies involving countertrade commitments and for financing any related unforeseen costs, is qualified as an asset.

Consumer and luxury goods, or any other product, equipment, machinery, or technology for which no foreign exchange outlay has been planned—either because the goods are considered non-essential to the importing country's economy or because they have come to the attention of prospective end-users too late to be included in annual purchasing plans—may require 100 per cent countertrade arrangements.

Chapter 7

ORGANISING FOR COUNTERTRADE

In the initial stages of involvement with countertrade some firms will assign responsibility for developing the company's countertrade programs or for suggested initial steps to one of its management officers. Many other companies getting involved in countertrade rely on the services of a single-salaried specialist, who has a background in trade and marketing involving experience with imports as well as exports. The salaried specialist acts as a coordinator between the sales and purchasing departments, consulting on countertrade activities. His trading expertise is expected to assist the company in locating outside buyers, such as end-users or trading houses, for countertrade products that cannot be absorbed within the company. The specialist may assist in identifying financial institutions that provide credit for countertrade transactions.

Consultants

Other companies starting in the countertrade field may hire the services of a consultant. The consultant's responsibilities include advising the company on countertrade policies, and planning the most appropriate organizational structure and guidelines related to countertrade, formulating countertrade negotiation strategies. Consultants having extensive knowledge of countertrade related matters are few in number and more difficult to secure than traders or marketing specialists.

Marketing Plan

The development of a marketing plan which takes into consideration countertrade as one of the optional recourses is a definite asset for a company expecting to encounter such obligations in its export market. The plan should identify goods potentially available as counter-deliveries by type and quantities, should detail preventive measures, and suggest approaches and strategies, methods and sources of financing, in-house matrix management procedures (i.e., across divisional lines), and logistical requirements. The plan should be treated as a marketing tool for the enhancement of the company's exports or as a profitable source of supplies.

The Western/Japanese exporter may also assist the foreign country importer to raise the foreign exchange needed to transfer his countertrade obligations to a broker against payment of a subsidy or premium.

After a review is made of the company's assets for countertrade, i.e., its current ability to cope with such obligations, the company can decide where improvements are in order and decide on the costs of undertaking them.

The following alternatives present themselves: to engage in countertrade transactions only when it is possible to transfer all such obligations to third parties; organize the company's own in-house countertrade unit; a corporate decision to organize a permanent in-house countertrade unit will have to be taken; the unit's location within the firm's command-and-review chain, delineating its functions and staffing, and determining sources and budget allocations for its operations.

The countertrade unit be established at corporate level to oversee and provide expertise, services and necessary liaison to divisions engaged in countertrade. The goods available for countertrade may be finished products and not components, intermediates, unfinished goods or raw materials of the type and quality sought by a company's purchasing organization. If the company avails itself of a large volume of steady supplies from abroad, the leverage provided by the imports could be used by the purchasing department during its negotiations for the annual procurements to offset any countertrade obligations that the company's exports might incur in that country. Corporate development division is an advantageous position from which to oversee the countertrade unit.

The undertaking of any countertrade project involves three interdependent areas of activity. Structuring the transaction so that its costs, potential problems, and realistic returns are identified in the early phases of the project financing of the transaction by relying on the structuring effort to make it bankable, as to the risks and exposures involved.

Marketing the counter-deliveries by relying on the structuring effort to identify prospective end-users or brokers for the goods, as well as to evaluate the subsidies to be paid to these companies for disposing off the goods.

In the areas of finance and trade, brokering with considerable expertise and service are available to exporters, while expertise in the area of transaction structuring (especially those related to countertrade), is more difficult to locate and less available within most exporting firms. It is in this domain that a countertrade unit may evolve the bulk of its activities in support of the parent company's marketing efforts.

Thus a company that designates marketing support as the main function of its countertrade units activities should be prepared to find the units' operations as a cost/profit centre within the company's overall export promotion programme. Some typical functions that could be performed by the countertrade units are to:

—secure sustained commitment by top management to the company's countertrade programmes;

—define manageable risks and limiting conditions acceptable when engaging in countertrade transactions, and set related guidelines for the company's sales force.

—assist with long-range marketing strategy plans in markets requiring or likely to require countertrade obligations, taking into account the countries' changing economic and political conditions as well as the export-related regulatory policies and competitive circumstances in these markets, perform an inventory of the company's foreign sourced supplies, identify new potential suppliers in countries where the countertrade factor, for use in fulfillment of the firm's countertrade obligations required by these countries, and as leverate for future company exports;

—participate in negotiations involving countertrade requirements with contract authority.

—identify and enlist the necessary support from third parties (potential to assist the company with its countertrade commitments on a transaction-by-transaction basis, and act as a one-stop information source within the company for all countertrade-related issues);

—coordinate internal clearing of debits and credits within the company resulting from sales by a division and purchases by another division which offset the former division's countertrade obligations;

—manage cash flows to a subsidy fund endowed by one, several, or all the exporting divisions of the company, which is intended to create an incentive and to subsidise countertrade imports by any division of the company and evaluating expected costs resulting from the company's involvement with countert-rade transactions.

The countertrade unit will strive to provide flexibility of alternatives for individual export markets. The countertrade unit would recommend to the firm's top management, at various stages of market penetration, alternative marketing approaches spanning direct sales, licensing, co-production, and joint ventures with a local partner or with another foreign firm. It is the growth dynamics and characteristics of the importing country, as assessed by the countertrade unit, that condition the evolving marketing strategy of the company, rather than individual, uncoordinated initiatives by any of its divisions, including those of any trading subsidiary. It also acts as a catalyst, facilitating strategic conceptual information flows from top down, and concrete and practical information flows from bottom up.

Another proposed function for the countertrade unit is to assist management in the development of corporate policies involving the firm's participation in countertrade transactions and to translate these into guidelines for the company's divisions. The role of the unit would gradually shift from overseeing and actively participating in such transactions, to providing only requested support services, information and liaison with outside firms, which can assist the company with the handling of individual countertrade commitments. The countertrade unit's staff may range from one or a few professionals in some firms, to tens of specialists in a trading subsidiary. Other factors affecting the size of the unit are its operational cost and any logistical problems related to integrating the activities of the unit with those of other divisions within the company.

Some countertrade subsidiaries have indeed been formed by major Western/Japanese companies in the belief that countertrade is somewhat akin to regular trade. In trading transactions, supply and demand conditions prevail, while in countertrade transactions only excess, unmarketable supply is most often the norm. These companies' decisions reflect the increasing difficulty in marketing counter-deliveries in the current international trading environment.

The size of the budget allocated to the operations of the countertrade unit depends on the unit's size. Funding countertrade units directly by divisions operating on a profit and loss basis has not gained acceptance, given the overall "corporate" image associated with the countertrade units' functions but height change.

Companies that do not contemplate involvement with countertrade on a regular basis or are just starting in the countertrade field may turn to the services of countertrade consultants or trading houses.

A trading house will, therefore, consider countertrade transactions as alternative sources of supply, provided that the countertraded goods can be sold, that their volume does not disrupt the trading house's own commodity or product flows, that adequate profit margins are provided and that the value of the transaction is above the house's lower limits.

Less than 30 major trading houses in the world conduct large scale operations which encompass multiple commodities, products, and geographical areas.

Basic Functions

There are four basic functions that can be performed by a trading house These are marketing, including representation; transpor-tation, including warehousing and insurance; finance, including investment management and credit extension and manufacture, including upgrading of commodities.

Japanese Sogo Shoshas (General Trading Companies) generally specialise in all the four areas. A trading house's main assets are its specialists, financial resources, established market positions and international marketing network commercial intelligence.

Firm commitments to an exporter to market countertraded goods in low demand whose deliveries extend beyond one year may rate subsidies as high as 10 to 15 per cent depending on the volumes involved. Trading houses will provide advice to exporters on the type of products that are saleable on world markets. Trading houses may succeed in allocating the countertrade obligations of an exporter against their own import accounts, thus reducing or eliminating the countertrade obligation of the exporter. Trading houses are becoming increasingly selective in their involvement in such transactions. These houses are committing their assets, specialists and market positions, only when the returns on their investments are commensurate with the risks of the transactions at hand.

For exporters who do not intend to participate in countertrade on a regular basis or for those adopting a staged approach in organizing for countertrade, and for companies which are faced with counter-deliveries too large or too varied to be handled by the firms' own means, the benefits of enlisting the services of a reputable trading house should be investigated.

Bank's Role

Major banks have lately been supplementing their export-related services with countertrade advisory ones that banks can provide: advisory services on countertrade related issues where they can act as middlemen in matching among their clientele exporters with importers, they may provide credits and guarantees in support of a countertrade transaction; and they may manage on a retainer basis, the clients; countertrade transactions by securing the assistance of appropriate brokers and monitor contracted performances.

Major U.S. Banks have also been intrigued by the potential new business opportunities that countertrade transactions offer, and are thus looking upon the practices with increasing interest.

Several commercial banks operating in the United States have established in-house countertrade departments, Citibank, Chase Manhattan Bank, European American Bank and J. Henry Schroker Bank. These Departments' activities revolve mostly around advisory services, bringing buyers and sellers together for a fee, processing letters of credit, and providing short-term countertrade financing. The banks rely on trading houses for assistance in discharging the countertrade obligations of their clients.

Lacking the ability to advise on how best to handle counter-deliveries or lacking the willingness to assume the financial risks of most countertrade transactions proposed by clients, some US Banks' efforts are gradually shifting to providing one-stop countertrade management services to exporters for a substantial fee. To hedge on its inability to assess on its own, the viability of countertrade transaction, the bank will report on the credit worthiness, trade record, and reputation of its client. As banks become more comfortable through experience with countertrade arrangements and are able to combine their traditional expertise in securing funds with an understanding of the trait necessary in trading, they will probably end up dominating the countertrade business. The Export Trading Company Act of 1982, which allows bank holding companies to set up export trading firms, affords banks a unique opportunity to achieve this goal.

Legislation's purpose is to increase US exports by liberalizing export finance restrictions, allowing bank holding companies to invest in export trading companies and by nullifying the application of anti-trust laws to certain export trade. The act provides American business with a tool—the successful exploitation of which depends on the ingenuity, initiative, and resourcefulness of the participating firms.

The basic functions of an ETC are to aggregate an appropriate mix of resources and to apply them effectively and profitably, in order to enhance the export capabilities of its members and clients.

The trading company must possess several basic capabilities in order to perform properly :

—Access to financial funds, resulting in the ability to extend credit or arrange for credit extension to customers.

—A staff experienced in international trade and able to carry out sales and distribution functions as well as export-support services.

—An efficient communications market intelligence system with access to international commercial information and domestic export-support services provided by other firms and a product or service that is marketable internationally.

It is important that the ETC have the capability and necessary contacts to supplement its own services with those from other sources, according to the requirements of individual transactions.

The configuration of an ETC defined by the range of goods, services and expertise that the own membership contributes, depends upon the purposes to be served. The intent in assembling such an organization may vary from solely providing trade support services to exporters at large, to fostering the trade of the ETC's own membership; geographical spread criteria, product criteria, and client criteria.

In the highly competitive, protectionist, sluggish world trade environment, both types will have a rough going in securing market positions abroad. This might be particularly true in the case of newcomers to the trading scene such as ETCs.

In favour of the American alternative is the ETC's unique combination of flexibility resulting from choice of size, area of operations, and form of assembly; the potential they provide for innovative approaches, adaptable to individual trade problems the opportunity offered to concentrate exclusively in export-growth areas such as the service and high technology sectors; and the competitive drive to survive and succees they breed, which is peculiar to newcomers who have to make do on their own wits. As more sophistication and experience is gained by those ETCs which survive the test of the market-place, these organizations will carve out their own niche of trade specializations which may complement or compete with those of established trading houses — and in the process will help American business become more competitive in world markets.

Business across the United States have taken steps to create, or have already set up, new export trading houses. These include Sears, Roebuck and Co., K-Mart Corporation and J.C. Penney Co., Bank of America and Los Angeles' Security Pacific; small export associations; management and distributor firms; and port authorities such as that of New York and New Jersey.

Compensatory arrangements in international trade have increased in importance. Compensatory transactions are not confined only to tied imports and exports of goods between two parties (countertrade), although such practices represent today a major portion of countertrade. Given the sluggish world trade growth rates and the dim prospects for a return to the open market policies of the 1960s and early 1970s in both developed and developing nations, it is in the broader definition of compensatory transactions that these practices will most likely register expansion in the 1990s.

The Third World countries have been looking upon countertrade, as a means to balance incremental imports through offsetting exports. Compensatory arrangements are increasingly becoming an accepted option in the planning processes of both the Western/Japanese exporters and the developing countries. This trend is not likely to be reversed in the foreseeable future, as governments continue to treat international commerce as an extension of national economic policies and prefer to deal with trade competition through bilateral accommodations favouring their own exporters.

The longevity of compensatory practices, the accumulated and growing debt of Third World countries, aggravated by the credit constraints on additional loans to many of these countries and the mounting number of requests for debt reschedulings; the developing countries' continued need for economic growth and technology which is dependent on sustained import levels as well as on export expansion in order to service debt and to hedge against mounting unemployment and related domestic political instabilities; and the uneven recovery rates in the industrialised countries, together with protectionist attitudes towards many bulk imports from the Third World are aggravating recourse to countertrade. The roots of these problems are deeper than any short-lived or tentative world economic scenario could indicate.

Most developing nations are aware of the inherent limitations of such practices which emphasize the temporary needs of the economies over the orderly, long-term development of selective export positions in individual foreign markets. Yet these countries appear to have accepted these arrangements as a means to cope with both the short medium-term problem of penetrating markets.

Yet many Third World countries with steadily deteriorating economies and with limited industrial bases have had to rely on light industry manufactures, raw materials, semi-manufactures and commodities for indirect compensation, counter-deliveries, although these transactions are becoming increasingly difficult to implement.

Direct-compensation arrangements, whereby counter-deliveries are manufactured using the imported technology and according to know-how and specifications, are expected to increase more rapidly, especially when involving the processing and assembly of goods and the manufacturing of components within already existing production capacity.

Direct-compensation arrangements are expected to become the preferred countertrade practice in a majority of transactions, and this will likely accelerate the shift in production locale for many light industry goods or components to the more advanced and stable among the developing countries.

Solutions to operational problems will also have to be addressed by Third World authorities. These may include promoting special investment incentives as well as organizing and ensuring the proper operation of compensatory coordinating structures at ministerial levels to facilitate, indirect-compensation linkages of counter-deliveries from the entire spectrum of the country's production.

When organizing for compensatory arrangements especially for countertrade, companies will have to take into account the dynamic nature of the practice—a tool intended to subsidise the changing needs of the developing countries' economic growth in terms of credit constraints. Such involvement may increasingly include investments of capital in addition to exports and technology transfers to foreign countries. As production quality improves and production capacity increases, the prevailing tendency may well be to produce countertrade goods made to order for the exporters, rather than providing him with unrelated products manufactured in the country.

The most challenging area of future application of compen-satory arrangements lies in the financing of major projects which involve requirements for funds in the hundreds or thousands of millions of dollars (development of mines, industrial complexes, or aircraft sales). For these projects with insufficient funding, advance planning and analysis is crucial, especially when the purchasing country's export profile and its industrialisation stage do not allow extensive use of countertrade or of domestic content production.

The planning would have to entail creative approaches and consider such options as piecing together sources of finance, services; and its industrialization stage do not allow extensive use of countertrade or of domestic content production.

If convertible currency credit—which, as in recent decades propelled international commerce to current levels is to remain constrained in trade with Third World countries— exporters and their bankers will have to come up with innovative ideas for using soft currencies, if established trade levels are to be maintained. Exporters will have to weigh its distaste for such unorthodox options against the benefits it expects to derive from the export projects, it may want to curtail the scope of its exports or shelter its participation by engaging in the transactions as a member of a consortium of companies.

Large-scale projects undertaken in future years in developing countries will undoubtedly result in a larger responsibility for risk falling on the shoulders of Western/Japanese suppliers. Such transactions will also require the increased availability of government finance and especially guarantees, from both the supplier's and the customer's countries. The transactions may require collateral in the form of trust funds held in banks for the purpose of sheltering revenue streams derived from the marketing of goods that the importing country has allocated to create initial funds for the proposed project.

If the uniform high growth rates fo the world economies and of international trade that were experienced prior to the onset of the energy crisis and the delinking of the dollar to gold were just a flash in history, during which wealth was created through the availability of cheap energy and easy credit, then future years will require adjustments and more realistic growth expectations. Provided that the accumulated debt problem of developing nations can be resolved without major repercussions on the international financial system, and that credit will be gradually resorted albeit under more restricted criteria to support trade to most or all of the world's developing nations, the developing countries will have to live with more stringent constraints of their trade balances than in the past. This implies, however, an ability to supplement financial transfers obtained through trade—related credits with market transfers extracted through countertrade impositions.

As the need for compensatory trade management services increases, it is hoped that the forthcoming assistance, the expertise of which is not rooted in precedents, experience, or established theory will measure up to the task as the markings of affordable errors for a developing nation are small indeed.

The developed nations of the world will have to come to terms with present realities and adapt past practices to current needs, which for an increasing number of developing nations are finding expression through compensatory impositions. With all the shortcomings of compensatory arrangements, they have acquired the status of a market phenomenon. Countertrade has the potential to make full use of the international financial system and trade interdependence established since 1945. While the adoption of compensatory arrangements will not by itself alleviate problems created in the past, it could narrow future trade imbalances, encourage investments and technology transfers, and pave the way for trade that in the absence of credit, could not occur.

The challenge of the 1990s will lie in devising internationally accepted criteria and in standardizing the application of countertrade through multi-lateral negotiations, so that uniformity and predictability can be restored to international trade alongwith finance/credit.

Chapter 8

ASSESSMENT OF THE EFFECTS OF BARTER AND COUNTERTRADE TRANSACTIONS — A GLOBAL VIEW AND COUNTRY EXPERIENCES

During 1980-87, international trade has witnessed a marked increase in the number of countries and intensity of efforts involved in actively promoting barter and countertrade as a means of conducting international exchanges of goods and services. As many as 61 governments encourage such techniques to some degree. A growing number of governments have become direct, active participants in countertrade transactions. Others have levied requirements for countertrade on some aspects of privately conducted trade. Few governments collect or publish data specifically to identify such transactions.

Since 1980-81, the world has seen a marked increase in efforts to promote and expand countertrade in various forms. A great variety of nations use countertrade—Israel, Jamaica, and Turkey; oil rich developing nations (Indonesia, Malaysia, Mexico and Saudi Arabia), newly industrialising nations (S. Korea and Singapore), and such traditional users as the East-Europeans (Rumania, the GDR, the Soviet Union, Czechoslovakia, Poland, Bulgaria etc.), developed market economies such as Australia, Belgium, Canada and Japan have become important players.

Reasons given for the expanding international emphasis on countertrade include the international debt and balance of payments problems of many nations, forcing upon them the need to find non-hard-currency ways of paying for important imports; (2) national budget problems which dictate a need to economise on and even recoup the costs of major military import purchases; and (3) political pressures to maintain economic development and employment-expansion programmes despite budget and payments deficits and intensifying competition in export markets.

During the 1980-82 recession, the average current account deficit of all non-oil-producing developing countries ranged between US $ 65 to US'$ 80 billion dollars annually, whereas that of industrialised countries collectively averaged US $ 36 billion. International commercial lending to many of the more indebted countries has remained severely curtailed in the eighties, especially those heavily dependent upon imported resources, have resorted to countertrade as a means of conserving foreign exchange.

Countertrade transactions consist of three major elements: the export sales agreement; the obligation agreements and the fulfillment or implementation of the obligations. Often, final agreement on the obligations lags behind the sales agreement by six months or more. Final fufillment of the obligations, the third element in a countertrade transaction, may take as many as 10 years or more to complete.

US Expei ience

The US military-related export sales having associated offset obligations and those corporations with foreign sales involving other types of countertrade involving other types of countertrade involving US $ 7.1 billion or 5.6 per cent linked countertrade obligations. The total value of associated U.S. countertrade obligations peaked in 1984, equivalent to over two per cent of exports. There has lately been an increasing interest in countertrade with China and in the aerospace sectors.

Item	1980	1982	1984
Sales Agreements involving countertrade:			
Military-related (offsets)	6568	732	5890
Non-Military	1846	983	1249
Total	8414	1715	7139
Countertrade Obligations:			
Military related (offsets)	414	439	2182
Non-Military	467	479	580
Total	881	918	2762

Almost US $ 5.5 billion of US exports resulted from countertrade (excluding offsets) agreements dring 1980-84, and approximately US $ 4.6 billion worth of goods and services were planned for exports during 1985-1990.

The US exports associated with non-offset countertrade increased almost four-fold, from 1980 through 1984. They represented 84 per cent of the total exports committed under sales agreements signed during the 1980-84 period. The actual time of delivery of the export products ranged from several months to several years after the contract signing and delivery may have been spread out over several years.

Imports from non-offset countertrade totalled US $ 1.8 billions dollars during 1980-84. Imports associated with non-military-related countertrade accounted for virtually all of countertrade imports in 1980 and for about 80 per cent of the total in 1984. The US imports received in such countertrade fluctuated annually between US $ 323 million and US $ 420 million and totalled US. $ 1.8 billion during 1980-84.

Annual trade surpluses are expected in countertrade transac-tions, because most countertrade agreements permit associated purchase obligations to be less than the full value of the export contract, to be carried out over several years, and to involve arrangements other than imports into the country. The US imports against the US countertrade obligations are generally much less than the associated exports and lag well behind obligations values. Military offset arrangements accounted for 80 per cent of all the US counter-purchase obligations in 1980-84, and for most of their increase in the period. Offset ,obligations fluctuated from loss of more than US $ 400 billion in 1980 and 1982, to a peak of US $ 3.2 billion in 1983. From 1980 to 1984, their value increased more than five-fold. Military offset obligations resulted primarily from foreign purchases of major weapons systems made in the United States.

The record high levels in 1983-84 reflect major arms updates— mainly by NATO countries and increased weapon systems pro- curements by other US partners. The US military exports sales in- creased steadily, nearly doubling between 1980 and 1984, to more than US $ 11.2 billion. Military-related export sales are much more likely to include a countertrade obligation than are non-military transactions. A decline in foreign purchasing power associated with the high US dollar between 1982 and 1984 accelerated foreign government demands for offsets. Increased emphasis is on development of domestic arms industries, through various means that offset agreements can provide, including technology transfer, co-production, joint ventures, and counter-purchase arrangements. The US non-military countertrade commitment accounted for only 20 per cent of the total US countertrade obligation for the period 1980-84.

In the 1980s world demand for countertrade grew markedly in the face of multiple economic problems, including recession, international debt crisis, and domestic budget stringencies. Developed nations were among the most numerous to resort to countertrade techniques. Latin American countries, which were among the most active in attempting to expand their countertrade, were a minor element in the expansion of the US countertrade involvement. Military purchases have continued unabated in the Middle East despite the end of Iran-Iraq War. Arab-Israeli tensions are mounting as also the easily disturbed situation in South Asia. Countertrade obligations entered into by the US companies with European countries registered a four-fold increase, reaching almost US $ 1.4 billion in 1984 compared with US $ 285 million in 1980. Europe's share of the total US countertrade obligations rose from 32 per cent in 1980 to 50 per cent in 1984. Most of the increases in obligations with Europe resulted from increases in military sales to NATO member-countries. NATO countries in Europe accounted for 44 per cent of the total US countertrade obligations during 1980-84.

Asia's share of the total US countertrade obligations increased slightly from 34 to 35 per cent. Most of the increased obligations resulted from offsets associated with military-related export sales. The largest increases in 1981 and 1984, were related to large US military sales to Israel. Saudi Arabia has also become a major player. In non-military countertrade transactions with Asia, China's foreign trade liberalisation, Indonesia's mandates, Malaysia's new countertrade requirements and Philippines foreign debt and exchange reserve problems have stimulated countertrade transaction increases. Africa and Latin America are major players.

Europe accounted for a much higher ratio of obligation to sales. Increased US competition for military sales to Europe is the primary force for driving up the share of obligations to sales. Sales contracts for aerospace products by the US companies that included countertrade obligations were valued at US $ 20.2 billion, equivalent to 70 per cent of all exports sales agreements involving countertrade (including offsets). Countertrade (including offsets) obligations to be fulfilled by contracting abroad for aerospace products were valued at US $ 20 million or 7.6 per cent of the total countertrade obligations.

For 1980-1984, 25 per cent of the US $ 79.8 billion in the US aerospace exports had associated countertrade obligations. This high concentration is attributed, in part, to the then US exchange rate at the time and cost of aerospace purchases. Other export sectors in which countertrade was important were defence products, communications and electronics, construction projects, minerals and chemicals. Sales agreements with counter-purchase obligations accounted for US $ 5.7

billion or 91 per cent of all sales agreements in which a non-military countertrade was negotiated during 1980-84.

Imports from Eastern Europe accounted for 70 per cent of total non-military countertrade imports in 1980. During 1981-84, the Eastern European share fell to 33 per cent in 1982 before climbing to 50 per cent in 1984. The share of total non-military countertrade imports accounted for by Latin America grew from zero in 1980 in 1980 to 36 per cent of the total in 1982 before declining to 12 per cent in 1984 in the wake of the deepening debt crisis.

In-house Component of Countertrade

Of the US $ 1.8 billion in imports making up non-military countertrade during 1980-84, 46 per cent were absorbed in-house for use by the US companies involved in the countertrade agreements. In 1980, in-house use of countertrade imports accounted for 33 per cent of the total non-military countertrade imports. In-house countertrade imports grew to 64 per cent of total non-military countertrade imports in 1982. The growth of in-house use of products received in countertrade is a reflection of the trend towards importing more sophisticated, and, therefore, more usable products into the United States.

Direct/Indirect Offset

Direct offset obligations (those that involve sub-contractor production, co-production and the licensed production of products that are linked to the product being sold, avionics for aircraft were valued at US $ 4.8 billion during 1980-84 compared with indirect offset obligations of US $ 3.6 billion. 61 per cent of the direct offset obligations will be satisfied through sub-contractor production in foreign countries. The production of avionics for a particular aircraft involved in an offset agreement may be shifted to the country buying the aircraft. The planned fulfillment of much (74 per cent) of the indirect offset obligation was unspecified, whereas most of the remainder of the indirect offset will be satisfied through some forms of countertrade.

Sub-contractors assumed US $ 977 million dollars of their prime contractors' offset obligations during 1980-84. One half (US $ 507 million) of these obligations were or will be fulfilled through indirect offset arrangements. The sub-contractor may be asked to join in a predetermined commitment, such as participation in disposing of or using in-house products that the prime supplier has already agreed to accept from the buying country; or the sub-contractor may be given the opportunity to negotiate its own obligation agreement with the buying government, which would be done on behalf of the prime contractor. The majority of respondents engaging in countertrade and military offsets indicated that they have been able to maintain or increase existing levels of employment and plant capacity because of new business generated by such sales agreements. Other benefits include larger and more efficient production runs, lower unit costs, increased capital formation, and the development of new technology. Countertrade has not adversely affected the competitiveness of the US companies, both among those engaging in countertrade and those that are not.

Countertrade is made up of several forms of reciprocal trade—

1. The period for flilling the counter-purchase compensation obligation is rather short-term, one to five years.

2. The value of goods offered by the foreign government or company is usually less than 100 per cent of the original sales contract value.

3. The counterpurchase requirement is contractually agreed upon, either in the original sales contract or as a separate, parallel contract.

Penalties usually range from 5 to 25 per cent of the value of the company's counter-purchase obligation. The other contracting party is expected to fulfill its part of the agreement to purchase the specified production during a definite period or in the case of default, pay an agreed-upon hard currency penalty. Where counterpurchases are required by an Eastern European country or an LDC, a contracting company is frequently offered a limited list of products from which it can select.

Evidence Account

By means of evidence accounts, which are usually opened with the foreign trade bank or a private bank of the importing organization, a company's purchases are automatically credited against its current or future counter-purchase obligations that can be satisfied by past purchases. Evidence account contract stipulates the value of sales and purchases by the contracting company and the magnitude of purchases that must offset the sale. Evidence accounts are not required to be in equilibrium each year. Companies dealing in raw materials, chemicals and other basic commodities are more likely to engage in evidence accounts. They are generally restricted under evidence accounts from transferring their counter-purchase obligations to a third party such as an independent trading house.

Buy-back

Referred to as "buy-backs", compensation agreements entail the sale of plant, equipment, and/or technology in return for resultant products. Evidence accounts result from an agreement to buy and sell goods from an LDC or a centrally planned economy over a given period. Such sales and purchases are recorded in evidence accounts. These accounts are used because individual countertrade transactions do not necessarily balance. Most early compensation deals involve the sale of technology and machinery for large-scale petro-chemical facilities and mining operations.

Characteristics of compensation transactions are:

1. The average value of transactions is usually much higher compared with those of other forms of countertrade, with the exception of offsets.
2. The typical period of product take-back is relatively long —5 to 20 years.
3. The value of product buy-back during the contract period usually equals the aggregate value of the plant, technology, and/or equipment, plus compensation for interest expense incurred during the period of take-back.

Compensation arrangements have been used by East European countries, the USSR, China and several less developed countries to obtain sophisticated foreign technology without depleting scarce hard-currency reserves. Such agreements provide the country receiving the plant, technology, and/or equipment with a supply of much needed production capacity and guaranteed exports. Compensation agreements allow the host country to take advantage of the foreign firm's marketing expertise to dispose off the resultant products, against compensation arrangements provided by the supplier of the plant. They proceed in a typical compensation agreement, project financing is arranged either through a Western/Japanese bank or a foreign State Bank.

Barter

Barter is the contractual direct exchange of goods or services between two principles without the use of foreign currencies. Barter agreements are frequently consummated over a short period of time, usually less than one year, so that world price fluctuations do not generally favour either side. Transfer of goods is usually accomplished through a single contract. Third parties are rarely involved in marketing the product, since most barter is done on government-to-government basis. Since

World War II, transactions of this sort have been common in trade within the Soviet bloc, between LDCs or between LDCs and the centrally planned economies. In the 40s and 50s India bartered hessian/sugar bags against Wheat and Sugar purchases from Argentina, Cuba and Brazil.

Barter transactions between governments are often accomplished by the use of "clearing agreements". The clearing/ payments agreement specifies the goods to be exchanged, the ratio of exchange, and the period for affecting the exchange. The goods are offered at an agreed upon ratio similar to that previously described in barter transactions. If market conditions change and the imported product cannot be absorbed in the home market, the importing country has two options—(i) it may suspend the importation of the product, (ii) risking an imbalanced account or it may sell its purchase option to a third party. The products are often turned over to international trade specialists called switch traders.

Switch Trade

Switch trading, typically associated with East-West countertrade, occurs after counter-deliveries of products begin. The switch trader may find a buyer in a soft-currency country or in a country in which the Central Government has imposed hard-currency transfer restrictions.

If the potential buyer is unable to pay for the goods with hard currency, the seller may be offered payment in goods produced in the buyer's home country. The switch trade usually offers a portion of the original discount in order to make the deal more attractive. Most of the switch trading organizations are located in Western Europe, Miami, Singapore, Hong Kong, (especially in Vienna, Amsterdam, London, Lausanne and Hamburg) and deal primarily in East European goods. Companies committed to a counter-purchase can easily dispose off countertrade obligations to a switch-trading house. The disadvantages are that a company transferring its obligation to a trading house is often looked upon unfavourably by the country supplying the countertraded goods because such an action is seen as an insincere attempt to establish a long-term trade commitment. East European foreign trade organisations prefer a Western/Japanese company that uses countertrade goods either for internal consumption or as transfer shipments to its subsidiaries or its suppliers.

Offsets

An offset arrangement takes place between a firm in an industrialised country and a foreign government. Offsets help recover the hard currency drain resulting from the purchase and, more importantly, provide desired transfer of technology and local employment. Although aircraft sales usually constitute the largest volume in offsets, communications equipment, electronic components and accessories, and guided missiles and parts are also frequently involved in offset arrangements.

The industrial and commercial compensation practices required to offset the purchase of military-related exports generally include-

1. Co-production: Overseas production based upon a government-to-government agreement that permits a foreign government or producer to acquire the technical information to manufacture all or part of the US origin defence articles.
2. Licensed production.
3. Sub-contractor production: The sub-contract does not necessarily involve licence of technological information and is usually a direct commercial arrangement.
4. Overseas investment: Investment arising from the offset agreement, usually taking the form of capital invested to establish or expand a subsidiary or joint venture in the foreign country.
5. Technology transfer: As a result of an offset agreement, research and development may be conducted abroad; technical assistance may be provided to the subsidiary or the joint venture partner; or other activities under direct commercial arrangement.
6. Direct offsets include any business that relates directly to the product being sold; generally, the foreign vendor seeks local contractors in joint ventures, to co-produce certain parts.
7. Indirect offsets include all business unrelated to the product being sold; generally the vendor is asked to buy a country's goods or invest in an unrelated business; or
8. A combination of direct and indirect offsets.

According to industry sources offsets do not result in artificial pricing, because companies do not view offsets as a subsidy or financial loss, but rather as a means of incorporating a completed product or investment into their operations. Extra costs associated with offset arrangements do result in lower profit margins. A typical agreement requests that 20 to 100 per cent of the invoice value of the original product be offset, and competition may even causes the offset offer to be sometimes higher than 100 per cent of the sale spread over time. The implementation of an offset is difficult and time consuming, sometimes taking upto 20 years to complete. "Offsetters" often try to use the products themselves.

Sales agreements involving countertrade with Asia grew at a greater rate than those with the NATO countries of Europe. Sales agreements principally with Canada and Australia, accounted for 31 per cent of all countertrade sales agreements. Aerospace products were the single largest group of products involved in export sales agreements associated with countertrade (including military offsets). During 1980-84, the total countertrade obligation of US $ 11.0 billion, West Europe accounted for both the largest share of the US countertrade obligations, with 52 per cent (US $ 5.8 billion) of the total obligation, and the largest share of total sales agreements involving countertrade.

Virtually all the NATO obligations involved offsets associated with military related exports. Military offsets also made up a substantial portion of the obligations of non-NATO Europe, Asia and all other countries. The value of countertrade obligations accounted for by Asian countries reflected the high percentage of aerospace products associated with countertrade (including military offsets) sales agreements, aerospace products represented only 20 per cent of the total countertrade obligations. The large percentage of the aerospace product obligation fulfilled is, in part, attributable to the fact that during the early period of the time-frame investigated, the obligations were heavily weighted towards aerospace products.

The largest concentration (27 per cent) of non-military countertrade sales agreements were with Asian countries, followed by Europe. Although counterpurchase agreements are sometimes difficult to negotiate and complete, they have become more prevalent because they usually require less time and effort on the part of the Western/Japanese firms than other types of reciprocal trade/sales agreements.

The countertrade obligation is a commitment to perform some reciprocal trade transactions, for example, buy and/or market the foreign country's goods and services, transfer technology, or take back the resultant product. Counterpurchase obligations were by far the most frequently mentioned type of non-military countertrade obligation.

Between 1982 and 1984, the average ratio was over 90 per cent. These ratios reflect a trend towards smaller and more numerous contracts in which the countertrade obligation constituted a significant portion of the sales agreement. The increase in the ratio over the five year period reflects a higher countertrade obligation because of increased demand and international competition willing to countertrade.

During 1980-84, the US Military export sales increases steadily from US $ 7.0 billion (1980) to US $ 11.2 billion (1984) or by 61 per cent. The severe annual fluctuations in the value of reported military related export sales is a result of the sporadic flow of major weapons system purchased by foreign governments. In 1982, there was a notable decrease in the value of exports sales contracts and associated offset obligations that paralleled the worldwide recession.

Offset demand increased, in part, in order to help purchasing countries balance deteriorating current accounts and check the outflow of foreign exchange. Other reasons for increased offset demands include the desire for economic development through technology transfer and the desire for development of an industrial base.

The average fulfillment time allowed for all offset obligations was 61 months.

The increase of more than 100 per cent in the total face value of the sales contracts during 1980-84 and reflects increased sales by the United States arms manufacturers of the components and services used for weapons systems developed by foreign industries, particularly, the established arms industries in Western Europe and the newer arms-exporting nations in Asia.

There is a trend for virtually all new export sales agreements to contain some type of offset requirements, the offset requirement will either be negotiated to extend over a longer implementation period or subsequently negotiated out of the sales agreement. Communication equipment accounted for the largest category of products involved in sales agreements associated with offset obligations of US $ 2 million or less.

More US firms were accepting larger obligations in the face of increased international competition for military-related export sales. Annual sales agreement fluctuations are, in part, a result of periodic sales or major weapons systems and updates. This increase reflects, in part, the spreading use of offsets in the area, the difficulty of paying for imports through conventional means, external debt problems, and a desire for transfer of technology.

Aircraft, guided missiles and space vehicles and parts were the category of products most likely to be involved in the offset obligation, just as they accounted for the greatest portion of the face value of the sales agreement. The US firms were accepting larger offset obligations in the face of increased international competition for military-related export sales.

The increase is also related to the growing demand of many foreign aerospace industries for state-of-the-art production technology. The third phase in an offset agreement after the signing of the initial export sales contract and agreeing to an offset obligation, is the fulfillment of the obligation. Most of the direct offset fulfillment was accounted for by sub-contractor production in foreign countries and about one-third was accomplished through co-production arrangements with foreign-based entities. This shared arrangement is often advantageous for both the prime and the sub-contractor. The sub-contractor may often negotiate an offset obligation directly with the buyer on behalf of the prime firm.

The largest number of new or enhanced sources of non-defence-related goods and services occurred in the area of electronic components and accessories, where seven new sources emerged mainly in Australia, Israel, Hongkong, Singapore, and the Republic of Korea. For defence-related goods and services, new or enhanced sources emerged mainly in the manufacture of aircraft and parts, electronic components and accessories and turbines and engines. Australia and Israel together accounted for many of the new sources, followed by Denmark, Norway and the United Kingdom. The fulfillment of offset obligations resulted in 26 new or expanded competitors to sub-contractors and 32 new or expanded markets, mainly in the aircraft and parts industry.

Offsets are increasingly being required by both industrialised and developing countries in all areas of international trade.

Offset deals create new business activity where it otherwise might not exist and also create new trading partners. Companies accept offset arrangements to enhance their business activities to gain market share and/or access to markets, generate greater profits, and/or improve operating efficiencies by enlarging production runs. The enhanced business activity leads, in turn, to lower costs of those goods and increased employment, and a better balance of payments. Military sales play an important role in increasing private sector employment throughout the economy, especially in manufacturing.

Offsets also increase tax revenue, since foreign military exports are treated as sales to foreign customers. Co-production agreements serve to assist allies in improving their non-military-related industrial capability and, therefore, their overall defence posture as well. Other benefits of co-production include standardisation of military hardware, establishment of secondary sources for potential use for follow-up and logistical support, and after-sales service.

Purchasing governments are turning to offsets to reduce the impact of military equipment purchases on their domestic budgets and trade accounts. Purchasing countries view offsets as a means of revitalizing their economy and building up their defence capabilities while limiting the outflow of scarce foreign exchange.

Offset arrangements allow LDCs to purchase military equipment that they could otherwise not afford. These countries hope to expand employment and increase the competitiveness of local industry by acquiring technology through offset agreements. The purchasing country can continue to utilize the technology and manufacture components even after offset obligations are fulfilled. They can force other countries to make investments in their economies that would not normally occur and receive assistance in the marketing of their exports. One drawback that offsets may present to the purchasing country is that the price of exports may have to be reduced in order to compensate the producer for the risks and inconvenience associated with the offset obligation. Another is that offset goods may displace sales in traditional, non-restricted markets and may not lead to a net increase in earnings from trade.

The economic and political difficulties that arose in many debtor countries as a result of trade problems and efforts to correct them led many debtor country governments to make use of the leverage they had as importers. By insisting on countertrade, debtor country governments, and in some instances private LDC firms, channeled back the pressure that their creditors imposed on them through the system of multilateral settlements. Many debtor-country governments saw countertrade as an opportunity to halt the deterioration of their current account deficits by balancing every transaction and assuring imports deemed vital for the functioning of their economies regardless of costs. Competition among Western/Japanese multi-national firms and the ability of these companies to adjust to new situations and absorb inefficiencies has helped proliferate international countertrade.

IMF Conditionality Restraints

Six specific factors that, in addition to non-oil producing LDC and non-market economy government policies face to increase the role of countertrade are conditions attached to International Monetary Fund (IMF) assistance; commercial bank lending restrictions; LDC import restrictions through exchange-rate policies and restrictions on hard-currency repatriation; export promotion; competition among Western/Japanese firms and absorption of countertrade into corporate business practices; and growth in commodity movements traditionally not accompanied by monetary transactions.

The major qualitative change that occurred in the worldwide use of countertrade during the 1980-82 and 1985-87 world recession was that in many LDC that previously had not relied heavily on these trading methods, began to do so. The non-market economies had always sought bilateral arrangements leading to countertrade in their foreign commercial relations. Their effort to sustain the flow of Western imports since 1980 further increased their interest in countertrade. In 1980-82 and 1985-87 recession that handicapped the restoration of external equilibriums of debtor nations, reinforced incentives for and commitments of debtor countries to rely on countertrade. In '89-90 also commodity prices are weakening.

The present world-wide protectionist pressure may also have contributed to this growth. The capital movements that resulted in large-scale external debts during the period 1973-80 had two major directions; from the non-oil producing to the oil-producing nations following the 1973-74 energy crisis and from the West to non-oil-producing LDCs and Eastern European non-market economies later during and after 1970s.

To a considerable extent, the industrial countries were able to finance their post-oil shock deficits by attracting direct inflows of OPEC funds and by borrowing in the international bond markets. Non-oil-producing LDCs and Centrally planned economies began to build up their foreign debts by borrowing from Euro-markets, Western Official lenders, and international organisations. Although these countries borrowed to finance short-term current account deficits and structural adjustments initiated by the industrialised countries, much of their borrowings served only to finance balance-of-payments without any significant capital formation.

The lack of foreign exchange associated with the deterioration of current account balances of non-oil-producing LDCs and non-market economies was the probable underlying cause that led to the proliferation of international countertrade. The following fac-tors were crucial in the current account balance, deterioration of non-oil-producing LDCs and Eastern European Centrally planned economies during 1973-80:

1. Deterioration in the overall terms of trade for non-oil producing LDCs and Eastern European non-market economies;
2 moderation in the growth of industrialised nations;
3. increases in the costs of financing from international capital markets;
4. domestic factors in non-oil-producing LDCs and Eastern European Centrally planned economies that constrained external adjustment policies.

Several debtor nations are under obligation to the IMF to conserve their foreign exchange reserves for the purpose of reducing their payments arrears. Such an obligation adds as an incentive for debtor nations to shift from currency based trade to countertrade, by increasing both exports and imports through countertrade at the expense of currency resources while requesting debt rescheduling.

If a given debtor country's economy is heavily dependent on imported resources, countertrade helps to maintain its level of domestic production and employment. The improvement of trade balances is one of the IMFs conditions for supporting stabilisation programmes in debtor nations. If the capital goods acquired through countertrade play a crucial role in a developing country's export development programme, countertrade may indeed help in improving the country's trade balance in the short term. Intentions by debtor nations to comply with these requirements for fear of losing the IMF's support have contributed to the spread of countertrade in international commerce.

Commercial Bank-lending Restrictions

The debt crisis reduced funds available for financing North-South and East-West trade from Western/Japanese commercial banks. This reduction was the result of the commercial banks' perception of risks associated with the acquisition of short-term, customarily high-interest bearing assets from countries in financial crisis. Regulatory measures by some Western/Japanese governments may have also played a part in lending restrictions by Western/ Japanese commercial banks and acted as an incentive for traders to engage in countertrade, since these trading methods allowed the stretching of funds available for trade financing.

Trading houses may assume part of the loan needed for the transaction or, by depositing in escrow account the proceeds from an advance sale of bartered and countertraded goods for the Western/Japanese seller, the LDC or non-market economy partner may have a positive balance in a Western/Japanese commercial bank. This helps an LDC or Centrally planned economy firm to retain its hard-currency earnings in addition to facilitating future commercial loans. The high real rates of interest caused by a relatively low supply of funds had also contributed to the spread of international countertrade.

Import restrictions through exchange-rate policies have been an integral part of efforts by debtor nations to correct their external imbalance. If LDC importers succeed in getting better deals through countertrade then they would, by importing with expensive foreign currency, they may in fact, be selectively revaluing their country's currency. To the extent countertraders get better deals than they would, by importing with currency, they create their own import subsidy programme.

Over-valuation and exchange controls create the need for the rationing of the country's sparse foreign exchange reserves. Although foreign exchange policies are part of a large variety of import restricting systems, any potentially effective system creates an incentive for private LDCs and Western/Japanese firms to circumvent it through countertrade. Obstacles to hard currency repatriation by certain LDC governments have led Western/Japanese firms to engage in countertrade deals. Blocked currency reserves are spent by Western/Japanese firms to acquire goods from the local market for resale in world markets or in the home-country market. A Western government's assistance to its exporters facing countertrade demands is forthcoming if the goods to be acquired through such deals are also vital for the country's economy. Development for Import (DFI) programme may be a convenient counter trade arrangements to secure supplies from another country.

The availability of inexpensive government credit to the Western/Japanese supplier of a foreign development project may itself be an incentive to a Western/Japanese firm to accept countertrade demands from foreign partners. Western/Japanese governments may also be forced to accommodate the countertrade demands their exporters face in LDCs because non-market economy countries generate competition for them through efforts to develop long-term bilateral relations with these countries. Western/ Japanese competition contributes to the increase of countertrade. In order to shore up their competitive positions, multinationals have engaged in a competitive acceptance of countertrade demands by LDCs and Centrally planned economies. Some Western/Japanese firms may transfer some of their most advanced technology through buy-back agreements to these countries.

Many large, successful Western/Japanese firms have integrated countertrade into their business routine. Some of them openly use countertrade as a marketing tool and allegedly use some of the acquired commodities as a hedge against instability in financial markets. Some Western/Japanese firms have also found that countertrade reduces their risks of non-payments by importers, especially in the case of heavily indebted countries. The relatively high costs of countertrade transactions compared with currency-based trade has created a profit incentive in Western/Japanese corporate business life to improve the efficiency of these trading methods.

Multi-laterisation of Countertrade

Innovative new schemes such as the London-based countertrade data centre or the creation of International Trading Certificates (ITCs) tend to make countertrade multilateral. The increasing expertise and expanding contacts of trading houses specializing in countertrade, and the in-house countertrade units of multinational corporations may themselves have become a factor contributing to the growth of international countertrade.

Long before the onset of the current worldwide growth of countertrade, a distinct opportunity to obviate monetary transactions had been recognised. Inter-firm production cooperation and the transportation of homogeneous goods, under bilateral (or multilateral) industrial cooperation arrangements, firms from different countries may at least partially assume the control of industrial plants under unified management. Since deliveries under such cooperation agreements will be similar to deliveries within an industrial firm, the role of monetary transactions will be relegated to settling balance at the end of the stipulated periods.

The growing number and variety of international micro-economic links create opportunities for economizing on monetary transactions. Growth in output produced under such cooperation agreements also means growth in countertrade.

Swaps

Barter arrangements among suppliers of homogeneous goods, crude oil, metals, chemicals, and agricultural products to save transportation costs are termed "Swaps". Efforts to restrain the growth of countertrade; efforts to restrain the growth of countertrade have taken place in the context of the OECD where a consensus of members has been sought on limiting use of these techniques.

During 1980-82, the number of countries either requiring countertrade (including military offsets) for both the private and public sectors of their economies, (2) pursuing countertrade on a bilateral basis, or (3) establishing bilateral payment agreements has grown dramatically. Only 23 countries were involved in offset obligations with military-related export sales. A hundred countries were particularly active in countertrade.

The US firms reported that they engaged in non-military countertrade and military offsets primarily because it was required by a foreign government. Such agreements were entered into because they provided a market share. The US countertrade including offsets occurred with most European countries except France. Most cooperative efforts, co-production and direct offsets occur within NATO member countries and other West European nations, which have the infrastructure to absorb offsets, but most indirect offsets occur with non-NATO countries. Several countries—Spain, Greece, Finland, and Yugoslavia have demanded fulfillment of offset obligations with tourism (an indirect offset) in contrast to large capital projects and high technology offsets associated with the remaining West European countries.

Prior to 1980, countertrade played a supporting function in trade with Eastern Europe, since Western banks provided generous lines of credit to their East European counterparts for financing imports. East European countries instituted countertrade requirements for products that were difficult to market in Western nation and in cases where East European countries had exhausted their credits from bilateral trade, but yet desired continuing imports.

East European countries were forced to resort to countertrade not only with LDCs, but also to increase the use of countertrade transactions with Western/Japanese corporations. The use of such transactions by East European countries has increased significantly owning to:

Deteriorating quality and product design of Eastern European Products that Western/Japanese firms must accept in countertrade;

lack of availability of desirable countertrade products, which forces Western/Japanese companies to purchase other less marketable goods;

risking countertrade quotas, which oblige Western/Japanese companies, in some cases, to accept more than 100 per cent worth of goods in countertrade;

increasing unsuitability of East European suppliers;

risking price levels in East Europe-Foreign Trade Organizations-FTOs use of "unrealistically high domestic price levels to calculate prices of counterrade goods", and increasing use of third-country-limitation clauses in sales contracts, as well as the use of contract clauses preventing barter houses from fulfilling contracts, both of which act to reduce competition.

Rather than exporting raw materials, most East European nations now promote the export of finished goods, such as machines and high technology products, and services. Selling raw materials is a more efficient means of earning hard currency in the short-term because of the lower amount of local currency used to produce a product of quality that compares with those produced outside Eastern Europe. Finished goods require a higher local currency input and are frequently more difficult to sell in market economies because of their generally perceived inferior quality design.

USSR

The Soviets promote five types of countertrade—
(1)   Natural resource/raw-material cooperation agreements with partial or full payments in the resultant products;
(2)   industrial cooperation agreements (ICAs) with partial payment in the resultant products;
(3)   ICAs with partial payment in unrelated products;
(4)   licensing agreements with partial payment in the resultant products; and
(5)   barter arrangements or products and equipment.

Industrial cooperation agreements, outside of natural resource/raw-material arrangements, are business arrangements that extend over a period greater than two years, provide for the transfer or production technology, and involve close managerial contacts.

The large increases in military obligations in 1981-84 were primarily a result of large-scale US military sales to Israel. The extent to which countertrade is used in the Middle East countries varies among countries. Turkey permits countertrade transactions only on a government-to-government basis.

Jordan, used its primary export-phosphates/potash—barter transactions: Israel mandated countertrade in early 1983, particularly in cases involving government purchases. Israel also receives trade offset arrangements from the United States in its FMS (Foreign Military Sales) purchases.

Saudi Arabia

Saudi Arabia has not mandated countertrade, but in early 1983 a formalised offset policy was established for contracts under its "Peace Shield" defence programmes. The Saudis will spend US $ 1.2 billion for a ground-based air defence command and control and communications system. A large countertrade deal was negotiated for purchase of aircraft from the UK.

The size of the offset obligation has not yet been determined but is expected to be implemented over the next 10 years. Saudi Arabia has begun to use countertrade involving petroleum for goods/services. In mid-1984, the Saudi Government concluded a barter deal of approximately US $ 1 billion in petroleum for 10 aircrafts from a major US aerospace company.

Pakistan and other Asian Experiences

Pakistan does not officially sanction countertrade, but some state trading organizations have used countertrade intensively to finance certain imports. Bangladesh and Burma specially have limited experience with such trade.

India

Although India does not have a formal policy on countertrade, it has engaged in such transactions through bilateral trade and link—special trading and countertrade agreements through state trading agencies and a new apex trading organisation has been set up to balance canalised imports against exports.

Thailand

Thailand, through a parastatal trading company, has engaged in government-to-government countertrade exchanges for agro-products.

Philippines/S. Korea

The Philippines and the Republic of Korea have also engaged in countertrade transactions.

Indonesia

Indonesia, since early 1982, has encouraged countertrade for public-sector purchases with foreign suppliers. After 1983-84, the Indonesian Government relaxed the restrictions imposed on foreign suppliers.

Malaysia

In early 1983, Malaysia expanded countertrade to be included in government purchases involving foreign suppliers and recently began strict enforcement of these laws.

China

China persues countertrade transactions primarily to acquire priority products aerospace high-tech and sophisticated manufactures/equipment

Latin America

Countries with such policies include Brazil, Columbia, Costa Rica, Bolivia, Ecuador, Honduras, Jamaica, Mexico, Venezuela, and Uruguay. Although Brazil's official policies do not specifically mandate countertrade, Brazilian state-owned enterprises engage in countertrade and the Government of Brazil has signed bilateral clearing arrangements. In early 1985, Brazil signed a barter agreement with Nigeria to exchange Brazilian goods for Nigerian petroleum worth upto US $ 1 billion. Mexico also does not mandate countertrade; however, in its December 1982 "Exchange Controls Decree" Mexico established the legal foundations for countertrade.

Although Argentina, Chile, and Peru do not have official policies or laws legitimizing countertrade, they have in the past engaged in such activities. Argentina has engaged in government-to-government countertrade. Chile has no formal policy on countertrade, but the government recognizes countertrade as a mechanism for preserving foreign exchange.

In a number of Latin American countries, countertrade appears to be concentrated in state-owned enterprises and in government-to-government transactions and in others, countertrade appears principally in the private sector, in Mexico, Columbia, Honduras, Ecuador and Uruguay.

In these countries, regulations and legislations governing countertrade encompass traditional exports (typically agricultural commodities or natural resources) and generally specify that transactions involving these products are to be used to generate hard currency or foreign exchange, with non-traditional exports goods to be generally used in countertrade transactions.

There have been a number of actions taken by Latin American nations to facilitate countertrade transactions among them. In July, 1984, Mexico, Argentina and Brazil negotiated a three year agreement to suspend tariffs and import licences on a tripartite basis and to expand the use of unconventional trade mechanisms, especially countertrade. The three countries are members of the Association of Latin American Integration (ALADI), an organization that has adopted a pro-countertrade posture. Bolivia, Peru and Brazil negotiated an agreement to restrict the use of the US dollars in their tripartite trade, thus emphasizing unconventional financing, particularly countertrade. In August, 1984, delegates from the Andean Pact signatories Columbia, Venezuela, Ecuador, Bolivia and Peru met in Caracas, Venezuela to discuss formally the use of countertrade in restoring declining regional trade. Latin America's foreign debt amounts to $ 450 billion and a reverse flow has been in evidence lately.

Africa/Australasia

Countertrade expanded significantly during 1983-84 in various countries in Africa, Australia and Oceania. Major trends include the increasing emphasis of expanding countertrade transactions to include light consumer and industrial manufacturers and the increasing use of countertrade in government procurement programmes. Despite Stabex and ACP the African economies have deteriorated sharply.

African nations opposition to countertrade has begun to soften in the face of economic pressures to reduce external debt. Incentives to countertrade include decreased development funds from developed nations, depressed commodity prices and a deterioration of commercial sources of financing. A number of African Nations have engaged in countertrade transactions with East European countries and the Soviet Union and some developing countries through bilateral trade and clearing payment agreements.

Australia/New Zealand

Like Indonesia and Malaysia, Australia and Newzealand have acquired offsets in the procurement of major weapons systems. Countertrade (including military offsets) has been practiced more extensively in certain sectors of the economy than others. Exports of these industries were most affected by countertrade, aerospace, construction projects, electronics, defence, minerals and chemicals.

The United States maintains a competitive advantage in each of the above-mentioned high-technology industrial sectors. Countertrade of agricultural products occurs frequently among Third World countries. Countertrade obligations were undertaken primarily in the following industries—aircraft and parts, communications and electronics equipment and engines and turbines. New sources of supply and competitors for certain products are being created by countertrade particularly in military offset arrangements for newly created defence and non-defence sources of supply. The product areas of these new sources of supply include metal processing and fabrication, weapons, engines and turbines, aircraft and parts, communications and electronics equipment, and related computer and data processing services. Commercial aerospace offsets for tourism exist with Finland and Yugoslavia. Greece is reportedly interested in tourism offsets for promoting business conferences. Imports resulting from countertrade tend to disrupt domestic markets.

In the case of military export sales, a number of the US companies stated that there would have been no sales agreement without accepting the offset obligation. Presently more US multi-national corporations are using, or plan to use in-house trading operations to handle their countertrade arrangements. These in-house organizations differ both in the size and scope of their operations. Majority of the products obtained through contracts in which a non-military countertrade was negotiated were primarily used in-house.

42 per cent were absorbed in-house, and 23 per cent were sold by trading companies. Export sales related to military offsets do not have an adverse impact on domestic employment; such sales agreements have either helped maintain stable employment levels or increased them. Without the military export sales agreements with the accompanying offset obligation, there would have been a probable overall reduction in the work required and jobs available. Offsets represented, in many instances, a means of maintaining existing plant capacity and employment. Military export sales associated with offsets have resulted in more efficient utilisation and improvement of existing plant and equipment with stable and/or increased production.

Impact

Major benefits derived from such sales have ben larger production lots/runs, lower costs, capital expansion, increased employment and the development of new technology. Competitiveness has been maintained and prices have remained stable.

War-time surplus capacity has not been adversely affected because of military export sales involving offset obligations. Surge capacity is constrained by lead times on raw materials, parts and purchased equipment, and by plants and equipment limitations, rather than by offset obligations.

A few of the larger US multinational corporations have set up trading companies as independent subsidiaries with the expectations that the trading subsidiary will generate enough revenues and earnings to become a self-supporting, profitable enterprise. These trading companies supply services such as market research and development, importing and exporting, customs, documentation, financing, and product distribution for a fee to their parent companies as well as to others, usually smaller firms.

One of the primary functions of the trading company is to dispose off goods that the client firm is under contract to receive in a countertrade deal. It must find a buyer for the goods either through its own network of contacts in world markets or by engaging an agent or broker to arrange more complex deals. The in-house trading company may not act simply as a procurer of goods for its clients. It may take part in setting product specifications and delivery schedules to ensure that the countertraded goods are of comparable quality and compatible technology with those of other suppliers and that the availability of these products meets the needs of the client. When the client company cannot use the countertraded goods internally, the trading company must search elsewhere for a buyer. The in-house trading subsidiaries also generate revenues and earnings.

They use their trading expertise and networks to locate products to meet certain demands and to locate markets for certain products. These trading companies are active in trade among the LDCs and the Eastern bloc countries and collect fees for their services. Other activities of in-house trading companies may include purchasing certain goods outright and then reselling them at a profit and entering into joint ventures with manufacturing companies in which the trading company acts as a worldwide organisation.

The cost-profit centre trading organisation is a part of the company that is concerned primarily with satisfying the company's countertrade obligations. Some in-house organisations are devoted almost exclusively to finding buyers for countertrade goods supplied by foreign countries. They participate in any negotiations that are likely to involve countertrade and help the negotiators select the best available countertrade products. In-house trading organisation is responsible for choosing the most saleable products. Once the contract has been finalised, it is the responsibility of the trading organisation to market those goods.

Another type in-house marketing organisation works as an information broker, purveyor supplying details on products and services that are available in countries with which its company has countertrade commitments. Whenever an international trade transaction results from information or assistance provided by this trading organisation, the value of the transaction is credited towards the company's countertrade obligations. This type of trading organisation generally deals only with the products offered in trade and provides no specifications for these products. Many of these items are not marketable in the developed countries because of quality, style or technological considerations, this orgnisation deals with many third-party agents and buyers in LDCs.

A third type of in-house countertrade organisation seeks to satisfy its company's countertrade obligations by locating countertrade products suitable for the use within the company and not for resale. Large manufacturing organisations require many kinds of raw materials and supplies, ranging from bauxite and crude oil to work gloves and machine tools. The in-house trading organisation can choose countertraded goods to fill an existing need and satisfy the company's countertrade commitments. Again, the trading organisations must ensure that the countertrade goods are cash generating and that the delivery schedule is compatible with the company's needs.

The trading organisation has to be familiar with the potential markets and market values of the countertraded goods as well as with the products themselves, their quality, and the reliability of supply. Often the products offered in countertrade are overvalued by the producer.

The Trading company may try to negotiate a lower value that would more closely approximate to market value.

In order to determine the amount that the countertraded goods must be discounted, the countertrade organisation must have extensive knowledge of market values, market dynamics, and the product itself. On the basis of the expected market value and any costs associated with disposing off the product, the trading organisation estimates how much, if at all, the countertraded goods should be discounted. The trading organisation takes into account the fact that the market value at the time of negotiations may not be the same as at the time of the delivery of the goods. The trading organisations must build these risks into the price structure of the contract.

When the countertrade contract has been finalised, the company that has accepted goods in countertrade is faced with the task of disposing them off. If the product is one that the firm can use internally, it may replace supplies purchased for cash with countertraded items. Some are inputs into the production process, such as raw materials and semi-finished manufactured goods that the firm can turn into finished products. Others are items that can be used in the operations of the company. These include tools, machine parts, and office and work force supplies. The company receiving the countertraded goods has to overcome resistance within the company to giving up traditional suppliers.

Products that cannot be absorbed by the receiving company have to be sold elsewhere. This can be done either through an in-house trading organisation or through an agent or broker. Selling outside the company has the advantage of eliminating the risk of in-house acceptance problems. Distribution channels are already in place for similar items and may be used for countertraded goods as well. There is also the possibility that related products could be sold to sub-contractors.

There are some serious risks in selling countertraded goods that are closely related to the company's products. This is especially true ·if countertraded products are distributed through the same channels as the company's own products. Another danger is that the countertrade goods will cause an over-supply in the market-place. This would result in lower prices and profits and might cause the company's primary products to lose market share.

If the products accepted in countertrade are unrelated to the company's lines of business, disposal is a much more complex matter. To successfully market these goods, a wide range of knowledge and a large network of contracts are necessary. The technical expertise to find products that are marketable and the marketing expertise to find buyers for these products are not usually found within the company. They are likely to be found in a large, independent, in-house trading subsidiary or a third-party agent or broker. If opens up many more countertrade opportunities, because the company is not limited to a certain group of products.

The recent surge in countertrade as an alternative to cash has prompted many organisation to develop countertrade operations and new trading companies to be formed, following the enactment of the Export Trading Company Act of 1982. Fifty new US trading firms came into being, and another 50 are expected to start operations soon. There has been a similar growth in financial and legal services and in in-house trading. Each of these new organisations is looking for opportunities to market its particular expertise and carve out its own market niche. Several multinational corporations have established independent trading subsidiaries that are expected to be profit-making ventures. They arrange countertrade deals for other companies as well as their parent corporations. The primary selling point of these subsidiaries is that they can draw on the parent corporations for whatever market expertise and networks they can provide. To enhance their services they may also hire outside expertise to gain experience or knowledge not available internally or, in extremely complex deals, they may employ a broker or an agent.

Established, independent trading companies are adding countertrade units to their staffs, and new trading companies are springing up to meet the needs of aspiring exporters and countertraders. The independent trading company usually has more trading experience over a broader range of markets and a wider information and distribution network.

Commercial banks are well-suited to handle countertrade transactions, since they are already in the business of financing international
trade. Commercial banks are using countertrade as a financing
alternative. Commercial banks have an advantage, because their
customers are accustomed to coming to them for financing and may
trust them more than an untried trading company. Banks use their
international network of customers and contracts for countertrade deals.
Some banks seek the help of trading companies to consummate deals
and further broaden the scope of their business. There are some
difficulties for banks engaging in international trade—they usually have
little practical product experience.

Established law firms have also added countertrade units. The US
Government will not oppose the US companies' participation in
countertrade arrangements unless such action could have a negative
impact on national security;

The US Government will provide advisory and market intelligence
services to the US Business, including information on the
application of the US trade laws to countertrade goods;

The US Government will exercise caution in the use of its barter
authority, reserving it for those situations which offer advantages
not offered by conventional market operations.

The Treasury Department conducted a study of offset arrangements
in cooperation with the Aerospace Industrial Association and the
Electronics Industry Association. Two laws encompass offset practices;
the Arms Export and Control Act and the Defence Security Assistance
Agency guidelines on Memorandums of Agreements (MOAs),
Memorandums of Understanding (MOUs), and Defence Cooperation
Country Agreements (DCAs). The foreign government played a
paramount role in negotiating the offset obligation either as sole
negotiator or as an active participant in the negotiations.

The US Government barter programmes were first provided for in
the Commodity Credit Corporation (CCC) Charter Act of 1949 and
later incorporated into the Agricultural Trade Developed and Assistance
Act of 1954. The CCC did not enter into contracts with foreign
governments to deliver designated strategic materials or supplies and
services originating in specified countries, but rather with commercial
firms. During 1950-62, most barter transactions were called strategic
material contracts. These transactions involved exchanges of CCC-
owned commodities for strategic materials.

Such barter was for the procurement of foreign produced supplies and services for overseas military installations and for projects of the AID, rather than for procurement of strategic materials. These barter contracts were called offshore contracts for example, (the recent US-Jamaican barter agreement).

In November 1981, the President directed the Federal Emergency Management Agency to procure approximately 1.6 million tonnes of Jamaican bauxite for the national defence stockpile. This was the first major US Government barter agreement since 1967. This agreement partly replenished the US stockpiles of bauxite. It also permitted the CCC to dispose off surplus dairy products after consultation with the traditional suppliers (Canada, France and New Zealand) of such products to Jamaica. On November 17, 1983, another US-Jamaican barter agreement was signed that called for a total of 1 million tons of Jamaican bauxite to be exchanged for CCC-owned diary products and wheat valued at US $ 34 million. Delivery of all the products included in the agreement was to be completed in 1985.

The only other barter agreement that has been formally proposed to the United States was an arrangement whereby CCC-owned non-fat dry milk would be exchanged for fluorspar from Mexico. In late 1984, the Dominican Republic expressed interest in the barter of bauxite for CCC-owned dairy products. In mid-1984, Kenya discussed with the US Department of Agriculture a possible exchange of pyrethrum (an insecticide) for rice. The stockpiling of these materials is to preclude a costly and dangerous US dependence upon foreign sources of supply in times of national emergency.

During the 98th Congress, at least 26 bills were introduced to encourage barter or to expand existing barter legislation. Development of new markets was to be encouraged and the negotiation period of transactions to be shortened. No definitive barter bills were enacted during the 98th Congress. The 98th Congress expressed interest in certain types of countertrade by including section 309 in the Defence Production Act Amendments of 1984 on April 17, 1984.

During the 99th Congress, a number of bills that have sections dealing with the US Government barter or offsets were proposed and in some instances enacted. Eleven Bills dealt with the US Government barter in promoting the export of the US agricultural commodities through the CCC for the purpose of expanding markets or acquiring strategic materials. Many debtor countries reacted to the deterioration of their current account balances by turning to countertrade.

The Governments itself engage in countertrade deals. The Government's role in countertrade activities varies according to the

State's economic control in the country. It can include procuring supplies needed for its administrative functions (e.g., Brazil, Indonesia and Mexico). In some countries (e.g., India) State Trading Companies purchase commodities for distribution to private firms through commercial channels.

Governments Mandated Countertrade Deals

A Government commitment to improve the country's external imbalance through countertrade may result in bilateral trade agreements providing that imports into the country must be linked to purchases by the seller, or by the seller's government (e.g., Columbia, Ecuador and Malaysia). Non-market economy countries' countertrade activities increased after 1980, partly because of increases in centrally planned economy trade and partly because of stepped-up non-market economy countries efforts to do business with Western/Japanese and LDC partners through these trading methods.

In non-market economy countries trade is essentially conducted on an annually balanced barter basis, and it is predicated on the assumption that no structural imbalance will develop among the trading partners. Production requirements specified by the sum total of bilaterally balanced trade agreements are built into national economic plans and broken down to firm level. For an individual centrally planned economy, the production requirements arising from trade with non-market economies are as amenable to planning as domestic production targets. To the extent non-market economy trade grows, international countertrade also grows.

Centrally Planned Economy Trade Expansion

The non-market economies seeking non-NME trade, prefer trade relations that conform to their domestic economic mechanism. Active search for comprehensive trade protocols involving bilateral clearing and industrial cooperation agreements (maximizing the countertrade deals under such agreements) with non-NME countries is a major characteristic of NME foreign trade policies.

The growth of countertrade received a major impetus through West-East industrial cooperation when the NMEs embarked on their moderanization programme in the early 1970s. The NMEs have also expanded their trade with the LDCs under bilateral protocol and clearing agreements since the early 1970s.

In the LDCs the State generally has a greater direct role in economic management than in the West/Japan. LDCs are more amenable to concluding countertrade agreements with the non-market economies than are Western countries and Japan. Given the non-convertibility of NME currencies and the willingness of the MNEs to accept LDC currencies as payment for their export, trade protocols and clearing agreements between LDC and NME governments allow those countries to minimize the balances to be settled in hard currency. The current numbers of bilateral clearing agreement between LDCs and NMEs is 130, and the volume of LDD-NME trade turnover under the agreement has risen perceptibly since 1980s.

Non-market economies efforts to expand long-term bilateral relations with the LDCs are further strengthened by the opportunity that bilateralism provides to increase the role of planning in the Third World. The developed countries also employ countertrade when economic reasons justify it. Canada, Australia and New Zealand procure certain imports through countertrade. In the Western military equipment trade, offsets represent countertrade arrangements.

Deterioration in the Overall Terms of Trade for Non-oil Producing LDCs and Eastern European NMEs

Terms of trade for the non-oil-producing LDCs fell by an average of two per cent per year during 1972-82. The deterioration was clearly tied to oil price increases and the effects of such increases on national economic conditions and on international trade. Whereas the terms of trade of this group of countries during 1963-72 improved at an average rate of 0.5 per cent per year, the decline in theirterms of trade was 7.6 per cent in 1974-75 and 7.3 percent in 1980-82. Estimates clearly indicate that the dynamic pattern of deterioration in the combined hard-currency terms of trade of this group was similar to that of other oil-importing regions. The terms of trade deteriorated in 1985-86 with modest change in 1987. The reverse flow to developed countries has increased in last four years.

After 1973, the developed Western nations and Japan initiated a structural adjustment in their production, re-allocating resources from traditional industries to energy-producing, energy-saving, and high-technology industries. Non-oil producing LDCs and NMEs that embarked upon efforts to make structural adjustments in their economies saw a constant increase in the cost of Western/Japanese plant and equipment that were necessary for these adjustments. Thus, Western inflation contributed to the overall deterioration in their terms of trade. The deterioration in terms of trade continued in 1985-86 and even the modest recovery in metals/cereals was largely accounted for by dollar depreciation and has flattened out lately.

Growth in the West slowed after the energy crisis, reducing their import absorbing capacity of industrialized countries. The average growth rate of imports of industrialised countries fell from 9 per cent (1963-72) to 3.6 per cent (1973-82). Tariff preferences granted to LDCs and to some NMEs and a redirection of LDC and NME exports to oil-producing countries mitigated somewhat the declining demand for their products by the industrialised world.

Reasons for Western inflation after 1973—cost-push inflation as a result of delinking of dollar from gold, global inflation, energy and other shortages and structural shifts, demand stimulus through expenditure increasing policies to assure full-employment, and the wage-price spiral through the traditional, society-wide, Eastern bargaining process. The weighted average rate of increase in consumer prices for the group of 10 countries which includes Belgium, Canada, the Federal Republic of Germany, France, Italy, Japan, the Netherlands, Sweden, United Kingdom and the United States plus Switzerland was 5.0 per cent in 1972 and 13.7 per cent in 1974. Inflation came down in 80s but is again causing concern in UK, Italy, USA, Canada.

Servicing external debts did not represent a serious problem for many non-oil producing LDCs until 1978. Interest rates on capital markets climbed to post-war highs and the export prices of goods from these countries began to weaken. Expenditure increasing fiscal and monetary policies created fiscal deficits in many non-oil producing LDC countries.

Hungary's Economic Reforms

In NME only Hungary embarked on the implementation of a market-oriented economic reform aimed at correcting the causes of its current account deficit. The USSR and other East European countries have lately been attempting reforms and China followed a more liberalised policy in agricultural produce area. G.D.R. is entering into a monetary union with F.R.G.

GATT

GATT codes do not cover military defence trade. Consequently, the GATT rules do not apply to countertrade transactions between private parties or to offset arrangements, for government purchases of defence materials. The general view, however, is that countertrade *per-se* does not constitute a violation of the GATT; countertrade imposed by government law or regulation can be inconsistent with the GATT rules.

Countertrade arrangements have usually been organized in response to immediate economic problems—liquidity crisis, shrinking of export outlets for primary products, and disturbance of their patterns following the imposition of import controls.

Developing countries are using countertrade to increase exports to enable them to obtain hard currency and improve their competitive position. The heavily indebted developing countries are trying to reestablish their external balance through a reduction of their imports and a parallel expansion of their exports. Developing countries generally propose primary and semi-processed products as compensation for their imports. Countertrade operations presumably allow these countries to offer a concealed discount on the selling price, either directly or indirectly.

Requests for countertrade do not emanate exclusively from the developing countries. Western/Japanese firms suggest these procedures to countries that close their borders to their exports. These tendency may well continue as a large number of developing countries are facing problems of liquidity and indicating that countertrade is the only means of maintaining trade with these countries.

Summary of Country Experiences

Some of the country summaries support the following conclusions:

1. Countertrade figures most importantly in the foreign trade of non-market economies;
2. governments in the developing world generally prefer to restrict the use of countertrade to the importation of goods vital for the functioning and the development of their economies and to the promotion of their non-traditional exports and to gaining incremental markets for their traditional exports;
3. Western/Japanese firms are not beyond initiating such deals when their economic interests so demand it and
4. countertrade legislation and policies vary greatly from one nation to another.

Austria

The country's private firms are heavily involved in countertrade with the NMEs, particularly in Eastern Europe. The government has, on a occasion exerted pressure on Western Automobile manufacturers to engage in counterpurchase and co-production agreements with Austrian firms as a pre-condition for obtaining preferential tariff treatment for their auto sales in Austria. The government has succeeded in concluding several offsets in the purchase of military equipment. Austria has emerged as a local point for East-West trade.

Bulgaria

Bulgaria's countertrade requirements in commercial contracts with the West are among the highest of the non-market economy countries with levels from 30 to 100 per cent. Countertrade requirements are lower in transactions involving high priority imports for which hard currency has been set aside. Foreign Trade Organisations (FTOs) are given considerable flexibility in negotiating commercial contracts involving countertrade. Among the products that Bulgaria attempts to market through countertrade agreements are electrical and transport equipment, chemical products, textiles, and foodstuffs. Bulgarian authorities place increasing emphasis on joint ventures with Western firms. Bulgaria countertraded agro-products for its machinery/equipment imports.

Czechoslovakia

Czechoslovakia requires countertrade on all items except hard-currency producing imports and energy/technology products. Since 1983, countertrade demands for over 100 per cent have been reported. Imports include high technology, energy equipment, mining equipment and food packaging machinery.

Denmark

There is no government countertrade programme *per-se* in Denmark. Denmark has been involved with military offset arrangements in the production of the F-16 aircrafts.

East Germany (GDR)

East Germany countertrade agreements, especially counter-purchase and compensation deals, are an integral part of the country's trade with the West. This is likely to undergo change after the monetary union with F.R.G.

France

The French Government has expressed serious reservations about the use of government-mandated countertrade. A countertrade policy and trade facilitation unit (Service de Compensation) has been organised within the Trade Ministry's Foreign Trade Relations Unit. The government has established an organisation known as SODIMEX which is responsible for encouraging purchases of French high technology products by countries with heavy foreign debts. A semi-official organisation known as the Association Pourla Compensation des Exchanges Commerciaux (ACCO) was established in 1978 by various trade associations and five major banks to provide countertrade consulting services to its members which include France's top exporting companies. France has bilateral clearing agreements with Algeria, China, Iraq, Syria and Vietnam. Products which have reportedly been purchased through countertrade include coal, phosphates, textiles, agricultural products, coffee, rice and manioc. France has reportedly sold anti-aircraft defence systems, fertilisers, wheat, flour, butter, insecticides and rice mill through countertrade or offset arrangements.

Greece

The Government of Greece requires offsets, including countertrade, under its government procurement policy. Each year the Ministry of National Economy issues an extensive list of Greek products available for countertrade. International Trade Co. (ITCO), a government-owned export trading company was organised to promote the export of Greek products. ITCO has negotiated export agreements with West Germany, Sweden, Albania, Iran, Bulgaria and Egypt. ITCO is the only government-controlled company authorised to negotiate countertrade contracts with Eastern Europe and China.

Hungary

Countertrade had been practiced less frequently in Hungary than in the Soviet Union, Poland, or Rumania. Countertrade demands vary according to the type of import and individual FTO involved in the arrangement. Since 1983, Hungary has increased its countertrade demands in order to improve the country's hard currency position. A large variety and volume of Hungarian goods are offered in countertrade and long-term cooperation agreements are sought in the areas of electrical power, chemicals, machinery and food processing. Hungary has pushed through major economic reforms of recent late.

Poland

The country's difficult external finances in the 1980s have been a major factor in generating countertrade between Western and Polish Firms. Poland leads the countries of Eastern Europe in the volume of trade conducted through countertrade arrangements. Polish countertrade demands are estimated to range from 30 to 50 percent of the contract value of total exports. The countries requirements for countertrade are particularly strong in the purchase of capital goods. The Western exporting firms can often counterpurchase Polish goods from other ETOs rather than exclusively from the buyer of its goods. Poland has also liberalised its venture policies to attract investments.

Rumania

In 1980, Rumania became the first East European nation to legally mandate the use of countertrade. A compensation quota of at least 100 per cent is initially required of all Western/Japanese firms engaging in countertrade with Rumania. Products which are frequently offered by Rumania in countertrade include machinery and vehicles, chemical products, and electrical equipment. Penalties for non-fulfillment of countertrade obligations range from 20-30 percent on machinery and vehicles to 15 per cent on chemicals.

Soviet Union

The Soviet Union is the world's largest countertrader in:

1. Natural resource/raw material cooperation agreements with partial or full payments in resultant products,
2. industrial cooperation agreements with partial payments in resultant products,
3. industrial cooperation agreements with partial payment in unrelated products,
4. licensing agreements with partial payments in products and
5. barter arrangements of products and equipment.

Soviet countertrade demands are the highest for chemicals and consumer goods. Buy-back arrangements have been used to finance large capital projects, particularly in the chemical and gas sectors. Since 1983, approximately 45 large industrial projects have been commissioned on this basis. The Soviet Union has engaged in extensive barter arrangements with Middle-Eastern countries, exchanging weapons and consumer goods for oil. These transactions have been conducted mainly with Iran, Iraq and Libya.

Under a system of five year barter arrangements initiated in 1951, the Soviet Union and Finland maintain balanced trade accounts with each other. The Soviet Union is guaranteed a market for energy exports and a source of high quality goods. Other countries with which the Soviets have reportedly concluded countertrade bilateral/clearing and payments deals include Brazil, Guyana, Peru, India, Austria, Rumania and F.R.G.

Spain

Countertrade is a relatively new practice in Spain. The majority of Spanish countertrade deals have been conducted with LDCs in Africa and Latin America and to a limited extent with Eastern Europe. The Ministry of Defence has instituted offset requirements for major Spanish military purchases.

Sweden

In June, 1984 the Government acquired a controlling share in SUKAB, a private-sector trading company established during World War II which has now become parastatal. Countertrade is expected to account for more than 8 per cent or more of total Swedish trade by the end of the decade. Approximately 20 per cent of Sweden's sales to Eastern Europe are affected by countertrade. Sweden has also concluded buy-back arrangements with China and Brazil and link agreements with India and Bangladesh. Offsets are a growing factor in Sweden's trade with OECD countries, particularly with regard to Military and Telecommunications Equipments.

Federal Republic of Germany

In practice, the government realises that West German companies must engage in countertrade in order to maintain foreign sales in countries faced with foreign exchange shortages. The government is willing to accommodate East-West countertrade rather than North-South countertrade. West Germany has reportedly exchanged auto technology, machine tools, chemical plants, steel and equipments for engines gas and oil. Nigeria, Libya and Saudi Arabia have also required countertrade in conjunction with deliveries of machinery. At least five major barter companies have been established in West Germany. Siemens and Mettalgessalgs fact, Krupp, have large countertrade units.

Yugoslavia

A system of semi-governmental community organisations of "Size" has developed to monitor such arrangements. Countertrade arrangements are also managed at the provincial level. Requirements are higher for consumer than for capital goods and range from 40 to 100 per cent. Imports which have been associated with Yugoslavian countertrade deals include aircraft, crude oil and petroleum products.

China

Since 1978, China has emphasised compensation and buy-back arrangements. Administrative regulations were drafted in 1979 and revised in 1981 that establish an approval process for countertrade deals and give special customs tariff incentives for compensation transactions. China has concluded hundreds of these agreements with Western nations and Japan. The majority of compensation arrangements undertaken thus far have involved projects in light industry, electronics, and foodstuff, located primarily in the coastal provinces and in Special Economic Zones and lately in automobiles, aircraft, sport shoes, etc. The Chinese have also negotiated joint venture that involve buy-back and exports derived from new production capacities and offsets against aerospace supplies.

Indonesia

The policy of using countertrade in government procurements had been
strictly applied. All government imports in excess of 500 million
rupiahs must be compensated by Indonesian products. The major items
of import through countertrade are fertilizers, electrical plants, textile
manufacturing machinery, diesel locomotive, other railroad and
telecommunications equipment, cement and raw materials. The
government offers to its potential sellers about 33 products. Goods
include rubber, coffee, pepper, tobacco, manioc, cement, sawn timber,
plywood, textile products, garments, etc. Lately exports of garments
specially wood have greatly increased.

West Germany, Japan, the United States, Singapore and Rumania
are the country's major countertrade partners.

Iran

Japan, the Soviet Union, Brazil, India, Pakistan and Taiwan are some
of Iran's significant countertrade partners. Oil is the country's chief
countertrade commodity.

Iraq

The seven year war with Iran had forced the country to make limited
commitments to use oil in settling obligations with French, South
Korean, Italian and Indian companies. Iraq occasionally countertrades oil
for military equipment and is now engaged in post-war reconstruction
programmes.

Israel

The Industrial Cooperation Authority within the Ministry of Industry
and Trade is responsible for administrating the country's countertrade.
Authorities emphasize long-term industrial cooperation as the most
beneficent form of countertrade for the country's economy.

Japan

In trade with the NMEs debtor and LDC countries, Japanese firms are
being confronted with strong demands to engage in countertrade, which
is mainly organised through the nine large general trading companies
(Sogo Sosha) like Mitsui, Mitsubishi C. Itoh, Marubine Nissho-Iwai,
Sumifonro.

Republic of Korea

The Government has a comprehensive official offset programme. The countertrade Promotion Committee within the Ministry of Commerce and Industry, monitors countertrade developments. The General Trading Co's—Daewoo, Samsung, Hyundai, Lucky and Goldstar are actively engaged in countertrade deals.

Malaysia

The government will engage in countertrade with any of the following five groups of countries:

1. Countries that supply goods for major Malaysian development projects;
2. countries with which Malaysia is experiencing persistent trade deficits;
3. developing countries that are important and growing markets for Malaysian commodities facing sharp competition ;
4. specialist countries experiencing similar difficulties ;
5. oil producing/exporting countries that obtain their imports in proportion to purchases of oil from them.

A special Government Agency within the ministry of Trade and Industry called *Unit Khas Countertrade* of the International Trade Division is in-charge of countertrade:

(i) Formulating and implementing policies and guidelines on countertrade;

(ii) collecting and disseminating information on products available for countertrade and on potential sellers and buyers of countertrade goods;

(iii) handling and approving proposals for countertrade deals from domestic firms as well as from foreign governments and firms;

(iv) advising other government agencies on the use of countertrade in their purchases; and

(v) monitoring implementation of the countertrade deal, Bills of lading, packing list, commercial invoices, customs declarations in Malaysia and letters of credit are accepted evidence of performance by a foreign partner.

All government agencies must include countertrade conditions in tender documents for certain Government procurements. National Petroleum Co., and firms producing cocoa and palm oil also export commodities through countertrade. The following commodities may be acquired through countertrade:

Rice, wheat, sugar, iron ore, cotton, coal, animal feeds, chemical products, fertilizers, machinery and equipment, defence equipment and vehicles.

Malaysian footwear, textiles, articles of rubber and wood, foodstuffs and electrical goods and components are among the manufactures and semi-manufactured goods that the government lists as available for countertrade. The government restricts the use of primary commodities in countertrade when such goods can be easily moved in international markets or when the purchasing country has demonstrated foreign exchange to purchase such goods.

The countertrade goods must be destined to the country of origin of the tenderer, although a different destination may be approved on a case-by-case basis; and the countertrade goods must not displace exports for free currency, they must be directed to new markets and must not involve goods that may otherwise be sold for free currency on world market.

Pakistan

Pakistan has bilateral trade agreements with several NMEs. These agreements entail countertrade to an extent which has grown of late.

The Philippines

The raw materials vitally important for the national economy, goods in scarce supply and goods that can be readily sold to a third party are allowed to be imported through countertrade. A special trading company negotiates and administers deals with the NMEs. The country's major countertrade products include food products, tobacco, petroleum, chemicals, manufactured goods, and machinery and transport equipment. Various countertrade agreements were ensured into with Japanese, Korean Co's.

Saudi Arabia

The country has a formal policy requiring offsets on certain defence and aerospace contracts. There is interest in the country to institute a coun-tertrade policy designed to promote non-traditional exports of sulphur, downstream petro-chemicals and fertilisers.

United Arab Emirates

Countertrade appears to be limited to transactions involving payments for petroleum and petroleum products and for vital imports.

Argentina

The government's involvement with countertrade in the past has been limited to clearing arrangements with several countries including the Soviet Union, China and Iraq. Products that have reportedly been exported in countertrade deals include grain, wine, wool, beef and other foodstuffs.

Bolivia

The government uses countertrade for the acquisition of capital goods required for the completion of infrastructural development projects. The Chamber of Commerce and the Chamber of Industry (Trade Associations) pool information for the Government on the availability of Bolivian goods for countertrade. Minerals, coffee and wool are the country's major countertrade goods. The United States is one of Bolivia's most important countertrade partner.

Brazil

Its state-owned company (Petrobras) has engaged in countertrade with oil-producing countries through its subsidiary (Interbras). Since 1983, Brazil has attempted to pay for oil imports with other means than cash. The majority of Brazil's countertrade agreements, including one with Nigeria, have involved the exchange of Brazilian goods such as sugar, salt, cotton, chemicals and construction materials for imports of petroleum. Brazil has also signed countertrade agreements with Ecuador, the Soviet Union, Angola, China, Iraq, the United Arab Emirates and Indonesia involving iron and steel, petroleum derivatives, agricultural and textile products. In November, 1984, Brazil passed legislation requiring offset concessions for aircraft purchases.

Columbia

In 1984, the government instituted several regulations governing special trade practices such as barter and compensation. These regulations were modified by a temporary law in February, 1984 which mandated countertrade as a pre-condition for the importation of some 30 products. Emeralds and coffee have been countertraded for transport equipment/machinery.

Ecuador

The National Monetary Board, determines policy guidelines and general rules on countertrade. Only goods that are difficult to move on international markets will be countertraded. Oil, cocoa, tuna, shrimp, coffee and fishmeal are currently excluded from the list of countertraded goods. Bananas may be used only if the countertrade deal helps open up new markets. The United States, West Germany, France, the Soviet Union, and Eastern European countries are the country's major countertrade partners.

Jamaica

The Jamaican Government supports the use of countertrade. Jamica's two major state-owned trading companies (the Bauxite alumina Trading Company and the Jamaican Commodity Trading Company) are both heavily involved in countertrade. Jamaica's major countertrade goods are bauxite, alumina, bananas, sugar and tourism. The United States, Yugoslavia and European countries are Jamaica's major countertrade partners.

Mexico

The Government of Mexico permits commercial (non-governmental) countertrade. Barter and countertrade transactions must be authorised by the Bank of Mexico and approved by the Ministry of Trade and industrial Promotion (SECOFIN). Products which have reportedly been exported under countertrade deals include coffee, honey, fluorspar, and sulfur and occasionally oil.

Nicaragua

Most of Nicaragua's countertrade arrangements have been carried out with neighbouring countries such as Guatemala. Commodities such as textiles and processed oats may be countertraded, but coffee and cotton cannot be involved in countertrade deals.

Peru

Peru has engaged in a limited number of countertrade deals with Western countries and several NMEs. The single largest countertrade deal was a 1976 agreement between Peru and Japan to build the trans-

Asean Oil pipeline. The agreement included an extended payment period for the pipeline and a supply contract for oil. Commodities which have been exported in conjunction with countertrade agreements include copper, fishmeal cotton and canned fish.

Uruguay

Major criterion is that Uruguayan exports incidental to barter and countertrade deals should not result in the loss of export revenues. The Foreign Trade Office often acts as an information broker/adviser between potential foreign sellers and Uruguayan producers. Uruguay has concluded various countertrade contracts.

Venezuela

Outside the petroleum sector, the Venezuelan Institute of Foreign Trade and the Venezuelan Exporters Association are developing expertise in countertrade in order to increase non-traditional exports from the private sector. Japan and West Germany are among Venezuela's major countertrade partners. Venezuela has exported aluminium under a major buy-back arrangement.

Australia

Since 1970, the Australian Government has required offsets on all overseas military and civilian purchases where government funding or decision-making is involved. The primary purpose of Australia's offset programme, which is administered by the Department of Defence Support, is to upgrade the technology of its local industries.

Ghana

Countertrade has been an important feature of Ghana's foreign trade policy of the past 25 years. In 1960s and 1970s Ghana undertook countertrade deals with the USSR, Czechoslovakia, Poland and China. Ghana has signed several large scale compensation deals with the German Democratic Republic, Bulgaria, and Egypt. The government has established an administrative system for negotiating and monitoring countertrade deals. Products which Ghana most frequently offers in countertrade are cocoa, tropical timber, rubber, frozen and canned fish and seafoods, gold, manganese and bauxite.

Ivory Coast

The main commodities offered by the Ivory Coast in countertraded deals have included bananas and coffee.

Libya

The country offers surplus oil and oil products in countertrade. Counterpurchase arrangements are the preferred forms of countertrade. Libya's principal countertrade partners are the Mediterranean countries.

Mali

The Government has instituted a number of local content requirements. Performance requirements such as increasing exports and restricting imports may also act as incentive to increase countertrade.

New Zealand

The New Zealand Department of Trade and Industry is responsible for examining countertrade proposals and in monitoring such sales. In 1982, this agency concluded a US $ 150 million arrangement with Iran in which oil was exchanged for lamb. Since 1980, the government purchases exceeding NZ $ 2 million need to have invited the tenderers to submit proposals that would offset the procurement costs through domestic manufacturing or counter-purchase arrangements. Offset proposals that relate to the development of primary processing in sectors such as forestry, fishing and horticulture are given special preference. Counter-purchases of horticulture products and exports of fish and derived products are encouraged if they will lead to new markets. A number of countertrade deals have entered with Gulf countries.

Tunisia

Trade agreements and protocols with the NME's have increased the role of countertrade in Tunisia's foreign trade. France has also concluded major countertrade deals with the country. Primary goods and semi-manufactures are Tunisia's chief countertrade exports.

Zimbabwe

Zimbabwe has the most detailed countertrade policies and rigorous enforcement of these regulations. Zimbabwe prefers government-to-government deals. The government examines countertrade proposals on a case-by-case basis and plays a major role in assisting firms with countertrade negotiations. The export product must be one that is hard to market. The price of both the imported and exported goods must be "acceptable". The government prefers countertrade deals involving exports of raw materials against imports of industrial raw materials and semi-finished goods.

Less than 10 countertrade deals have been concluded with Rumania, the German Democratic Republic, Bulgaria, the United Kingdom and others. The commodities that Zimbabwe has exchanged through these transactions include ferro-chrome, nickel, high-nicotine tobacco and maize surpluses.

Specific and detailed countertrade case examples as practised by various countries are appended. These are based on data collected by the author from United Nations Conference on Trade and Development, Geneva which is the only UN body mandated to deal with countertrade and the Association of State Trading Organisations headquartered in Yugoslavia and the author's own sources, extensive travels and global studies in Vienna.

Chapter 9

THE LEGAL FRAMEWORK*

Transactions Covered

Countertrade transactions dealt with in the legal guide are those international contractual arrangements under which one party supplies goods, services or technology to the second party, and in return, the first party purchases or procures the purchase of an agreed amount of goods, services or technology from the second party, or from a party designated by the second party. (For the sake of simplicity, the legal guide will refer only to "goods" as the subject-matter of countertrade transactions, although the subject-matter of a given transaction may include services or technology). A distinctive feature of these transactions is the existence of a link between the supply of goods in the two directions in that the conclusion of the contract or contracts for the supply of goods in one direction is conditioned upon the conclusion of the contract or contracts for the supply in the other direction. When the parties enter into contracts in opposite directions without expressing such a link between them, the contracts, as regards contractual rights and obligations of the parties, cannot be distinguished from straightforward independent transactions. Therefore, the legal framework deals only with transactions that express in a contractual form such a link between the contracts constituting the countertrade transaction.

Beyond this basic definition, countertrade transactions display a number of differing features. The differences concern such matters as the contractual structure of the transaction, the time sequence of conclusion of the component contracts, the underlying commercial interests of the parties, and other commercial and technical characteristics of the transactions. The legal framework takes into account that countertrade

* United Nations General Assembly, United Nations Commission on, International Trade Law Twentythird Session, New York, June 1990.

transactions display these differing features and that these features will affect the drawing up of the various contracts.

A countertrade transaction may be contractually structured in different ways. Often, the supply of goods in each direction is covered by a distinct contract. In such a case the link between these segments arising from the fact that the conclusion of the contract in one direction is conditioned upon the conclusion of the contract in the other direction may be expressed in an agreement separate from those contracts. In other cases that link may be expressed in a contract clause that is integrated into one of those contracts. In yet other cases, the whole transaction, that is, the reciprocal supplying of goods and the stipulation expressing the link between the segments of the transaction, is incorporated into one contract (e.g., a barter contract). The legal framework discusses the implications of the choice of a particular contract structure or the choice of a particular contract form.

Furthermore, the contracts for the supply of goods in the two directions may be concluded at different points of time or they may be concluded simultaneously. When they are concluded at different points of time, which is often the case, the parties conclude an agreement expressing a commitment to conclude the future contract or contracts for the supply of goods. Such an agreement may be entered into together with the conclusion of the initial contract for the supply of goods in one direction or it may be entered into prior to the conclusion of any supply contract. When the parties agree simultaneously on the supplies in both directions, the agreement between the parties would not include a commitment to conclude future contracts, but would establish a relationship between the performances due from each party. The legal framework refers to the particular sequence of the conclusion of the supply contracts when this is required by the context of the discussion.

Another aspect of the variety of countertrade transactions is the degree of interest the parties may have in the different segments of a countertrade transaction. In some transactions one of the parties is interested only in the export of its goods and would prefer to be free to decide whether to import goods from the other party. In other transactions, the parties consider the supply of goods in the two directions as being in their mutual interest. There are also transactions in which, at the outset of the transaction, a party perceives a commitment to conclude future contracts as a concession to the other party, but subsequently comes to regard that commitment as a benefit. The legal framework takes into account such possible differing degrees of interest that the parties may have in the different parts of the countertrade transaction and the impact that such differing degrees of interest may have on the contract or contracts.

Furthermore, a broad distinction among countertrade transactions may be made depending on whether the goods supplied in one direction are used in the production of the goods to be supplied in the other direction or whether no such technological link exists between the reciprocal deliveries. The legal guide will cover both of those varieties of countertrade and will make reference to a particular variety whenever appropriate.

A further distinction may be made on the basis of the number of the parties involved in a transaction. In some cases, the reciprocal deliveries of goods under the transaction are carried out between the same two parties. In other cases, on one side of the transaction, or on both, the roles of the seller and of the buyer are assumed by different persons. The legal framework addresses the contractual issues that are raised by the involvement of more than one party on either or both sides of a transaction.

Terminology

Terminology used in practice and in writings to describe countertrade transactions and the parties involved in them varies greatly. A prevailing terminology has not developed. The following establishes a terminology used in the legal framework for different varieties of countertrade transactions, parties and contracts in countertrade.

Varieties of Countertrade

The discussion in the legal guide is relevant to different commercial types of countertrade. In most instances, the contractual issues addressed in the legal framework are the same for all commercial types of countertrade transactions, and the discussion in the legal framework generally does not distinguish among types of countertrade. However, in some contexts the discussion is particularly relevant to a commercial type of countertrade. Therefore, the terms used to denote such types of countertrade are explained below. The criteria used to distinguish the types of countertrade are based on commercial technical and legal aspects of the transaction.

Barter

In practice the term "barter" is used with different meanings. The term may refer, for example, to countertrade transactions in general, to an intergovernmental agreement addressing mutual trade in particular goods between identified partners, or to countertrade in which trans-border flow of currency is eliminated or reduced or where a single contract governs the mutual shipments of goods. The legal framework uses "barter" in a strict legal sense to refer to a contract involving a two-way exchange of specified goods in which the supply of goods in one direction replaces, entirely or partly, the monetary payment for the supply of goods in the other direction. Where there is a difference in value in the supply of goods in the two directions, the settlement of the difference may be in money or in other economic value.

Counter-purchase

This term is used to refer to a transaction in which the parties, in connection with the conclusion of a purchase contract in one direction, enter into an agreement to conclude a sales contract in the other direction, i.e. a counter-purchase contract. Counter-purchase is distinguished from buy-back in that the goods supplied under the first purchase are not used in the production of the items sold in return.

Buy-back

This term refers to a transaction in which one party supplies a production facility, and the parties agree that the supplier of the facility, or a person designated by the supplier, will buy resultant products from the purchaser of the facility. The supplier of the facility often provides technology and training and sometimes component parts of materials to be used in the production.

Offset

Transactions referred to in the legal framework as offsets normally involve the supply of goods of high value or technological so-phistication. Under the "direct offset" the contract for the supply of goods in one direction is combined with an agreement that the supplier will purchase from the other party component parts of, or products related to, those goods. Sometimes the supplier would also agree to provide technology or investment for the production by the other party of the component parts. Such direct offsets are also referred to as industrial participation or industrial co-operation. The expression "indirect offset" typically refers to a transaction where a governmental agency that procures, or approves the procurement of, goods of high value requires from the supplier that counter-purchases are made in the procuring country or that economic value is provided to the procuring country in the form of investment, technology or assistance in Third markets. The counter-export goods are not technologically related to the export goods (i.e., they are not components of the export goods, as in direct offset, and they are not resultant products of the facility provided under the export contract, as in buy-back). The governmental agency often stipulates guidelines for the offset, for example, as to the industrial sectors or regions that are to be assisted in such a way. However, within such guidelines, the party committed to counter-purchase or to providing such assistance is normally free to choose the contracting partners.

Parties to Countertrade Transaction

Exporter or counter-importer. The term "exporter" or "counter-importer" is used for the party who is—under the first contract to be concluded—the supplier, that is, the exporter of goods, and who has entered into a commitment with the other party to purchase, that is, to counter-import, other goods in return. One or the other term is used depending on the context in which the party is mentioned. It should be noted that in some countertrade transactions the exporter and the counter-importer are the same party, while in others the exporter and counter-importer are different parties.

Importer or counter-exporter. The term "importer" or "counter-exporter" is used for the party who is—under the first contract to be concluded—the purchaser, that is, the importer, of goods, and who has entered into a commitment with the other party to supply, that is, to counter-export, other goods in return. One or the other term is used depending on the context in which the party is mentioned. As in respect of the exporter and the counter-importer, in some countertrade transactions the same party is the importer and the counter-exporter. Sometimes, however, one party imports and another party counter-exports.

In some writings the term "exporter" is used to denote the party from an economically developed country, who often supplies goods of technological context that normally cannot be obtained in the other party's country. The term is used irrespective of whether the "exporter" supplies first and agrees to purchase later or whether the "exporter" makes an "advance purchase" from the other party in order to enable that other party to raise funds needed for a subsequent purchase of goods from the "exporter". The term "importer" is used in those writings to denote the party from a developing country. To underline that meaning, such writings may use terms such as "primary" or "Western exporter" or "developing country importer".

A distinction based on economic or regional considerations is not used in the present legal framework. One reason is that the guide covers both intra-regional and inter-regional countertrade. Thus, distinctions used in discussions of inter-regional countertrade, in which the issues tend to be considered primarily from the perspective of one of the parties, would not be suitable since the legal frame advises both parties whatever may be their relative economic strength or background. Furthermore, terms based on the time sequence of the conclusion of contracts are more suitable since, for the purpose of discussing the contractual role and interests of parties, the question of primary significance is whether the party has already sold its goods and has promised to purchase goods from the other party, or whether the party, having purchased goods, has not sold its goods yet.

Purchaser, supplier or party. The legal frame frequently uses the term "purchaser", "supplier" or "party" to refer to parties purchasing and supplying goods in a countertrade transaction. When reference is made to a party who is committed to purchase or supply goods but has not yet done so, the legal guide may use the terms "party committed to purchase goods" and "party committed to supply goods". Such terminology is employed when the discussion in the legal guide is relevant to the contractual position of a party purchasing or supplying goods irrespective of whether the purchase or supply in one direction takes place before or after the purchase or supply in the other direction. The order in which the shipments take place would not affect the contractual position and risks of the parties when the parties commit themselves o conclude contracts for the supply of the goods without stipulating the sequence in which those contracts are to be concluded. Such terminology also covers cases in which the contracts for the supply of goods in the two directions are concluded concurrently and in which the sequence of the contracts cannot serve as a terminological criterion.

Component Contracts of a Countertrade Transaction

Countertrade agreement. The countertrade agreement is the basic agreement which sets forth several stipulations concerning the type of countertrade transaction being entered into and the manner in which it is to be implemented. In practice, the countertrade agreement is referred to by a variety of names, such as "frame agreement", "countertrade protocol", "letter of intent". "umbrella agreement", "memorandum of understanding", "letter of undertaking", or "counterpurchase agreement". The countertrade agreement usually contains the commitment of the parties to enter into the future contracts required to fulfil the objective of the transaction ("countertrade commitment"). In addition to the countertrade commitment, the countertrade agreement is likely to contain other stipulations on issues such as the type, quarterly and quantity of the goods, price of the goods, time period of fulfilment of the countertrade commitment, payment, restriction on resale of goods, participation of third persons in the transaction, liquidated damages or penalties, security for performance, interdependence of obligations in the transaction, choice of law, and settlement of disputes. The countertrade agreement may be embodied in a discrete instrument or it may be included in a contract for the shipment of goods. When the parties agree simultaneously on the terms governing the supply of all the goods in both directions, the countertrade agreement would contain a stipulation expressing the link between the concluded contracts and possibly other stipulations, but would not contain a countertrade commitment.

Countertrade commitment. This term is used to refer to the commitment of the parties to enter into a future contract or contracts. Depending on the circumstances, those future contracts may relate only to the shipment in one direction or to the shipments in both directions. The degree to which the countertrade commitment is definite depends on the amount of detail contained in the countertrade agreement concerning the terms of the future contracts.

Export, import, counter-export, and counter-import contracts. The contracts for the supply of goods entered into by the parties would be referred to by names consistent with the names of the parties, that is, "export" or "import" contract for the first contract entered into, and "counter-export" or "counter-import" contract for the contract entered into subsequently. The contracts in each direction may be referred to in the singular even though there may be several such contracts on both sides of the countertrade transaction.

Supply contracts. In the cases mentioned above where no clear criterion exists for distinguishing between the exporter and the importer, or where the context requires a general reference to any party to the countertrade transaction, and in which the term "party" or "parties" to the countertrade transaction may be used, the contracts for the supply of goods between the parties may be referred to as "supply contracts".

Countertrade transaction. This term is used to refer to the whole countertrade arrangement containing the related supply contracts and any countertrade agreement.

Focus on Issues Specific to Countertrade

The contracts for individual supplies of goods under a countertrade transaction generally resettle contracts concluded as discrete and independent transactions. In some cases, however, the content of a contract is affected by the fact that it forms part of a countertrade transaction. For example, when the proceeds of a contract in one direction are to be used to pay for the contract in the other direction, the two supply contracts may contain payment provisions particular to countertrade. Therefore, the frame does not deal with supply contracts except to the extent that they contain provisions typical of countertrade.

The questions specific to or of particular importance for international countertrade are concentrated in the countertrade agreement. The legal frame focuses on questions raised in drawing up the countertrade agreement. Where necessary reference is made to drawing up a provision in a supply contract that is influenced by the fact that the contract is part of the countertrade transaction.

Some of the issues dealt with in the legal guide are essential in establishing a countertrade transaction. The parties would have to choose a contracting approach, express in appropriate form their commitment to engage in reciprocal trade, and specify the extent of the commitment. Solutions to certain other questions dealt with in the legal guide, while not necessarily essential, would help to ensure proper implementation of the transaction. Such questions include: the time period for the fulfilment of the countertrade commitment, type, quality, quantity and price of the countertrade goods, payment mechanism, participation of a third person in the fulfilment of the countertrade commitment, restrictions on resale of countertrade goods, security for performance, liquidated damages and penalties, possible effect on the countertrade transaction of problems arising in an individual contract for the supply of goods, choice of law, and settlement of disputes. The parties intending to enter into a countertrade transaction are advised to address the essential questions. As to the other questions that are not necessarily essential but may be helpful in the implementation of the transaction, the parties will have to judge whether and to what extent the contractual solutions discussed in the legal frame are relevant to the circumstances of the given case.

Governmental Regulations

In some countries countertrade is subject to governmental regulations. Such regulations, which may derive from international agreements, are closely linked with national economic policies and as a result vary from country to country and are likely to be changed more often than rules of contract law. Governmental regulations may promote or restrict countertrade in a variety of ways. It may be provided that certain types of imports must be paid for only through a countertrade arrangement, that state trading agencies are to explore the possibility of countertrade when negotiating certain types of contracts, that certain types of local products are prohibited from being offered in countertrade, or that foreign currency payments into the country must not be restricted. Other such rules may relate to exchange controls or to this authority of an administrative organ to approve a countertrade transaction. Some regulations may be specifically oriented to countertrade, while others may be more general, but with an impact on countertrade. Some regulations are directed to one contracting party only and do not directly affect the contents or the legal effect of the contract concluded by that party. In other instances the regulation may limit the parties' freedom of contract.

The legal guide advises parties to take into account such governmental regulations. Since the regulations are disparate, and are often changed, advice is given, in the form of a *caveat* rather than in any detailed discussion of the substance of the applicable regulations.

Universal Scope of Legal Guide

The legal frame treats the legal issues arising from countertrade at the universal level, in view of the fact that the motives for engaging in countertrade, the interests of the parties involved, and the private law questions do not reveal regional particularities. To the extent there exist regional differences in contract practices, they concern in particular the frequency of use of certain commercial types of countertrade and the elaborateness and refinement of contractual solutions.

Contracting Approach*
Choice of Contract Structure

A preliminary question the parties have to address is the contract structure of the countertrade transaction. The parties may embody the obligations in regard to the shipments of goods in the two directions in one contract or they may incorporate those obligations into separate contracts.

---

* United Nations General Assembly, United Nations Commission on, International Trade Law Twentythird Session, New York, June 1990

Single Contract

Under a single contract approach the parties conclude one contract for the flow of goods in the two directions. Such a single contract may take the form of a barter contract or the form of a merged contract that contains all contractual terms governing the reciprocal shipments.

Barter Contract

"Scope and terminology of legal frame", the legal guide uses the term barter in its strict legal sense to refer to a transaction involving an exchange of goods for goods, so that the supply of goods in one direction entirely or partly replaces the monetary payment for the supply of goods in the other direction. In a barter contract there is no need for a countertrade commitment since the parties agree at the outset of the transaction on all the contract terms for the shipments in the two directions. If the goods to be supplied in one direction are agreed to be of the same value as the goods to be supplied in the other direction, no monetary payment would be made. If the values are agreed to be different, the difference may be settled by monetary payment or by further delivery of goods. The parties may or may not express the value of the goods in monetary terms. If they do so, the attachment of a price to the goods serves to compare the value of the deliveries. The parties may have to express the value of shipments in monetary terms due to customs or other administrative requirements.

A factor that is often the main reason for using barter is that the use of barter eliminates or reduces the need for currency transfers. It may be noted, however, that the avoidance of currency transactions may also be achieved through the use of other structural forms, namely, the parties may conclude separate sales contracts in each direction and agree to set off their commitments.

There are several considerations that the parties may take into account in deciding whether to cast their countertrade transaction in the form of a barter contract. One consideration is that the conclusion of a barter contract implies a comparison between the values of the goods to be exchanged, which in turn implies that the type, quality and quantity of the goods should be specified at the time of conclusion of the contract. Conclusion of a barter contract would not be feasible when the parties are not in a position to agree at the same time on the type, quality and quantity of the goods to be shipped in the two directions.

Another factor to be considered is the possible reluctance of a party to ship the goods before being certain that the other party will ship goods. payment against the presentation of shipping documents or the opening of a documentary letter of credit, devices used with other types of contracts to address such a concern, cannot be used in barter since neither delivery is payable in money. Simultaneous deliveries, which might be a solution to take care of this kind of concern, are seldom feasible in international commerce. As a result, a party may delay shipping until the other party has shipped because of a concern that the other party might not ship. Such a delay may cause an inconvenience to both parties: to the party that has planned to deliver the goods at the agreed time and is burdened with the possession of the goods and to the party who does not receive the goods in time. The parties may overcome these concerns by providing for a guarantee or a stand-by letter of credit to assure the party who has shipped, of compensation in the event that the other party fails to ship (the use of guarantees or stand-by letters of credit).

A further consideration is that under a barter contract the value of the goods to be shipped in one direction is often measured by the goods to be shipped in the other direction, rather than in terms of the market price for each shipment. The absence of a price in a barter contract or the use of prices that do not reflect the market prices might cause a difficulty when non-conforming goods are delivered under a barter contract. If in such a case monetary compensation is regarded as the appropriate relief, the absence in the contract of a market price, or of any price at all, could lead to disagreement over the amount of the compensation. The stipulation of a price other than the market price may also give rise to a difficulty in calculating customs duties when they are based on the market value of the goods.

Merged Contract

The term "merged contract" is used to describe the case in which the parties embody in one contract all the terms covering the obligations of the parties to ship goods to each other and to pay for the goods they have received. If the parties agree to set off their claims for payment under a merged contract, the difference between a merged contract and a barter contract, under which one shipment constitutes compensation for the other shipment, would be diminished. As in barter, there is no need in a merged contract for a countertrade commitment since the deliveries to be made in the two directions are covered by definite contract terms.

Many legal systems appear to give weight to the contract structure of the transaction in determining whether the obligations are interdependent. In such a system, if the mutual obligations are merged into one contract, the mutual obligations are likely to be considered as interdependent so that non-delivery, refusal to take delivery, or non-payment relating to a shipment in one direction may be invoked as a reason for suspending or refusing performance in the other direction. Furthermore, termination of an obligation in one direction, whether or not a party is responsible for the termination, may be interpreted as entitling a party to terminate an obligation in the other direction. If the parties using a merged contract approach wish to keep the obligation to ship goods in one direction and the corresponding payment obligation independent from the obligations relating to the shipment in the other direction, they should use unambiguous language to that effect.

Separate Contracts

When the parties use separate contracts for the shipments in the two directions, they would use one of the following approaches: (a) the export contract and the countertrade agreement are concluded simultaneously and the counter-export contract is concluded subsequently; (b) the countertrade agreement is concluded prior to the conclusion of any definite supply contracts; and (c) the separate supply contracts for the shipment in each direction in the countertrade agreement establishing a relationship between them are concluded simultaneously.

The obligation to ship goods in a particular direction in a countertrade transaction may be fulfilled by two or more different contracts, which may involve different buyers and sellers. While such a situation affects the contractual structure of a given transaction, it does not affect the nature of the discussion in the chapter. Therefore, references in the singular to a supply contract, as well as to an export or counter-export contract, also cover the situation in which more than one contract is concluded for the shipment of goods in a particular direction.

Export Contract and Countertrade Agreement Concluded Simultaneously

The parties often finalize a contract for the shipment in one direction (export contract) before they are able to reach agreement on the contract for the shipment in the other direction (counter-export contract). Parties using this contracting approach may face a broad range of issues specific to countertrade. In order to assure conclusion of the counter-export contract, the parties conclude, simultaneously with the conclusion of the export contract, a countertrade agreement containing the commitment to conclude the counter-export contract. The primary purpose of the countertrade agreement in such cases is, in addition to stating the countertrade commitment, to outline the term of the future contract and establish procedures for concluding and carrying out supply contracts. Possible issues to be addressed in such a countertrade agreement are enumerated below.

The contents of the countertrade agreement would be influenced by the degree to which the parties are able to define the terms of the future contract. It is advisable that the countertrade agreement be as definite as possible concerning the terms of the future contract, in particular regarding the type, quality, quantity and price of the countertrade goods, in order to increase the likelihood that the countertrade commitment will be fulfilled. To the extent that the parties are not in a position to settle the terms of the counter-export contract in the countertrade agreement, they are advised to establish guidelines within which the terms are to be agreed upon the procedures for negotiation.

The content of the countertrade agreement would also be influenced by the degree of interest the parties have in the shipments in the two directions. In many cases the exporter is primarily interested in the conclusion of the export contract, and the countertrade commitment results primarily from a desire to secure the export contract. In other cases, the importer purchases goods from the exporter in order to enable the exporter to finance the counter-import. In yet other cases, each side is particularly interested in obtaining the goods being offered by the other side. Because the interests of the parties vary in such a manner, the content of the countertrade agreement may vary from case to case with respect to issues such as sanctions for non-fulfilment of the countertrade commitment, payment mechanisms, procedures for concluding the future contract and for monitoring fulfilment of the countertrade commitment, and interdependence of obligations.

The simultaneous conclusion of an export contract and a countertrade agreement is an approach frequently used in counter-purchase, buy-back or offset transactions. In the case of the counter-purchase transaction, the parties may not yet know what type of goods would be counter-exported. In the case of a buy-back, the parties may not be able to agree on such terms as price or quantity because of the long time period between the conclusion of the contract for the export of the production facility and the beginning of production of resultant products. In an offset transaction, the parties may not know what type of goods will be counter-exported or the identity of the counter-exporters.

The use of this contracting approach raises the question whether to include the terms of the countertrade agreement in the export contract or to embody those terms in a separate instrument. The choice of the parties in this regard may have an effect on the degree to which the obligations stipulated in the export contract and the obligations set forth in the countertrade agreement are considered to be interdependent. When there is such interdependence, a delay in the fulfilment or non-fulfilment of the countertrade commitment may provide the importer with a justification for suspending payment of the amounts due under the export contract or for deducting corresponding damages from the payment due under the export contract. Similarly, the exporter may regard a delay in payment for the export contract as a ground for delaying fulfilment of the countertrade commitment. Furthermore, delayed payment under the counter-export contract might prompt the importer to delay payment under the export contract.

If the obligations relating to the export and to the countertrade commitment are embodied in separate contracts, it appears that many legal systems would consider the two sets of obligations to be independent, except to the extent specific contract provisions establish interdependence. In other legal systems the export contract and the countertrade agreement may, despite the use of separate contracts, be considered to be interdependent on the ground that the obligations of the parties embodied in the two contracts form part of a single transaction. When the parties wish to avoid interdependence of obligations between the export contract and the countertrade agreement, or when they wish to limit interdependence to particular obligations, it is advisable that they embody the export contract and the countertrade agreement in separate contracts. When, despite the use of separate contracts, it is uncertain whether the obligations under the export contract and the countertrade agreement would be considered independent, it is advisable that the independence of the obligations be clearly expressed in the countertrade agreement.

The parties may wish to establish, by express contract clauses, an interrelationship between particular obligations arising out of the export contract and out of the countertrade agreement, while keeping other obligations independent. The parties may agree that refusal to take delivery under the export contract or termination of the export contract permits the exporter to terminate the countertrade agreement, and that non-fulfilment of the countertrade commitment by the counter-importer entitles the counter-exporter to deduct an agreed amount as liquidated damages or penalty from payments due under the export contract.

Countertrade Agreement Concluded Prior to Conclusion of Definite Supply Contracts

The conclusion of a countertrade agreement may be the first step in the transaction prior to the conclusion of any definite supply contracts in either direction. The aim of the countertrade agreement in such a case is to express the commitment of the parties to conclude supply contracts in the two directions and to establish procedures for concluding and implementing those contracts. In order to achieve the envisaged level of shipments in the two directions, it is advisable that the countertrade agreement be as definite as possible concerning the terms of the contracts to be concluded in the two directions. The parties may also wish to establish mechanisms for monitoring and recording the level of trade and to provide sanctions for a failure to fulfil the countertrade commitment. The need for such sanctions may be diminished if the parties agree that their countervailing claims for payment for the shipments in each direction will be set off rather than paid for individually. Such a payment mechanism would provide an incentive to both parties to order goods from each other and thereby attain the level of trade envisaged in the countertrade agreement. The incentive is derived from the fact that a party who has shipped goods and holds a trade surplus will be stimulated to order goods from the other party in order to be compensated for its own deliveries. These and other issues that the parties may wish to address in a countertrade agreement entered into prior to the conclusion of any supply contract are set out below.

Export Contract, Counter-export Contract and Countertrade Agreement Concluded Simultaneously

When the parties simultaneously conclude a contract for the supply of goods in the direction and another contract for the supply of goods in the other direction, and there is no indication in the contracts that there is a relationship between them, the contracts would appear on their face to be independent of one another even if one party or both parties regarded the conclusion of one contract as a condition for the conclusion of the other contract. When, however, the parties wish to give contractual effect to an intention that the conclusion of one contract be conditioned upon the conclusion of the other, that is, when they wish to structure the contracts in the two directions as a countertrade transaction, the parties should conclude a countertrade agreement expressing that relationship.

This contracting approach raises a limited number of issues since it does not involve a countertrade commitment. The main issue in this contracting approach is the manner in which the obligations of the parties with respect to the shipments in the two directions are to be linked by provisions in the countertrade agreement. There is no need to deal in the countertrade agreement with various issues related to the fulfilment of the countertrade commitment (in particular the type, quality, quantity or price of the countertrade goods, time schedules of fulfilment of countertrade commitment, security of performance or liquidated damages or penalties supporting the countertrade commitment). The issues that the parties may wish to address in a countertrade agreement concluded simultaneously with the definite supply contracts in the two directions are set out below.

Contents of Countertrade Agreement
Countertrade Agreement with Countertrade Commitment

Countertrade Commitment

The essential feature of a countertrade commitment is a stipulation by which the parties undertake to negotiate in order to conclude one or more supply contracts. In order to add definiteness to the commitment and to increase the likelihood of its fulfilment, parties often include in the countertrade agreement provisions concerning terms of the anticipated contract, negotiation procedure designed to facilitate fulfilment of the countertrade commitment, sanctions for the failure to conclude the contract, and other provisions to ensure the proper carrying out of the countertrade transaction. Negotiation procedures and means for providing definiteness to the commitment are discussed below. Other types of clauses that parties may wish to consider including in a countertrade agreement are enumerated below and elaborated in the following chapter of the legal framework.

Type, Quality and Quantity of Goods

In order for the countertrade commitment to be meaningful, it is particularly important that the countertrade agreement be as specific as possible as to the type, quality and quantity of the countertrade goods. Clauses in the countertrade agreement addressing these issues are discussed below.

Pricing of Goods

Since the parties are often not in a position to set the price of the countertrade goods at the time the countertrade agreement is concluded, they may establish guidelines and proceeds for setting the price at a later date. Such provisions help to prevent delays in the conclusion of supply contracts and provide pricing flexibility in long-term countertrade transactions. Issues relating to pricing clauses are addressed below.

Fulfilment of Countertrade Commitment

A basic question to be addressed in the countertrade agreement is the length of time to be allowed for fulfilment of the countertrade commitment. In some cases, the parties establish mechanisms for monitoring and recording fulfilment of the countertrade commitment. Provisions relating both to the length of the fulfilment period and to monitoring and recording mechanisms are set out below.

Participation of Third Persons

The parties may wish to involve third persons, either as suppliers or purchasers, or both, of countertrade goods. In such cases the countertrade agreement may contain provisions concerning participation by third persons. Those provisions could determine the manner in which the third persons would be selected and the legal effect of the involvement of third persons on the obligations undertaken by the parties to the countertrade agreement. Issues to be dealt with in the countertrade agreement relating to participation of third persons are discussed below.

Payment

When payments for the shipments in each direction are kept independent, no payment issues specific to countertrade are raised. However, when the parties wish to link the payments for the shipments in the two directions so that the proceeds of the contract in one direction are used to pay for the contract in the other direction, they would have to include in the countertrade agreement provisions on the manner in which payment is to be linked. A discussion of contractual aspects of various types of linked payment mechanisms is set out below.

Restrictions on Resale of Goods

The freedom of a party to resell goods purchased in a countertrade transaction may sometimes be restricted by contractual agreement between the supplier and the purchaser of the goods. The purchaser may be restricted as to the territory of resale, as well as to the terms of resale (for example, resale price or packaging). Clauses in the countertrade agreement concerning such restrictions are discussed below.

Liquidated Damages and Penalties

In order to limit disagreements as to the extent of damages resulting from a breach of the countertrade commitment, the countertrade agreement may stipulate a sum of money due from a party upon failure to fulfil the commitment to purchase or make available countertrade goods. The use of such clauses in a countertrade agreement is addressed below.

Security for Performance

The parties may use guarantees to support fulfilment of the countertrade commitment, as well as the proper performance of individual supply contracts concluded pursuant to the countertrade commitment. The use of guarantees to support the fulfilment of the countertrade commitment, or the obligation to pay under a liquidated damages or penalty clause, raises issues to be addressed in the countertrade agreement. In transactions in which the parties limit payments in cash by exchanging goods for goods or setting off countervailing payment claims, the countertrade agreement may stipulate the use of guarantees to cover liquidation of an imbalance in the flow of trade. Issues to be addressed in the countertrade agreement when the parties wish to use guarantees to support fulfilment of the countertrade commitment and liquidation of an imbalance in trade are discussed below.

Interdependence of Obligations

The parties may wish to address in the countertrade agreement the question of the interdependence of their obligations pertaining to the shipments in one direction with their obligations pertaining to the shipment in the other direction. This question becomes relevant when a difficulty arises in the conclusion or performance of a supply contract. These provisions are set out below.

Choice of Law

The parties may wish to agree upon the law to be applied to the countertrade agreement or to the supply contracts.

Settlement of Disputes

It examines issues to be considered in preparing dispute settlement clauses for countertrade agreements.

Countertrade Agreement without Countertrade Commitment

When the parties simultaneously conclude separate contracts for the entire supply of goods in the two directions, there is no need for a countertrade agreement containing either a countertrade commitment to conclude future contracts, or clauses on the type, quality, quantity or price of the goods, liquidated damages or penalties to be paid for failure to conclude supply contracts, or guarantees to support the countertrade commitment.

The primary purpose of the countertrade agreement in this case would be establish a link between the contracts in the two directions, namely, that the conclusion of a contract in one direction is conditioned upon the conclusion of a contract in the other direction. The countertrade agreement may provide that a problem in the performance of one contract would have an effect on the obligation to perform the contractual obligations in the other direction.

The parties may also establish a link between the contracts by structuring payment for the two contracts in such a way that the proceeds of the shipment in one direction would be used to pay for the shipment in the other direction. Linked payment mechanisms of this type are discussed below.

In addition, the countertrade agreement may address issues such as restrictions on the resale of countertrade goods, participation of third persons in the countertrade transaction, choice of law and settlement of disputes.

Countertrade Commitment

The degree to which the parties commit themselves to enter into a supply contract may range from a commitment to exercise "best efforts" to conclude a supply contract to a firm commitment to enter into a supply contract. Under a "best efforts" commitment, also referred to as "serious intention", the commitment of the parties is limited to negotiating in good faith and the parties retain the discretion to refuse all contract offers that they consider unacceptable.

If the parties wish to increase the likelihood that a supply contract will be concluded, they should include in the countertrade agreement procedures to be followed in their negotiations and clauses setting out, as definitely as possible, the terms of the future contract.

Negotiation Procedures

Countertrade agreements may set forth with varying degrees of procedural detail the manner in which negotiations are to be carried out. Specifying the negotiation procedures increases the probability that the negotiations will lead to a successful outcome. This would be particularly true where the nature of the negotiations is likely to be complicated, either because of the subject-matter of the eventual contracts or because of the number of persons who might be involved in those negotiations.

At a minimum, the countertrade agreement might provide that a party would be obligated to respond to contract proposals by the other party. More specific procedures would address issues such as: the party who is to submit a contract offer; questions to be covered by a contract offer; time periods for submitting it; the form, means or frequency of communication; the time period for reply; the time within which an agreement must be reached, and beyond which negotiations will be deemed to have failed. Furthermore, the parties may provide that in certain circumstances a party would be relieved of the duty to negotiate, when that party has made an offer meeting the agreed conditions and it has not been accepted, or, if the other party was to make the offer, when no such offer has been made.

The stipulation of negotiation procedures such as those mentioned in the previous paragraph may also increase the possibility that a party who has not negotiated in good faith could be held responsible for the failure to conclude a contract. Such procedures could enable an aggrieved party to demonstrate that the other party refused to negotiate, imposed conditions to negotiate that the party could not properly impose, used unfair dilatory tactics, reopened discussion on issues already agreed upon, negotiated with other parties when it was improper to do so, or prematurely broke off negotiations.

However, procedural stipulations alone do not ensure that negotiations will be successful or that a party interested in the conclusion of the contract will be able to obtain relief in the event the negotiations do not succeed. A party who refuses to enter into a contract can avoid liability by showing adherence to the negotiation procedures. The most

effective way to increase the likelihood of succeeding in the
negotiations and of having a basis for obtaining relief in the event the
negotiations fail, would be to increase the definiteness of the
countertrade commitment. This would be done by stipulating in the
countertrade agreement, to the degree possible, the terms of the future
contract.

Providing Definiteness to Countertrade Commitment—General Remarks

Commitments to enter into supply contracts often do not stipulate in a
definite manner the term of the contracts to be concluded. Frequently
the parties do not know the type of goods that will be the subject of the
future supply contracts or what the terms of delivery will be. Even if
the parties might be able to set out in the countertrade agreement terms
of the future supply contract, they sometimes forego doing so because
they expect each party to live up to the commitment to conclude a
future contract, though the terms of that contract may not be defined in
great detail in the countertrade agreement.

A lack of definiteness may result in delays or uncertainties in
negotiating a supply contract in view of the potentially broad scope of
the negotiations. Furthermore, it may be difficult to establish whether a
party who has refused a contract offer is in breach of the countertrade
commitment.

Sometimes the parties are not in a position to be more definite
about the terms of the anticipated supply contract than to provide that
the contract terms should be fair or in accordance with the prevailing
market conditions. Such provisions may be helpful when countertrade
goods of a standard quality are agreed upon, thereby enabling a fair price
to be ascertained. If, however, the type of countertrade goods is not
settled or if the countertrade goods are products that do not have a
standard price, such a "fair terms" commitment may not substantially
enhance the position of the party interested in the conclusion of the
contract. In such cases opinions may differ as to what contract terms are
fair, thereby protracting the negotiations and making uncertain the
success of a claim against the party refusing to conclude the contract.

Terms of a future supply contract may be specified in the
countertrade agreement, or the countertrade agreement may provide
guidelines for settling terms of the future contract. As the countertrade
agreement becomes more definite with respect to the terms essential for
the existence of an enforceable contract, the agreement approaches the
point at which the parties have settled all the terms of the supply
contract and postponed only the act of signing the contract.

Many legal systems contain rules to which the parties may resort in order to provide definiteness to a contract clause. For example, numerous legal systems provide a solution when the parties have not settled the price of the goods; the solution may be, for instance, that the price should be the one "generally charged at the time of the conclusion of the contract for such goods sold under comparable circumstances in the trade concerned" (Article 55 of the United Nations Convention on Contracts for the International Sale of Goods). Another example may be the rule on the quality of the goods to be delivered under the contract when the contract has not settled that issue; the rule in Article 35(2) (a) of the above-mentioned Convention is that the goods should be "fit for the purposes for which goods of the same description would ordinarily be used". In some legal systems the parties may, within certain limits, resort to a court for the purpose of determining such a contract element. In other legal systems, however, the courts are not competent to intervene in this manner in a contractual relationship.

Although such means for contract supplementation exist in many legal systems, they normally do not provide a solution in all cases of indefiniteness. The contract elements left indefinite in the countertrade agreement may not lend themselves to being made definite by reference to the applicable law. If the parties have not agreed on the type of goods to be counter-exported, it would probably be impossible to determine the type on the basis of the applicable law. Where the type of goods has been settled, the criteria provided in the applicable law concerning the price of the goods may not lead to a clear solution. Furthermore, such contract supplementation is subject to uncertainty arising out of divergencies among legal systems as to the techniques of supplementation, the role of the courts, the arbitral tribunal, or the parties in determining the missing term, or as to the judicial control over the result of the supplementation. In any case, reliance on such means for contract supplementation tends to be more useful for purposes of dispute resolution than it is for contract implementation. As a result, the parties may wish to consider the contractual means discussed below for providing definiteness to a contract term left open in the countertrade agreement.

Contractual Means of Providing Definiteness

The terms that are often left indefinite in the countertrade agreement and with respect to which contractual means for completing indefinite terms may be particularly useful are the type, quality, price and quantity of the countertrade goods. The contractual means that the parties may consider for completing any one or more of those terms are discussed below. In other parts of the legal guide, these contractual means will be referred to in specific contexts.

Standards or Guidelines

The parties may wish to provide standards or guidelines to be used in determining particular contract terms. The use of a standard would allow the parties to determine a contract term by computation or by some other objective method not dependent upon the discretion of the parties. Examples of such standards include a formula, tariff, quotation, rate, index, statistic, or some other criterion not influenced by the will of either party. The price of the countertrade goods may be determined by reference to the price at which goods of the same type are sold in a particular market or exchange, or the quality of the countertrade goods may be defined by reference to a particular national or international quality standard. Many legal systems recognize as valid a provision that the price or other contract term should be determined by reference to a standard.

Guidelines, set parameters within which the contract term is to be determined and involve a degree of latitude in arriving at a contract term. The countertrade agreement may set a range within which the parties are to negotiate the price or it may be agreed that the price must be "reasonable". If the type of goods has not been determined, the parties may agree on a list of goods on which the negotiations should focus or to which it should be limited. As to other terms of the future contract such as delivery, the parties may agree that the supply contract should be negotiated on the basis of prevailing market conditions. Where reference is made to market conditions, it is advisable that the parties refer to a specific market.

Because of the discretion left to the parties, the inclusion of a guideline in the countertrade agreement for a particular term in the future contract does not ensure the finalization of that term. Nevertheless, narrow range within which agreement should have been achieved, or clear guidelines limiting the latitude available to the negotiators, will not only make it more likely that a contract will be concluded but will also make it easier to show that a party refusing a given contract offer is in breach of the countertrade commitment.

Determination of Contract Term by Third Person

Sometimes the parties agree that a particular contract term will be determined by a third person. While such an approach provides a high degree of certainty that the term will be made definite, its infrequent use may be attributable to a reluctance by parties to relinquish their control over a contract term. When such a method is used, it is usually to determine the price of goods. The parties might be willing to agree on such a method of determining a contract term if clear guidelines are established within which the third person is to decide or if the third person intervention is the last resort after other agreed mechanisms, negotiations, application of an agreed standard, have failed. If the parties do not wish to entrust the decision on a contract term to a third person, but still want the benefit of the opinion of a third person, it may be agreed that the determination by the third person will only be a recommendation.

A number of legal systems recognize the right of the parties to entrust a third person with determining a contract term. In particular, reference by the parties to a third person for the determination of the price is a question frequently addressed in legal systems. There are, however, variations among the systems. For example, while some legal systems recognize that an arbitral tribunal or even a court may be entrusted with the determination of a contract term, others permit such a determination only if it is not performed as part of arbitral or judicial proceedings. Legal systems also differ as to the consequences of a failure by the parties to agree on the third person or of a failure by the third person to act. Under some legal systems, the parties would have no recourse to a procedure for designating or replacing the person, and would have to accept the consequences of the contract term being left undetermined. In other systems, if the third person was to determine the price, the case may be treated as if the parties had agreed on a reasonable price. There are also differing approaches to the availability and extent of judicial review of a decision by a third person.

The issues that the parties may wish to address in a stipulation empowering a third person to determine a contract term are enumerated below.

Person to Request Determination of Term

The parties may wish to address the question whether, at the time when the parties fail to agree on the term, either party would be entitled to request the third person to determine the term or whether the third person may act only upon the request of both parties.

The Identity of the Third Person or the Appointment Procedure

The parties may wish to name in the countertrade agreement the person who is to determine the contract term. In this case, the parties may also wish to provide an appointment procedure to be used in the event that the named person fails to act or is unable to act. If the parties do not wish to name the person who is to determine the contract term, it may be advišable for the parties to agree that they will appoint the third person at such time as they are unable themselves to reach agreement on the contract term. In such a case the parties may wish to agree on an appointment procedure, which is to become operative if the parties cannot reach agreement in the appointment of the third person.

Guidelines or Standards to be Observed by Third Person

The parties are advised to delimit the mandate of the third person by providing guidelines or standards to be observed in determining the contract term. Such guidelines and standards are discussed generally above.

Nature of Decision of Third Person

The parties may agree that the decision by the third person would be binding as a contractual stipulation of the parties. Another approach may be to provide that the determination of the third person would be treated as a recommendation to be considered by the parties in good faith.

Procedure for Challenging Decision by the Third Person

In some situations, where the binding determination by the third person involves a question of particular economic significance, the parties might wish to provide an opportunity for the decision to be challenged by resort to another person, a panel of persons, or an institution. As to the nature of the decision on the challenge, it may be provided that the decision would bind the parties or only be a recommendation. The parties may wish to stipulate the mandate that would be given to the person deciding on the challenge to uphold or reject the challenge, or to modify the challenged decision. The parties may wish to indicate how, in the event the challenged decision is set aside, the decision on the.

contract term is to be made, by the parties themselves or by the same or a different third person.

Determination of Contract Term by Contract Party

Sometimes the countertrade agreement leaves the determination of a contract term to one of the parties to the countertrade agreement. If such an approach is contemplated, the parties should take into account the restrictions legal systems provide concerning the validity of clauses empowering a party to the contract to determine a term of the contract. Generally, an arbitrary right given to one of the parties to determine a contract term is unenforceable. If the subject of the determination is the price, a number of systems would recognize such a right given to a party if its exercise is limited by such standards as reasonableness, good faith or fairness. Some of these systems would construe ambiguous agreements as implying a reference to such a standard. Other legal systems require the freedom to determine the price to be limited by a more definite standard.

General Remarks

A countertrade transaction is usually the result of extensive written and oral communications between the parties. Each party may find it desirable to establish a checklist of the necessary steps to be taken in negotiating and drawing up contracts constituting the transaction, the countertrade agreement and the supply contracts. Such a checklist could reduce the possibility of omissions or errors occurring in the steps taken prior to entering into the contract. A party may also wish to consider seeking legal or technical advice[*] in drawing up the contracts. While countertrade transactions can be expected to become routine for parties experienced in countertrade, even simple countertrade transactions may pose difficulties for newcomers to countertrade calling for legal or technical advice. For complex transactions, even experienced parties may require advice.

The process of establishing a countertrade transaction could be facilitated if the parties agree that before a first draft of the countertrade agreement and any supply contract is prepared, negotiations on the main technical and commercial issues are to take place. Thereafter, one of the parties could be asked to submit a first draft reflecting the

---

[*] United Nations General Assembly, United Nations Commission on. International Trade Law Twentythird Session, New York, June 1990.

agreement reached during the negotiations. A first draft may then be discussed and elaborated, resulting in a preliminary set of contract documents, which, after review and finalization, will govern the relationship between the parties.

The legal rules applicable to the countertrade agreement may require that a countertrade agreement be in written form. Even when written form is not required, it is advisable for the parties to express their agreement in writing to avoid later disputes as to what terms were actually agreed upon. If the parties decide that modifications of the countertrade agreement are to be in writing, it is advisable that this be stated in the countertrade agreement.

The parties may wish to clarify the relationship between the contract documents, on the one hand, and the oral exchanges, correspondence and draft documents which came about during the negotiations, on the other. The parties may wish to provide that those communications and draft documents are not part of the contract. They may further provide that those communications and draft documents cannot be used to interpret the contract, or, alternatively, that they may be used for this purpose to the extent permitted by the applicable law. Under the law applicable to the contract, oral exchanges and correspondence might in some cases be relevant to the interpretation of the contract even if they occur after the contract is entered into.

The parties should ensure that the contract terms as expressed in writing are unambiguous and will not give rise to disputes, and that the relationship between the various documents comprising the transaction is clearly established. Such precision may be of particular importance in countertrade transactions that are carried out over a long period and may have to be administered by persons who have not participated in the negotiations at the outset of the transaction, buy-back or offset transactions. Each party may find it useful to designate one person to be primarily responsible for supervising the preparation of the contract documents. It is advisable for that person to be a skilled draftsman familiar with international countertrade transactions. To the extent possible, it is advisable for that person to be present during important negotiations. Each party may find it useful to have the final contract documents scrutinized by a team having expertise in the subject-matter reflected in the documents in order to ensure accuracy and consistency of style and content.

The applicable legal rules may also contain rules on the interpretation of contracts and presumptions as to the meaning of certain expressions such as "reasonable price", "trust" and "compte fiduciaire", and "penalty", "liquidated damages and penalties". The parties are advised to select contract wording in light of the applicable law in order to ensure that the expressions used reflect the intended meaning. One approach is for the applicable law to be determined at a very early stage of the relationship between the parties, at the commencement of negotiations. The countertrade transaction may then be negotiated and drawn up taking that law into account. Another approach is for the parties to determine the applicable law only after negotiations have taken place on the main technical and commercial issues and have resulted in a measure of accord between the parties. They may thereafter review the first drafts relating to the transaction, which reflect that accord, in the light of the applicable law to ensure that the terms of the draft take account of that law.

The parties should take into account the mandatory legal rules of an administrative, fiscal or other public nature in the country of each party that are relevant to the countertrade transaction. They should also take into account such mandatory legal rules in other countries when those rules are relevant to the transaction. Certain rules may concern the technical aspects of the countertrade agreement, safety standards for the countertrade goods or rules relating to environmental protection, and the terms of the countertrade agreement should not conflict with those rules. Other rules may concern export, import and foreign exchange restrictions, it may be provided that certain rights and obligations are not to arise until export or import licences, approvals for payments or for the use of particular payment mechanisms have been granted. Legal rules relating to taxation may be a factor, and the parties may wish to include in the countertrade agreement provisions dealing with liability for tax.

The parties may wish to consider whether the countertrade agreement is to contain introductory recitals. The recitals may set forth representations made by one or both parties which induced the parties to enter into the agreement. The recitals may also describe the context in which the countertrade agreement was entered into. The extent to which recitals are used in the interpretation of the terms of the agreement introduced by the recitals varies under different legal systems, and their impact on the interpretation may be uncertain. Accordingly, if the contents of recitals are intended to be significant in the interpretation or implementation of the countertrade agreement, it may be preferable to include those contents in the operative provisions of the countertrade agreement.

The parties may find it useful to examine standard forms of countertrade agreements, general conditions, standard clauses, or previously concluded countertrade agreements to facilitate the preparation of contract documents. Such an examination may clarify for the parties the issues that should be addressed in their negotiations. However, it is inadvisable to adopt provisions appearing in those locuments without critical examination. Those provisions may, as a whole, reflect an undesirable balance of interests, or those provisions may not accurately reflect the terms agreed to by the parties. The parties may find it advisable to compare the approaches adopted in the forms, conditions or countertrade agreements examined by them with the approaches recommended in the present legal guide.

Language

The contracts constituting the countertrade transaction (that is, the countertrade agreement and the individual supply countries) may all be drawn up in only one language version (which may, but need not be, the language of either of the parties), or in the two languages of the parties where those languages differ, or the countertrade agreement may be drawn up in the language and the supply contracts in another language. Where the conclusion of the countertrade agreement precedes the conclusion of the supply contracts in the two directions, or where it precedes the conclusion of the counter-export contract), it is advisable that the countertrade agreement specify the language of the contracts. The specification of the language before the commencement of negotiations on a supply contract may facilitate preparations of the parties for the negotiations and avoid a disagreement.

Drawing up a contract in only one language version will reduce conflicts of interpretation in regard to its provisions. Drawing up all the contracts constituting the countertrade transaction in the same language will reduce conflicts between two contracts of related content. On the other hand, each party may understand its rights and obligations more easily if one version of the contract is in its language. In addition, where extensive or complex working instructions to personnel of one or both parties are derived directly from the contract, it may be of particular importance that the contract is in the language in which the instructions are to be given. If only one language is to be used, the parties may wish to take the following factors into account in choosing that language: that it is advisable for the language chosen to be understood by the senior personnel of each party who will be implementing the contract; that it might be advisable for the contract to be in a language commonly used in international commerce; that the settlement of disputes is likely to be facilitated if the language chosen is the language in which proceedings would be conducted or if the language chosen is the language or one of the languages of the country of the applicable law.

If the parties do not draw up the contracts in a single language version, it is advisable to specify in the contracts which language version is to prevail in the event of a conflict between the two versions. If the negotiations were conducted in one of the languages, the parties may wish to provide that the version in the language of the negotiations is to prevail. A provision that one of the language versions is to prevail might induce both parties to clarify as far as possible the prevailing language version. The parties may wish one language version to prevail in respect of certain segments of the transaction or in respect of certain contract documents (e.g. countertrade agreement or technical documents related to the countertrade agreement or a supply contract) and another language version in respect of the remainder of the contracts or documents. Where the parties provide that both language version are to have equal status the parties should attempt to provide guidelines for the settlement of a conflict between the two language versions. The parties may provide, for example, that the agreement is to be interpreted according to practices that the parties have established between themselves and usages regularly observed in international trade with respect to the agreement in question. The parties may also wish to provide that where a term of the contract in one language version is unclear, the corresponding term in the other language version may be used to clarify that term.

Parties to Transaction

Where a contract involved in the transaction (the countertrade agreement or a supply contract) consists of several documents, the parties may wish to identify and describe themselves in a principal document designed to come first in logical sequence among the documents that incorporate that contract. The document should set forth, in a legally accurate form, the names of the parties, indicate their addresses, record the fact that the parties have entered into a contract, briefly describe the subject-matter of the contract, and be signed by the parties. It should also set forth the date on which, and the place where, the contract was signed, and the time when it is to enter into force. Subsequent reference in the contract to the parties may be facilitated if the principal document would specify that in the subsequent text and in the subordinate documents the parties would be referred to by agreed abbreviations or by expressions such as exporter, importer, counter-exporter, counter-importer, trading house. A party may have several addresses, the address of its head office, the address of a branch (through which the contract was negotiated) and it may be preferable to specify in the documents the address to which notifications directed to a party should be sent.

Parties to countertrade transactions are usually legal entities. In such cases the source of their legal status incorporation under the laws of a particular country may be set out in the contract. There may be limitations on the capacity of legal entities to enter into contracts. Therefore, unless satisfied of the other party's capacity to enter into the contract, each party may wish to require from the other some proof of that capacity. If a party to the contract is a legal entity, the other party may wish to satisfy itself that the official of the entity signing the contract has the authority to bind the entity. If the contract is entered into by an agent on behalf of a principal, the name, address and status of the agent and of the principal may be identified, and evidence of authority from the principal enabling the agent to enter into the contract on its behalf may be annexed.

Notifications

In a countertrade transaction a party frequently has to notify the other party of certain events or situations. Such notifications may be required to initiate negotiations for the conclusion of a supply contract, to facilitate cooperation in the performance of the contract, to enable the party to whom notification is given to take action, as the prerequisite to the exercise of a right, or as the means of exercising a right. The parties may wish to address and resolve in their contract certain issues which arise in connection with such notifications.

In the interests of certainty, it is desirable to require that all notifications referred to in the countertrade transaction be given in writing, although in certain cases requiring immediate action the parties may wish to provide that notification can be given orally in person or by telephone, to be followed by confirmation in writing. The parties may wish to define "writing" and to specify the acceptable means of conveying written notifications—surface mail, airmail, telex, telegraph, facsimile, electronic data interchange (EDI). However, care should be taken not to so limit the means of notification that, if the means specified is not available, no valid notification could be given. The parties may also wish to specify the language in which notifications are to be given (that is, the language of the contract).

With regard to the time when a notification is to be effective, two approaches may be considered. One approach is to provide that a notification is effective upon its dispatch by the party giving the notification, or after the lapse of a fixed period of time after the dispatch. Alternatively, the parties may provide that a notice is effective only upon delivery of the notification to the party to whom it is given. Under the former approach, the risk of a failure to transmit or an error by the transmitting agency in transmission of the notification rests on the party to whom the notification is sent, while under the latter approach it rests on the party dispatching the notification. The parties may find it advantageous to select a means of transmitting the notification which provides proof of the dispatch or delivery, and of the time of dispatch or delivery. Another approach may be to require the party to whom the notification is given to acknowledge receiving the notification. It may be convenient for the contract to contain a general provision to the effect that, unless otherwise specified, one or the other approach with respect to when a notification becomes effective on dispatch or delivery is to apply to notifications referred to in the contract. Exemptions to the general approach adopted may be appropriate for certain notifications.

The parties may wish to specify the legal consequences of a failure to notify. The parties may also wish to specify the consequences of a failure to respond to a notification that requires a response. When the parties envisage a series of shipments, they may provide that if the supplier notifies the purchaser of a proposed shipment of a given quantity of the goods on a particular date, the purchaser is deemed to have agreed unless an objection is made.

Definitions

The parties may find it useful to define certain key expressions or concepts that are frequently used in the countertrade agreement or in the supply contract. Definitions are particularly useful in contracts between parties from different countries, even if they use the same language, because of the increased possibility that certain expressions or concepts may be used differently in the two countries. Definitions are also useful when the contracts are in two languages since they tend to reduce the likelihood of errors in translation. A definition ensures that the expression or concept defined is understood in the same sense whenever it is used in the agreement or the contract, and dispenses with the need to clarify the intended meaning of the expression or concept on each occasion that it is used. A definition is advisable if an expression which needs to be used is ambiguous. Such definitions are sometimes made subject to the qualification that the expressions defined bear the meanings assigned to them. Such a qualification takes into account the possibility that an expression which has been defined has inadvertently been used in a context in which it does not bear the meaning assigned to it in the definition. The preferable course is for the parties to scrutinize the contract carefully to ensure that the expressions defined bear the meanings assigned to them wherever they occur, thereby eliminating the need for such a qualification.

Since a definition is usually intended to apply throughout an agreement or contract, a list of definitions may be included in the controlling document. Where, however, an expression that needs to be defined is used only in a particular provision or a particular section of the agreement or contract, it may be more convenient to include a definition in the provision or section in question.

Expressions such as "countertrade agreement", "writing", "dispatch of notification", and "delivery of notification" may be defined. The parties may wish to consider the following:

Countertrade Agreement. "Countertrade agreement" consists of the following documents, and has that meaning in all the said documents: (a) the present document; (b) list of possible countertrade goods; (c) . . .

Writing. "Writing" includes statements contained in a telex, telefax, telegram or other means of telecommunication which provides a record of the content of such statements.

Dispatch of a Notification. "Dispatch of notification" by a party occurs when it is properly addressed and conveyed to the appropriate entity for transmission by a mode authorized under the contract.

Delivery of a Notification. "Delivery of a notification" to a party occurs when it is handed over to that party, or when it is left at an address of that party at which, under the contract, the notification may be left, irrespective of whether the notification is brought to the attention of the individual responsible to act on the notification.

The parties may find it useful, when formulating their own definitions, to consider the descriptions contained in the present guide of the various concepts commonly used in countertrade transactions.

Type, Quality and Quantity of Goods*
General Remarks

The parties may either identify in the countertrade agreement the type of goods that will be the subject of the future supply contract, possibly stating only broad categories of goods, or not stipulate the type of

---

* United Nations General Assembly, United Nations Commission on, International Trade Law Twentythird Session, New York, June 1990.

goods. The more precise the countertrade agreement is with respect to the ype of goods, the greater the possibility is of stipulating in the countertrade agreement the quantity and quality of the goods. Precision as to type, quality and quantity increases the likelihood that the intended supply contract will be concluded. Sometimes, even though the type of countertrade goods is identified in the countertrade agreement, the exact quality and quantity of the goods are left for later determination because the conditions on which the parties wish to base their decision on quantity and quality are not yet fully known.

Type of Goods

Various considerations may enter into the selection of the type of goods. The supplier would prefer that the goods be those that could easily be made available or those that the supplier wishes to introduce in a new market, while the purchaser would like to purchase goods that are needed or could be resold easily. The freedom of the parties to agree on the type of goods to be supplied in one or both directions may be affected by government regulations.

In some countries government regulations exclude certain types of goods from being offered for purchase in a countertrade transaction if the price of the goods is not to be remitted as in an ordinary sale. Such regulations are intended to ensure that goods that can be sold for convertible currency are not sold in transactions that restrict the transfer to the supplier of the convertible currency. Government regulations may also provide that the import of certain types of goods is permitted only if the exporter agrees to purchase goods in return.

The choice of the parties as to type of goods may also be restricted by government regulations requiring that the countertrade goods must originate in the country, or in a particular region of the country or must be purchased from a particular economic sector or group of suppliers. Such restrictions on origin and source are particularly likely to be encountered when the party requiring a countertrade commitment is a governmental entity. It is advisable that any restrictions on origin and source of goods be reflected in the countertrade agreement. Clauses in the countertrade agreement concerning origin and source restrictions are discussed below.

When the parties conclude a countertrade agreement without determining the type of goods, they may wish to include in the countertrade agreement a list of possible countertrade goods, the purchase of which would count toward fulfilment of the countertrade commitment. Where the countertrade agreement is concluded prior to the supply contracts pertaining to deliveries in both directions, there may be two lists, one for each direction in which goods will be shipped. The product list may be attached to the countertrade agreement at the time of signature or may be agreed upon later.

The countertrade agreement should be clear as to the nature and extent of the undertaking of the parties with respect to a list of possible countertrade goods. The supplier may undertake to make available all the types of goods on the list. In such a case the purchaser would be free to choose from among different types of goods appearing on the list, unless the countertrade agreement restricts the purchaser's choice. There may be a limit on the number of different types of goods that may be purchased or there may be minimum or maximum levels set for the purchase of certain types of goods.

The undertaking of the supplier as to availability may be limited to certain specified types of goods on the list. In such a case, the purchaser would be free to choose from among the goods that are identified in the countertrade agreement as being available. The possibility of purchasing any of the other types of goods, whose availability is not assured, would be left to subsequent negotiation.

It may be agreed that the purchaser's commitment is to be reduced to the extent the supplier fails to make available those types of goods that are identified in the countertrade agreement as being available. In addition, the supplier's commitment to make available goods appearing on a list may be supported by a liquidated damages or penalty clause "Liquidated damages and penalty clauses" or a guarantee "Security for performance"

When the supplier does not make an undertaking as to the availability of any particular type of goods appearing on the list, the determination of the types of goods actually available will occur in the course of the subsequent negotiations. If the supplier fails to make available any of the goods on the list, the purchaser would not be liable for the failure to fulfil the countertrade commitment "Fulfilment of countertrade commitment".

The parties may wish to state in the countertrade agreement that the purchaser is obligated to supply within a specific time period the specifications necessary to establish accurately the purchaser's requirements with respect to the goods to be purchased and to enable the supplier to make a corresponding offer. The countertrade agreement may indicate that specifications will be provided by a third party, a trading house engaged to purchase the goods, or an end-user.

Because countertrade agreements are often entered into for the purpose of developing new exports or new markets for existing exports, selection of the countertrade goods could be conditioned or a requirement that the goods be a non-traditional export of the supplier or, if they are a traditional export, that they be resold in a new market. Where the purchaser has made prior purchases from the supplier or has a prior commitment to purchase goods from the supplier, the countertrade agreement may stipulate that the purchase is to be of a new type of goods and must result in a level of sales higher than established levels in order to be counted towards fulfilment, concerning "additionality" as a factor in setting the quantity of goods. It is advisable that the countertrade agreement define the requirements as to new products or markets, either by identifying products and markets considered new or identifying those not considered new.

Establishing a procedure in the countertrade agreement for making decisions on the type of countertrade goods may be helpful, particularly in a long term countertrade transaction or one involving multiple parties. The parties may wish to form a joint committee that would meet at regular intervals to identify countertrade goods and to monitor fulfilment of the countertrade commitment. Procedures established for identifying countertrade goods should be coordinated with deadlines in the fulfilment schedule: "Fulfilment of countertrade commitment", "Contracting approach". Such a joint committee might also be utilized to settle the price of the goods, "Pricing of goods".

Quality of Goods

The question of quality of countertrade goods raises two main issues that the parties may wish to address in the countertrade agreement. The first involves specifying the level of quality that the goods must meet; the second involves establishing procedures to ascertain, before the conclusion of a supply contract, that goods being offered meet the specified level of quality (pre-contractual inspection). Agreement on both aspects of quality may help the parties to avoid disagreements over such questions as whether the party committed to purchase countertrade goods is obligated to purchase particular goods offered by the supplier or whether they are worth the price at which they are offered.

Specifying Quality

If the type of goods is not identified in the countertrade agreement, or is identified only by broad categories, precise statements of quality cannot be made. In such cases, the parties may only be able to state quality requirements in general terms such as "export", "prime" or "marketable" quality. When the type of goods is identified, it is advisable to be as precise as possible with respect to quality. General statements on quality may be sufficient if the goods are commodities or manufactured goods with standardized levels of quality, wire, steel sheets or petro-chemical products. Statements of quality can be made more precise, by referring to a particular country or market, to the purpose for which the goods must be fit, or to packaging, safety and environmental .re-quirements.

The parties may wish to address in the countertrade agreement the remedies of the purchaser in the event that goods delivered under supply contracts concluded subsequently do not meet quality standards stipulated in the countertrade agreement or in individual supply contracts. By including such provisions in the countertrade agreement, the parties could avoid negotiating the question of the purchaser's remedies each time a supply contract is concluded.

Pre-contractual Quality Control

Pre-contractual quality control, that is, quality control carried out before the conclusion of a supply contract by the party committed to purchase in order to establish whether the goods offered conform to the quality standards set in the countertrade agreement. Pre-contractual quality control allows the parties to avoid difficulties that may arise if, after a supply contract is concluded, the goods are discovered not to meet the agreed quality standards.

Identity of Inspector

The pre-contractual quality control may be conducted by an inspector designated either by the party committed to purchase or by the parties jointly. When the inspector is to be designated jointly the parties may wish to stipulate in the countertrade agreement criteria for the selection of the inspector. When the type of goods has been identified, the parties would be in a better position to name the inspector since the subjectmatter in which the inspector would need expertise would be known to the parties.

Inspection Procedures

The parties may wish to agree on various aspects of the inspection procedure such as: the location and time of inspection; the mandate of an inspector to be designated jointly; whether, in the case of an inspector designated by the purchaser, the supplier will be informed of the inspector's mandate; the inspector's duty of confidentiality; deadlines for submission of the inspector's report; a requirement that reason be stated for a finding that the goods are non-conforming;

whether sampling and testing procedures customarily used in a particular trade suffice or whether *ad hoc* procedures need to be established; additional inspections or tests when the result of an inspection is conducted. A further inspection to be conducted by a second inspector and that the second inspection would be controlling and cost of inspection.

Effect of Inspector's Finding

It may be agreed that the inspector's finding would be regarded as a statement of opinion on the basic of which the parties would consider what steps to take. Alternatively, it may be agreed that a finding by the inspector as to the quality of the goods would directly affect the contractual relationship of the parties. It may be agreed that a supply contract would be deemed concluded in the event that the inspector finds that the goods conform to the quality standard stipulated in the countertrade agreement; in the event of a negative finding, the supplier's offer to conclude a supply contract would be deemed not accepted and the rejection of the goods in question would not constitute a breach of the countertrade commitment. Where the countertrade agreement envisages various levels of quality, it may be agreed that the inspector's finding as to quality would be used in a formula for determining the price of the goods.

Quantity of Goods: General Remarks

When the countertrade commitment refers to goods of one specific type, the quantity of goods to be purchased may be stipulated in the countertrade agreement or left to be determined at the time of the conclusion of the supply contracts on the basis of the extent of the countertrade commitment. When the parties express the countertrade commitment as a monetary amount, rather than as a quantity of goods to be purchased, they may wish to postpone determining the quantity until the conclusion of the supply contract. Such a postponement would allow fluctuations in the unit price of the goods to be taken into account. An increase in the unit price would mean a reduction in the quantity of goods to purchased, while a drop in the unit price would mean an increase in the quantity to be purchased. When the countertrade commitment is expressed in terms of the number of units to be purchased, the parties may wish to stipulate a minimum monetary amount so that, in the event of a drop in the unit price, additional units would have to be purchased.

When a countertrade agreement provides for several possible types of goods, the quantity of each type of goods that will be purchased may be left to be determined at the time of the conclusion of the supply contracts. The overall value of the purchases would have to be in conformity with the extent of the commitment set in the countertrade agreement. The countertrade agreement may specify the minimum and maximum percentages of the countertrade commitment that may be fulfilled by purchase of each type of goods.

Where the parties are not in a position to determine quantity in the countertrade agreement, it may be useful for the countertrade agreement to set a deadline for agreement on quantity. The parties may refer to a specific date 30 days before the close of a subperiod of the fulfilment period or to an event in the contract in the other direction., in a buy-back transaction it may be agreed that quantity is to be determined upon the start-up of the plant delivered under the export contract.

It may also be agreed that at specified points in the periods for the fulfilment of the countertrade commitment, a party committed to purchase would be obligated to provide an estimate of the quantities of goods expected to be purchased in the upcoming period of time. Similarly, a party committed to supply goods may agree to periodically provide an estimate of the quantity of goods expected to be made available. The parties may wish to agree on a permitted deviation between the estimated quantities and the quantities actually purchased or made available.

When the proceeds of the export contract are to be used to pay for the counter-export contract, it is advisable that the parties ensure that the quantity purchased under the export contract is such that the proceeds of the export contract would cover payment for the counter-export contract. Payment mechanisms used in such cases are discussed below.

If the parties foresee the possibility of purchases of quantities beyond those stipulated in the countertrade agreement, they may wish to consider whether the purchaser's additional orders will be granted any preference over other potential buyers. A related issue is whether the additional quantities would be supplied on the same terms as the original quantities envisaged in the countertrade agreement.

The parties may leave the quantity of goods to be determined on the basis of the purchaser's requirements. In such cases, the parties may wish to consider whether the supplier is to be the purchaser's single source for the goods and whether the purchases are to fall within a range specified in the countertrade agreement. The quantity of the goods may also be determined on the basis of the supplier's output of a given product. This approach may be used, in a buy-back transaction. In this case too, the parties may wish to stipulate that the purchases are to fall within a range set in the countertrade agreement.

Additionality

When the purchaser has made prior purchases from the supplier of a given type of goods, the provisions in the countertrade agreement regarding quantity may contain a concept often referred to as "additionality". According to this approach, only those purchases that exceed the usual quantities purchased will be considered as fulfilling the countertrade commitment. The parties would normally be able to establish the threshold of additionality by agreeing on the quantity that is to be regarded as the usual or traditional purchase. When the parties do not identify the type of goods in the countertrade agreement, they may include a general stipulation that if the goods ultimately selected are of a type that the purchaser is already buying, only those purchases above existing levels would be counted toward fulfilment of the countertrade commitment.

Where the arrangement allows the purchaser to choose from a number of eligible suppliers other than the party to whom the countertrade commitment is owed, in an indirect offset transaction, the additionality threshold would not be passed on previous trade volume between the parties to the countertrade agreement, but on the trade volume with the suppliers selected or on the volume of previous purchases by the committed party in the suppliers' country. The parties may wish to identify the sources of any trade information to be used in setting the additionality threshold.

Modification of Provisions on Type, Quality and Quantity

A need for a review of provisions on type, quality or quantity of goods may arise due to the nonavailability of goods specified in the countertrade agreement, the desire to place additional products on a list, a change in the commercial conditions underlying the transaction, a shift in the commercial objectives of the parties or a governmental regulation affecting the choice of countertrade goods. It could be agreed, particularly in long-term transactions, that the parties would review the provisions on type, quality and quantity of goods either at regular intervals or in response to changes in circumstances stipulated in the countertrade agreement, a change beyond a certain threshold in the price of the goods. The review could be carried out within the framework of a mechanism for monitoring and coordinating fulfilment of the countertrade commitment, "Fulfilment of countertrade commitment".

In order to avoid a modification procedure, the parties may wish to provide that under certain conditions fulfilment credit would be earned by the purchase of goods other than those agreed upon in the countertrade agreement or appearing on a list of possible countertrade goods. It might be required that the purchases in question meet an additionality test, or it may be stipulated that they would earn fulfilment credit at a reduced rate.

Payment*: General Remarks

The parties may decide that the payment obligation under the supply contract in one direction is to be liquidated independently from the payment obligation under the supply contract in the other direction. When payments are independent, the payment under each supply contract is made in a way that is used in trade generally, such as payment on open account, payment against documents, or letters of credit. Alternatively, the parties may decide to link payment so that the proceeds generated by the contract in one direction would be used to pay for the contract in the other direction, thus allowing the transfer of funds between the parties to be avoided or reduced. The legal guide discusses only linked payment arrangements. It does not discuss independent payment arrangements since they do not raise issues specific to countertrade.

One reason the parties may have for linking payments is the expectation that it would be difficult for a party to effect payment in the agreed currency. Another reason may be to ensure that the proceeds generated by the shipment in one direction would be used to pay for the shipment in the other direction. Payment mechanisms designed to meet such needs include retention of funds by importer, blocking funds paid under the export contract through blocked accounts or crossed letters of credit to secure their availability to pay for the counter-export contract, and set-off countervailing claims for payment.

An aspect of linked payment mechanisms to be considered is the financing costs that result from the fact that linked payment mechanisms immobilize the proceeds of shipments made by the parties. The longer the interval between the time the proceeds are generated by the contract in one direction and the time those proceeds are used to pay

---

* United Nations General Assembly, United Nations Commission on, International Trade Law Twentythird Session , New York, June 1990.

for the contract in the other direction, the greater the financing costs are
likely to be.

The parties may wish to consider the possibility of interference by a
third party in the functioning of the linked payment mechanism. A
creditor of one of the countertrade parties may seize proceeds of a
supply contract or a payment claim of the debtor, the bank holding the
funds may become insolvent or governmental authorities may intervene
to prevent payment due to shortage of foreign exchange. Such
interference could result in the freezing of the payment mechanism until
the claim against the countertrade party is adjudicated or a governmental
measure lifted. A factor in assessing this risk is the degree of protection
the law applicable to the payment mechanism affords against third-party
interference. Furthermore, the longer funds are held in the payment
mechanism, or claims for payment wait to be set off, the greater the
risk of third-party interference.

It should be noted that payment mechanisms may require governmental authorization it they involve a delay in or an absence of
repatriation of the proceeds of a supply contract, the holding of funds
abroad or the holding of a domestic account in a foreign currency.

Retention of Funds by Importer

Sometimes it is agreed that the shipment in a particular direction
(export contract) is to precede the shipment in the other direction
(counter-export contract), and that the proceeds of the export contract are
to be used to pay for the subsequent counter-export. Such cases are
sometimes referred to as "advance purchase" in view of the fact that the
importer is to purchase goods in advance in order to generate financing
for the counter-export contract. In such cases, the parties may agree that
the proceeds of the export contract will be held under the control of the
importer until payment under the counter-export contract becomes due.

A consideration as to the acceptability of such an arrangement
would be the exporter's confidence that the importer will hold the funds
in accordance with the countertrade agreement. Such confidence is more
likely to exist when the parties have an established relationship.
Another consideration is the risk that the importer will become
insolvent or that the funds in the hands of the importer will be subject
to a third-party claim. Under ordinary circumstances the claim of the
exporter would have no priority over that of another creditor of the
importer. In some legal systems, the funds may enjoy a degree of
protection against the claims of third parties if the agreement
concerning the retention of funds places the importer in a fiduciary
position with respect to the funds. In common law systems, this might

be done by establishing a "trust" in which the importer acts as the "trustee" of the funds. Fiduciary mechanisms available in some other legal systems may offer similar protection.

Furthermore, if the countertrade agreement does not specify the type of goods to be counter-exported, or if no standard exists to measure the quality of the type of goods agreed upon, a disagreement may arise over the type, quality or price of counter-export goods. The possibility of such a disagreement increases the risk that for an unacceptable period of time the retained funds will neither be put to the intended use nor released to the exporter. When the parties are able to specify the type of goods, a consideration affecting the acceptability of retention of funds by the importer may be the length of time required to make the counter-export goods available. Retention of funds by the importer might be more acceptable when the goods to be purchased with the retained funds are available in stock and can be shipped quickly, and less acceptable when the goods have to be specially manufactured.

An appropriate balance needs to be established between two opposing objectives. One objective is to assure the exporter access to the funds if the counter-export did not take place. The other objective is to assure the importer that the funds will not be transferred to the exporter, at least not the full amount, if the exporter is in breach of the commitment under the countertrade agreement to counter-import. The first objective may be advanced by fixing a date by which the funds have to be transferred to the exporter in the event the counter-export has not taken place. The second objective may be advanced by authorizing the importer to deduct any liquidated damages or penalty that may be due to the importer for the exporter's breach of the countertrade commitment before the funds are returned to the exporter.

Depending upon the length of time the funds are to be retained under the control of the importer, the parties may wish to consider providing in the countertrade agreement for the payment of interest. If they do so, the parties may stipulate the manner in which the funds are to be deposited so as to earn the most favourable rate of interest.

Blocking of Funds: General Remarks

When the exporter does not wish to leave the funds generated by the export contract under the control of the importer, the parties may wish to use another payment mechanism designed to ensure that the proceeds of the first shipment are used for the intended purpose. The legal guide addresses two mechanisms of this type, blocked accounts and crossed letters of credit.

When the parties opt for a blocked account, they agree that the importer's payment is to be deposited in an account at a financial institution agreed upon by the parties and that the use and release of the money will be subject to certain conditions. After the funds have been deposited in the account, the importer counter-exports and obtains payment from those funds by personation of agreed upon documentation evidencing the performance of the counter-export contract to the institution administering the account. Accounts of this nature have been referred to as "escrow", "trust", "special", "fiduciary" or "blocked" accounts. The expression "blocked account" is used here in order to avoid unintended references to particular varieties of such accounts that may be encountered in different legal systems.

When the parties opt for crossed letters of credit, the importer opens a letter of credit to cover payment for the export contract ("export letter of credit"). The export letter of credit then serves as the basis for the issuance of a letter of credit to pay for the counter-export contract ("counter-export letter of credit"). Pursuant to the instructions of the parties, the proceeds of the export letter of credit are blocked in order to cover the counter-export letter of credit. The export letter of credit is liquidated when the exporter presents the required documents, including an irrevocable instruction that the proceeds should be used to cover payment under the counter-export letter of credit. Payment under the counter-export letter of credit, which is funded by the export letter of credit, is effected upon presentation of the required documents by the counter-exporter.

A blocked account or crossed letters of credit may be used when the importer does not wish to ship the counter-export goods until the availability of funds to pay for those goods is secured. In such "advance purchase" arrangements, both blocked accounts and crossed letters of credit provide security that the funds generated by the shipment in one direction, specifically designated to occur first, would be used to pay for the subsequent shipment in the other direction.

The financial drawbacks of blocking funds may be mitigated to some degree if interest accrues on the blocked funds. A bank holding funds designated for paying letters of credit may be less inclined to pay interest than a bank holding funds in a blocked account. For this reason, a blocked account may provide an interest-bearing vehicle for holding excess funds in anticipation of future orders. This may be helpful in cases where the parties are not certain at the outset as to whether all the proceeds generated by the export will be needed to pay for the counter-export.

Blocked Accounts

Some legal systems provide special legal regimes for blocked accounts if they are established in a particular legal form, "trust" account or "compte fiduciaire"). In those legal systems, a blocked account would be subject to general contract law if it is not established in such a particular form. When a special legal regime is applicable, the holder of the funds is subject to special fiduciary obligations with respect to the disposition of the funds and the funds may enjoy a degree of protection against seizure by third-party creditors.

Contractual provisions outlining the agreement of the parties on the blocked account will be found in the countertrade agreement. In addition, an agreement will have to be concluded between the bank and one or more of the countertrade parties ("blocked account agreement"). The provisions in the supply contracts concerning the blocked account will normally be limited to identifying the account to be used for payment.

Countertrade Agreement: Location of Account

The parties should consider stipulating in the countertrade agreement the location of the account. They may do so by identifying the bank, indicating the country in which the account is to be opened or providing some other criterion for selection of the bank. The choice of possible locations of the account may be limited if the legal system of the party whose shipment generated the funds restricts the right to hold currency abroad. In such a case the choice may be limited to establishing the account with a bank located in that party's country.

When the parties have a choice as to the location of the bank, they should bear in mind that the location of the account may determine the law applicable to the account. The suitability of the applicable law in a given location may be assessed in view of the security provided to the parties that the fiduciary obligations of the bank will be properly exercised. Furthermore, it is desirable that the applicable legal regime provide some protection against interference by a third-party creditor of one of the parties. A degree of protection may be available under some legal systems against claims of third persons.

Operation of Blocked Account

It is advisable that the countertrade agreement contain certain basic provisions to be incorporated in the blocked account agreement with the bank. Such provisions enable each party, upon agreeing to the use of a blocked account, to establish that the account will have the features it considers important. These provisions concern, in particular, procedures for the transfer of funds into the account, documentary requirements for transfer of funds out of the account, payment request using a prescribed form, bill of lading or other shipping document, certificate of quality and interest. In addressing the contents of the blocked account agreement in the countertrade agreement, the parties should be aware that the bank is likely to be accustomed to handling blocked accounts on the basis of contract forms or standard conditions.

The countertrade agreement may provide that payments into the account would be made through a letter of credit opened by the importer in favour of the exporter. It may also be agreed that disbursement of the funds held in the account would be carried out through a letter of credit opened by the counter-importer in favour of the counter-exporter. In such cases it is advisable that the countertrade agreement specify the instructions to be given to the issuing banks and the documents to be presented under the letters of credit. The beneficiary would be required to present, alongwith documents evidencing shipment, an irrevocable instruction that the proceeds should be deposited in the blocked account.

Other Issues

It is advisable that the countertrade agreement address issues such as amount of funds to be blocked, interest, transfer of unused or excess funds, and any supplementary payments. (For a discussion of various issues common to linked payment mechanisms that might be dealt with in the countertrade agreement see below).

Blocked Account Agreement

The blocked account agreement would contain instructions to the bank and specify the actions to be taken by the trading parties and the bank, as well as other provisions concerning the operation of the blocked account. The blocked account agreement would also address issues such as interest and bank charges. It is important to ensure that the blocked account agreement is consistent with the provisions in the countertrade agreement concerning the blocked account.

Parties

The blocked account agreement will be concluded between the bank holding the account and one or more of the countertrade parties. In some cases, an additional bank may be a signatory to the blocked account agreement. This may occur where the funds to be paid into the account are to be channelled, by agreement or by mandatory law, through a particular bank. Some legal systems require that a blocked account established abroad be held in the name of its central bank and that bank be a party to the blocked account agreement. In multi-party countertrade situations where the counter-exporter or counter-importer are distinct from the exporter and importer, the additional trading parties may also be parties to the blocked account agreement.

Transfer of Funds Into and Out of Account

The blocked account agreement would set out procedures customarily used by the bank in administering a blocked account. It is advisable that the parties make sure that their agreement as to the manner in which the funds are to be paid into the account and disbursed from the account to the counter-exporter is reflected in the blocked account agreement. It may be useful to indicate whether partial drawings are permitted, the manner in which the amount to be paid is to be determined on the basis of the face value of the invoice and whether notification of payment requests would be made to the party that deposited funds in the account. The blocked account agreement would also describe the conditions under which excess or unused funds should be transferred to the exporter, or applied according to his instructions. In the latter case, the blocked account agreement may indicate the terms on which funds would be held before instructions are received from the exporter.

It should be noted that the bank holding the blocked funds may require that its responsibility be limited for examining the conforming of the documents included in the counter-exporter's request for payment with the agreed upon requirements, rather than ascertaining whether the underlying contract has been performed. The bank may also require that the counter-exporter, who will be paid from the account, indemnify the bank against costs, claims expenses (other than normal administrative and operating expenses) and liabilities which the bank may incur in connection with the blocked account.

Duration and Closing of Account

In order to ensure the availability of the blocked account for the necessary period of time, the blocked agreement should specify that the account will remain open until a certain date or for a period of time following the entry into force of the countertrade agreement. The parties may wish to provide that the blocked account would remain operative for a period of time 60 days, following the end of the period for the fulfilment of the countertrade commitment. Such a time period would enable the transaction to be completed as planned in the event that shipment under the counter-export contract took place just before expiry of the fulfilment period or was delayed for justified reasons. The blocked account agreement could indicate circumstances in which the account would close, in addition to the passage of an agreed upon period of time. These could include an event such as rescission of the export contract or of the countertrade agreement. If the export letter of credit is payable at sight, the issuing bank is given an irrevocable instruction to retain the funds until a given date for the purpose of paying the counter-export letter of credit. If the export letter of credit is a deferred-payment letter of credit, the bank issuing the export letter of credit would be instructed that upon the date payment is due, the funds are to be used for payment under the counter-export letter of credit.

It is advisable that the instructions for the issuance of the export letter of credit stipulate that the proceeds of the export letter of credit would be paid to the exporter in the event the counter-export fails to materialize. Under an export letter of credit payable at sight, the proceeds would be paid to the exporter if by an agreed date the counter-export goods have not been shipped. If the export letter of credit is payable on a deferred basis, it could be provided that the proceeds will be paid to the exporter if, by the payment date, the counter-exporter has not presented the required documents. Payment to the exporter would also be in order when the proceeds of the export letter of credit exceed what is needed to cover the counter-export letter of credit. If such a situation is foreseen, it is advisable that the importer instruct the issuer of the export letter of credit to transfer to the exporter any proceeds of that letter of credit that are in excess of the specified amount needed to cover the counter-export letter of credit.

Expiry Dates

It is advisable that the counter-export letter of credit expire a reasonable period of time after the expiry of the export letter of credit. Where the two letters of credit have an identical or almost identical expiry date, insufficient time may remain for shipment and presentation of documents under the counter-export contract if shipment and presentation of documents under the export contract took place at the last minute.

Set-off of Countervailing Claims for Payment
General Remarks

The parties may agree that their mutual claims for payment based on shipments made in each direction would be set-off. Under such an arrangement, each party is compensated for its deliveries through deliveries of goods from the other party. Money is not actually paid except to settle an imbalance in the values of the shipments in the two directions.

A set-off approach may be utilized when only one shipment is to be made in each direction or when multiple shipments are to be made in the two directions over a longer period of time; record-keeping mechanism that the parties may wish to use to set-off payment claims of multiple shipments. Such a record-keeping mechanism, referred to in the legal guide as a "set-off account", is referred to in practice by various terms, including "compensation account", "settlement account" or "trade account".

A set-off account may be administered by the parties themselves or by a bank. The engagement of a bank may be prescribed by mandatory rules of law. Banks are also used because the parties may wish that the debit and credit entries in the set-off account be made on the basis of shipping documents examined in accordance with procedures customarily used by banks. Furthermore, banks engaged to administer a set-off account may agree to guarantee the obligation of a countertrade party to liquidate an imbalance in the flow of trade.

Under one approach to structuring a set-off account, two accounts are maintained for recording debit and credit entries, one at a bank in the country of one party and another one at a bank in the country of the other party. Another approach would be to use a single account administered by a single bank; other banks may be involved for the purpose of forwarding documents and issuing or advising letters of credit.

When two banks are involved in administering the set-off arrangement, it is probable that they will conclude an interbank agreement. This interbank agreement may cover some of the points already addressed in the countertrade agreement, as well as establish the technical arrangements relating to the set-off account. The countertrade agreement may refer to the interbank agreement, stating that the technical details of the operation of the accounts will be in accordance with an interbank agreement concluded between the participating banks. Although the countertrade parties are not normally signatories to an interbank agreement, it is advisable that the countertrade parties participate in the preparation of the interbank agreement in order to ensure consistency between the countertrade agreement and the interbank agreement.

The legal guide does not address state-to-state umbrella agreements for mutual trade within the framework of a clearing account between governmental banking authorities. Under such arrangements the value of deliveries in the two directions is recorded in a currency or unit of account and eventually set off between the governmental banking authorities. Individual traders in each country conclude contracts directly with each other but submit their claims for payment to their respective central or foreign trade bank and receive payment in local currency. Similarly, purchasers pay their respective central or foreign trade bank in local currency for their imports. Such clearing mechanisms, which might be part of economic measures designed to promote trade, fall outside the ambit of the legal guide since the individual supply contracts in one direction concluded under the umbrella agreement are not contractually linked to contracts concluded in the other direction.

Countertrade Agreement
Effecting Credit and Debit Entries

The parties may wish to agree that entries in the account will be made on the basis of documents. The countertrade agreement should stipulate the documents required to be presented by the supplier in order to obtain a credit. The type of documents stipulated depends on the point of time in the execution of a supply contract at which the parties wish to allow credit to be given to the supplier. These documents might include, invoices, packing lists, certificates of quality or quantity, bills of lading or other transport documents, evidence of the customs clearance of the goods in the receiving country or of their acceptance by the purchaser, and any other.

A similar provision may be included with respect to funds generated by the export that are in excess of the amount needed to cover the price of the counter-export contract. Transfer of unused funds is also an issue when the parties agree that only a portion of the proceeds of the export contract is to be retained, as a deposit towards payment for the counter-export, and that the balance due under the counter-export will be paid at the time it becomes due.

Supplementary Payments or Deliveries

The parties may anticipate that their shipments will not be of the same value or in the planned quantity so that the proceeds of the shipment in one direction will be insufficient to cover payment for the shipment in the other direction. In such cases, it is advisable to agree whether the difference would be settled through additional deliveries or through cash payments.

Bank Commissions and Charges

It would be advisable for the parties to address in the countertrade agreement the question of payment of banking charges for operation of the payment mechanism, including the cost of any related letters of credit. In order to simplify the operation of the payment arrangement, it may be agreed that banking commissions and charges will be recorded separately from entries pertaining to shipment of goods. Where a single bank is used which acts on behalf of both parties, it may be agreed that the banking charges will be shared equally. Where a bank is involved on both sides of the transaction, it may be agreed that the charges of each bank will be paid by its respective client. According to an alternative method of apportioning costs for letters of credit, charges for the issuance of a letter of credit are borne by the purchaser, while charges for negotiation and confirmation, if required, are borne by the supplier. Extensions or other amendments of letters of credit could be borne by the party responsible for such extension or amendment.

Payment Aspects of Multi-party Countertrade Transactions

General Remarks

A countertrade transaction may involve one or more third parties. In some cases, in addition to the exporter and the importer, a third-party counter-importer is involved ("three-party countertrade"); in other cases, in addition to the exporter and the importer, a third-party counter-exporter is involved ("three-party countertrade"); in yet other cases, in addition to the exporter and the importer, both a third-party counter-importer and a third-party counter-exporter are involved ("four-party countertrade"). "Participation of third persons" and the engagement of a third-party counter-importer may occur when the importer needs to sell goods in order to secure funds to cover the cost of the import, but the exporter is not interested in purchasing or is not able to purchase what the importer has to sell. A third-party counter-exporter may be engaged when the importer itself does not have goods of interest to the exporter.

If the parties agree that the payment obligations under the export contract and under the counter-export contract are to be settled independently, a countertrade transaction involving third parties does not raise payment issues specific to countertrade. Issues specific to countertrade are raised if the proceeds of the contract between one pair of parties (for example, importer and exporter) will be used to pay for a contract between a different pair of parties (importer and third-party counter-importer). In such cases, as described in the following two paragraphs, a party receiving goods does not pay or ship to the party supplying those goods, but instead pays or ships to a third party.

In a three-party countertrade transaction involving a third-party counter-importer, the importer, instead of transferring money to the exporter under the export contract, delivers goods to the counter-importer and is considered to have discharged the payment obligation for the import upto the value of countertrade goods delivered to the counter-importer. The counter-importer, in turn, pays the exporter an amount equivalent to the value of the goods received from the counter-exporter. Similarly, in a three-party transaction involving a third-party counter-exporter, the importer transfers funds to the counter-exporter to pay for the shipment to the counter-importer and the counter-importer (exporter) agrees that the claim for payment under the export contract is discharged by the value of the goods that have been counter-exported to him.

In a four-party countertrade transaction, where the counter-exporter is a separate party from the importer and the counter-importer is a separate party from the exporter, the exporter ships goods to the importer and the importer, instead of paying the exporter, pays to the counter-exporter an amount equivalent to the value of the goods received from the exporter. The payment from the importer to the counter-exporter compensates the counter-exporter for the shipment to the counter-importer. The counter-importer pays to the exporter an amount equivalent to the value of the goods received from the counter-exporter.

Payment in a multi-party countertrade transaction may be structured so that cross-border payment would not be necessary. This would be possible, as between an importer and an exporter, when the importer and the third-party counter-exporter are located in the same country or when the exporter and a third-party counter-importer are located in the same country. When both the counter-exporter and the counter-importer are third parties, cross-border payments may be avoided if both the exporter and the counter-importer are both located in one country and if the importer and the counter-exporter are both located in another country. Where cross border transfer of currency does not take place, payments would be made in local currency between parties on each side of the transaction.

In multi-party countertrade, in addition to the payment-related provisions in the countertrade agreement and the export and counter-export contracts, there would also be agreements between the exporter and the counter-importer or between the importer and the counter-exporter concerning payment in local currency equivalent to the value of the goods received by a given party and the payment of a commission. Furthermore, an agreement may be concluded between the participating banks concerning the payment mechanism.

The countertrade agreement should describe the performance for which each party is responsible, the sequence in which shipments are to take place, the manner and sequence of payments, and the instructions to be given to the participating banks. A multi-party countertrade transaction with a linked payment mechanism requires coordination of the actions of the participating parties and of the instructions given to the participating banks. It is advisable to have a single countertrade agreement, signed by all the participating parties. Where not all the parties to a multi-party transaction are parties to the countertrade agreement, it may be necessary to include in the individual supply contracts terms concerning the linked payment mechanisms.

Blocking of Funds in Multi-party Countertrade

As in countertrade involving two parties, blocked accounts and crossed letters of credit may be used in multi-party countertrade. Issues relevant to the use of blocked accounts and crossed letters of credit are discussed above.

When a blocked account is used in a four-party transaction, or in a three-party transaction involving a third-party counter-exporter, the proceeds of the export contract would be held in a blocked account until presentation of documents evidencing performance of the counter-export contract, at which point the funds would be transferred to the counter-exporter. In the event that by the deadline for presentation of documents evidencing performance of the counter-export contract, those documents have not been presented, the funds would be transferred to the exporter. In order to establish payment through a blocked account, the exporter and importer conclude a blocked account agreement with the bank selected to administer the account.

When crossed letters of credit are used in a three-party transaction involving a third-party counter-exporter, the counter-importer (exporter) opens a letter of credit in favour of the counter-exporter (counter-export letter of credit). Cover for the counter-export letter of credit is obtained from the proceeds of the letter of credit opened by the importer for the benefit of the exporter (export letter of credit). The exporter obtains access to the shipping documents relating to the counter-export goods by presenting evidence of shipment under the export contract and an instruction that the proceeds of the export letter of credit should be used to cover the counter-export letter of credit. Similarly, in the case of a three-party transaction involving a third-party counter-importer, the proceeds of the export letter of credit could be used to cover the counter-export letter of credit.

When crossed letters of credit are used in a four-party transaction, the importer, who obtains the issuance of the export letter of credit, deposits with the issuing bank of the export letter of credit the amount of the letter of credit. Upon the instruction of the exporter, the proceeds of the export letter of credit are not paid to the exporter, but are blocked to cover the counter-export letter of credit. Upon the presentation by the counter-exporter of shipping documents under the counter-export letter of credit, the funds deposited by the importer to cover issuance of the export letter of credit are paid to the counter-exporter; on the other side of the transaction, the counter-importer pays the exporter an amount equivalent to the value of the goods received by the counter-importer. If the counter-exporter does not present shipping documents under the counter-export letter of credit, the funds deposited by the importer to cover the export letter of credit would be transferred to the exporter.

Pricing of Goods: General Remarks*

It is advisable that the parties specify in the countertrade agreement the price of the goods that will be the subjectmatter of the future supply contract, if they are able to do so. When the parties are not able to set the price in the countertrade agreement, it is advisable to provide a method for determining the price at the time the supply contract is to be concluded. This deals with methods for determining the price after the countertrade agreement has been concluded. In addition, this discusses the currency in which the price is expressed and revision of price.

The parties may need to defer setting the price either because the type of goods has not been identified at the time of the conclusion of the countertrade agreement or because there is to be a long interval between the conclusion of the countertrade agreement and the conclusion of a given supply contract. Such an interval may prompt the parties to defer setting the price because of the possibility of price fluctuation or of a change in the underlying economic conditions during the interval. In some cases, the parties may set the price of an initial shipment, but leave the determination of the price of subsequent shipments for a later time. Providing a method for determining the

---

* United Nations General Assembly, United Nations Commission on, International Trade Law Twentythird Session, New York, June 1990.

price may help the parties avoid differences over what the appropriate price should be, which may delay or prevent the conclusion of supply contracts.

In a barter transaction, it may not be necessary to include a provision on price because the goods shipped in one direction constitute payment for the goods shipped in the other direction. Nevertheless, pricing issues may arise in a barter transaction if the parties decide to measure the relative value of their shipments in monetary terms, rather than merely in terms of volume and quality, or if the shipments are of different value and the imbalance is to be settled in money. Pricing would also be necessary when customs regulations require that goods entering a country indicate a monetary value.

In setting the price of the countertrade goods, it is advisable that the parties specify whether or not the price includes costs ancillary to the costs of the goods themselves, such as transportation or insurance, testing, or customs duties and taxes. Some of the elements of the price may be indicated by using an appropriate trade term such as those defined in the INCOTERMS of the International Chamber of Commerce.

The parties may wish to stipulate the point of time when the price is to be calculated, particularly in the case of goods whose price may fluctuate. When the countertrade transaction involves a single shipment or a number of shipments within a relatively short period of time, and the price is to be determined only once, a specified date may be agreed· upon. In some cases, the price setting mechanism may be set in motion by an event such as the start-up of a plant under a buy-back transaction or the placing of an order. When multiple shipments are spread out over a longer period of time, several dates for determination of price may be agreed upon or the countertrade agreement may provide a mechanism for revision of the initial price.

The parties should bear in mind that there may be mandatory rules that affect the level at which the price may be set. For example, if the price is set at a low level in relation to the market price, the goods may be subject to anti-dumping import restrictions.

Currency of Price

The currency in which the price is to be paid may involve certain risks arising from the fluctuation in the purchasing power of that currency and from the fluctuation in exchange rates between that currency and other currencies. If the price is to be paid in the currency of the supplier's country, the purchaser bears the consequences of a change in the exchange rate between that currency and the currency of the purchaser's country. The supplier, however, will bear the consequences of a change in the exchange rate between the currency of the supplier's country and the currency of another country in which the supplier has to pay for equipment, materials or services needed in the production of the goods. If the price is to be paid in the currency of the purchaser's country, the supplier bears the consequences of a change in the exchange rate between this currency and the currency of the supplier's country. If the price is to be paid in the currency of a third country, each party bears the consequences of a change in the exchange rate between this currency and the currency of its respective country. Where a financing institution has granted the purchaser a loan for the purchase of the goods, the purchaser may prefer the price to be paid in the currency in which the loan is granted.

In stipulating the currency in which the price is to be paid, the parties should take into consideration foreign exchange regulations and international treaties in force in the countries of the supplier and the purchaser, which may mandatorily govern this question. The parties should also take into account that under some legal systems the price in an international contract must be paid in the currency in which it is denominated, while other legal systems may permit, or even require, payments in the currency of the place of payment, even if the price is denominated in a foreign currency.

The countertrade agreement may denominate the price in a currency that the parties consider to be stable or in a unit of account that is not a national currency, but provide that it is to be paid in another currency. The effects of such an approach are similar to those achieved by a currency clause, and restrictions imposed by the applicable law in respect of currency clauses may also apply to such provisions. If this approach is used, it is advisable to agree in the countertrade agreement that the exchange rate is to be the one prevailing at a specified place on a specified date.

It is not advisable for the contract to denominate the entire price in two or more currencies, and allow either the debtor or the creditor to decide in which currency the price is to be paid. Under such a clause, only the party having the choice is protected, and the choice may bring the party having the choice unjustified gains.

Determining Price after Conclusion of Counter-trade Agreement Standards

The countertrade agreement may provide for a determination of price through the use of a standard see "Contracting approach". Such a method provides a price at the time of the conclusion of the supply contract in an objective manner not influenced by the will of the parties.

The parties may wish to include a procedure to apply in the event a standard they select proves to be unworkable, e.g. because a market price is not available as expected. The parties may provide that the price is to be determined by the use of an alternate standard or that the price is to be determined by a third person.

Market Prices for Goods of Standard Quality

When goods identified in the countertrade agreement are commodities or semi-finished products, grains, oil, metals, wool for which prices are regularly reported, the parties may agree to link the price of the countertrade goods to the reported price. Where the goods are traded on several exchanges or in several markets, the parties are advised to specify a particular exchange or market to which reference will be made. In order to protect against price fluctuations, the standard may call for an average of the prices reported at several agreed points of time, e.g. the prices reported on the first business day of the month for the six months preceding the date of the determination of the price.

Production Cost

The parties may agree that the price is to be based on the supplier's cost of producing the goods, plus an amount to cover the supplier's overhead and profit. Such an approach may be selected when the exact cost of various inputs cannot be anticipated at the time the countertrade agreement is concluded. In order to limit the purchaser's risk of having to pay an excessive price, it is advisable that, where possible, the parties stipulate in the countertrade agreement the quality of inputs, e.g. raw materials, energy and labour that will be required for the production of one unit of the goods. The parties may also wish to stipulate that the supplier should maintain records reflecting production costs in accordance with forms and procedures required by the purchaser, and that the purchaser shall have access to those records.

Competitor's Price

The price may be determined on the basis of the price charged by an identified competitor producing the same type of goods as those that will be delivered under the supply contract. If the countertrade agreement does not identify the competitor, it may establish criteria for the selection of a competitor, either geographical criteria or criteria related to the volume of production of the same type of goods. Because the competitor may sell a product at different prices in different geographical regions and markets, it is advisable that the countertrade agreement identify the market to which reference will be made. The price clause could also indicate how the price information will be obtained and the date as of which the competitor's price is to be determined. Furthermore, the parties may agree to exclude specially discounted prices charged to certain customers preferential prices e.g. the standard may exclude prices charged for the goods when they are purchased by disaster relief organization or by employees of the supplier.

A competitor's price may not be relevant, without adjustments, if it is based on a significantly larger or smaller quantity than the quantity intended to be purchased under the countertrade agreement. A competitor's price may also not be appropriate if the competitor's goods are of a different quality, if the competitor's price is based on payment conditions; deferred payment not being offered by the supplier of the countertrade goods, or if the amount of transportation costs, of insurance and public charges contained in the competitor's price differs from what is to be included in the price of the countertrade goods. It is therefore advisable to stipulate that the standard should take into account only prices for shipments that are comparable in quantity, delivery and payment conditions to the future supply contract, or that amounts should be added or subtracted from the competitor's price in order to compensate for differences.

The parties may agree that the price is to be determined on the basis of several competitors' prices. Such a clause may identify the competitors or it may provide that each of the parties is to obtain quotations from a specified number of competitors. If the competitors are not identified, it is advisable that a clause of this type specify the countertrade or regions from which the parties are to obtain the quotations. It is also advisable that the countertrade agreement indicate the manner in which the price is to be calculated, whether by calculating a mean or a medium price. The parties may wish to specify the period of time during which the quotations are to be obtained. In doing so, the parties should take into account the length of time necessary to obtain the quotations as well as the need to base the calculation on current prices.

When the party committed to purchase goods manufactures the same type of goods, the parties may agree that the price will be determined on the basis of the price charged by the purchaser or on the basis of the purchaser's own cost of manufacture. Such an approach might be used, for example in a buy-back transaction in which a producer of a certain type of goods sells a facility that produces that type of goods and agrees to buy back the resultant products.

Most-favoured-customer Clause

It may be agreed that the price of the countertrade goods will based on the lowest price at which goods of the same type are supplied by the supplier to other customers. In some cases, the parties may restrict the clause of a limited category of customers (that is, in a particular country or customers identified in the countertrade agreement). The parties may wish to indicate the means to be used to identify the most-favoured customer. The supplier could be required to provide specified types of information indicating the prices charged by the supplier to other customers. It is also advisable to ensure that the most-favoured-customer price is relevant to the shipments to be made pursuant to the countertrade agreement. The parties may also wish to specify the date as of which the most-favoured-customer price is to be determined. The parties may wish to specify any specially discounted prices (preferential prices) offered by the supplier to certain customers that should not be taken into account. The scope of the most-favoured-customer clause may be broadened by agreeing that the price will be determined on the basis of the lowest price charged by the supplier or by other specified suppliers of the same type of goods.

Use of more than One Standard

The countertrade agreement may provide that the price is to be determined by a formula involving two or more standards. The price may be determined by averaging the prices derived from the selected standards. Another possibility is for the price derived from a particular standard to be compared with prices derived from one or more other standards. If the difference between the price derived from the selected standard and the prices from the comparator standards does not reach a specified threshold, the price derived from the selected standard would apply. If the difference exceeds a specified threshold, the final price would be, based on the average of the price derived from the standards. Such techniques may be useful when it is desired to avoid the possibility that the price derived through the use of a single standard might not reflect the market value of a given product at the time the purchase is to be made.

Negotiation

The parties may agree that the price is to be negotiated. For a discussion of procedures the parties may establish for the negotiations, a "Contracting approach". It is advisable that, to the degree possible, the parties agree on guidelines for the determination of the price.

Such guidelines may establish minimum and maximum limits within which the price is to be negotiated. In establishing such limits, the parties may use price standards of the type described earlier. It may be agreed that the price should not be more than 5 per cent higher or more than 5 per cent lower than the price charged by a competitor.

Alternatively, guidelines may merely provide a reference price to be taken into account in negotiations. In formulating a guideline of this type, the parties may use price standards such as those described earlier. It may be agreed that the price will be negotiated taking into account the price of a particular competitor.

A negotiation guideline may also take the form of a statement that the price of goods is to be "competitive", "reasonable", or at a "world market" level. Such a clause might be acceptable when the goods are of a standard quality. A guideline of this type may be made more precise by specifying whether the price should be based only on prices paid to the supplier by other buyers or should also be based on prices charged by other suppliers, the period of time the parties should refer to in determining what is a "competitive", "reasonable" or "world market" price, and, if there are variations in prices in different markets, which markets, types of buyers or geographical territories are referred to.

Determination of Price by Third Person

Sometimes the parties provide for the price to be set by an independent third person, a market specialist in the goods in question. For a discussion, determination of contract terms by third persons, see "Contracting approach". Such an approach may also be used as an alternative price-setting method in the event that an attempt by the parties themselves to set the price proves unsuccessful.

It is advisable for the countertrade agreement to delimit the mandate of the third person by providing guidelines of the type discussed with respect to negotiation. The parties may wish to establish deadlines for referral of the matter to a third person, so that the price could be set in time to allow conclusion of contracts as planned.

Determination of Price by One Party

Sometimes it is agreed that the price will be determined by one of the parties to the countertrade agreement, see "Contracting approach". Legal systems that recognize determination of price by one party tend to require that such determination be subject to guidelines in order to be enforceable. In considering the type of guidelines to use, the parties should bear in mind that legal systems differ as to the degree of precision required. Under some legal systems the determination of the price by one party must be subject to a standard of reasonableness or fairness. When the parties do not refer to a standard of reasonableness or fairness, some of these legal systems will imply a reference to such a standard. Other legal systems require that the latitude of the party determining the price be subject to a standard more definite than reasonableness or fairness.

Revision of Price

When multiple shipments are spread out over a period of time, there may be a need to revise the price in order to reflect changes in the underlying economic conditions. It may be agreed that a revision would occur at specified points of time. Those points of time should be coordinated with the schedule for the fulfilment of the countertrade commitment, e.g. the revision is to take place four weeks prior to the commencement of a subperiod.

Under another approach, it may be agreed that a revision would take place in response to specified changes in underlying economic conditions, an exchange rate fluctuation beyond a certain percentage from a reference rate in effect on the date the countertrade agreement was concluded or changes beyond an agreed threshold in specified components of production cost such as raw materials or labour. Contractual provisions concerning price revision due to a change in the value of the currency in which the price is to be paid are mandatorily regulated under some legal systems. The parties should, therefore, examine whether a clause which they intend to include in the countertrade agreement is permitted under the law of the country of each party.

Yet another approach is to provide for a price revision at regular intervals, every six months, as well as for unscheduled revisions in response to specified changes in underlying economic conditions. In order to limit the frequency of price revision, it could be agreed that an unscheduled review could not take place within a specified period of time following a review, or within a specified period of time preceding a scheduled review. Yet another approach would be to set the price revision procedure in motion upon the delivery of a specified portion of the total quantity of goods to be purchased.

The countertrade agreement might provide for the price revision clause to apply only in cases' where its application would result in a revision exceeding a certain percentage of the price.

When the countertrade agreement contains a price revision clause, the parties may wish to specify the shipments to which the revised price is to apply. It may be agreed that the applicable price for a given shipment is the price in effect on the date the goods are ordered or on the date the letter of credit is issued.

Reapplication of Price Clause

The parties may stipulate in the countertrade agreement that the price is to be revised through the use of the same method as was employed to determine the initial price (standards to be determined by negotiation), determination of price by a third person or determination of price by one party

Index Clause

The purpose of index clauses is to revise the price of the countertrade goods by linking the price to the levels of the prices of certain goods or services prevailing on a certain date. A change in the agreed indices automatically effects a change in the price. In formulating an index clause, it is advisable to use an algebraic formula to determine how changes in the specified indices are to be reflected in the price. Several indices, with different weightings given to each index, may be used in combination in the formula in order to reflect the proportion of different cost elements, materials or services to the total cost of construction. Different indices may be contained in a single formula to reflect the costs of different types of materials and services. When the sources of the same cost element, labour or energy are in different countries, different indices may be found in a single formula for that cost element.

Several factors may be relevant in deciding on the indices to be used. The indices should be readily available, they should be published at regular intervals. They should be reliable. Indices published by recognized bodies (such as well-established chambers of commerce), or governmental or inter-governmental agencies, may be selected. The parties should exercise caution in using indices based on different currencies in a formula, as changes in the relationships between the currencies may affect the operation of the formula in unintended ways.

In some countries, particularly in developing countries, the range of indices available for use in an index clause may be limited. If an index is not available for a particular element of costs, the parties may wish to use an available index in respect of another element. It is advisable to choose an element whose price is likely to fluctuate in approximately the same proportions and at the same times as the actual element to be used. In cases where it is desired to provide an index for labour costs, a consumer price index or cost-of-living index is sometimes used if there is no wage index available.

Change in Exchange Rate of Currency in which Price is Payable
Currency Clause

Under the currency clause, the price to be paid is linked to an exchange rate between the currency in which the price is to be paid and a certain other currency (referred to as the "reference currency") determined at the time of entering into the countertrade agreement. If this rate of exchange has changed at the time of payment, the price to be paid is increased or decreased in such a way that the amount of the price in terms of the reference currency remains unchanged. For purposes of determining the applicable exchange rate, it may be desirable to adopt the time of actual payment, rather than the time when the payment falls due. If the latter time is adopted, the supplier may suffer a loss if the purchaser delays payment. Alternatively, the supplier may be given a choice between the exchange rate prevailing at the time when payment falls due or that prevailing at the time of actual payment. It is advisable to specify an exchange rate prevailing at a particular place.

The reference currency should be stable. The insecurity arising from the potential instability of a single reference currency may be reduced by reference to several currencies. The contract may determine an arithmetic average of the exchange rates between the currency in which the price is payable and several other specified currencies, and provide for revision of the price in accordance with changes in this average.

Unit of Account Clause

If a unit-of-account clause is used, the price is denominated in a monetary unit of account composed of cumulative proportions of a number of selected currencies. In contrast to a clause in which several currencies are used, the weighting given to each selected currency of which such a monetary unit of account is composed is usually not the same, and greater weight is given to currencies generally used in international trade. The unit of account may be one that is established by an intergovernmental institution or by agreement between two or more states and that specifies the selected currencies making up the unit and the relative weighting given to each currency. Special Drawing Right (SDR), European Currency Unit (ECU), or Unit of Account of the Preferential Trade Area for Eastern and Southern African States (UAPTA). In choosing a unit of account, the parties should consider whether the relation between the currency in which the price is payable and the unit of account can be easily determined at the relevant times, at the time of entering into the supply contract and at the time of actual payments.

The value of a unit of account composed of a basket of currencies is relatively stable, since the weakness of one currency of which the unit of account is composed is usually balanced by the strength of another currency. The use of such a unit of account will therefore give substantial protection against changes in exchange rates of the currency in which the price is payable in relation to other currencies.

Security and Performance* : General Remarks

The legal frame focuses on guarantees (also referred to in practice as "bonds" or "indemnities") in a countertrade transaction supporting the countertrade commitment. Such a guarantee may support the obligation of the party committed to purchase countertrade goods, as well as the obligation of the party committed to supply goods. Sometimes a guarantee supports the countertrade commitment by way of securing payment under a liquidated damages or penalty clause covering the countertrade commitment. Guarantees particular to countertrade may also be used to support liquidation of imbalance in the flow of trade. Guarantees supporting the performance of individual supply contracts are not specifically addressed since they do not raise issues particular to countertrade.

Requiring guarantees may have general advantage of preventing parties who are unreliable or who do not have sufficient financial resources from participating in the countertrade transaction. Guarantor institutions generally make careful inquiries about a party whose obligations they are asked to guarantee, and will normally provide guarantees only when they have reasonable ground for believing that the party can successfully perform the obligation. This may be of

---

* United Nations General Assembly, United Nations Commission on, International Trade Law Twentythird Session, New York, June 1990.

particular advantage to importers or exporters who are otherwise unable
to determine whether the proposed counter-party is reliable.

Depending upon its terms, a guarantee may be independent of, or
accessory to, the underlying obligation. Under an independent
guarantee, the guarantor's obligation to pay does not depend on whether
the obligated party (the "principal"), who procures the guarantee, has in
fact breached the underlying obligation, but on whether the party to
whom the obligation is owed (the "beneficiary") has complied with the
payment conditions of the guarantee. Upon meeting the payment
conditions, the beneficiary receives prompt payment even if there is
disagreement between the principal and the beneficiary as to whether the
underlying obligation has been breached. It would be up to the
principal, in an action for recovery of the amount paid, to prove that
the obligation had not been breached. Despite the fact that a guarantor's
obligation to pay may be independent from the underlying obligation,
the right of the beneficiary to claim under the guarantee may under the
law applicable to the guarantee be excluded in exceptional
circumstances, in particular when the claim by the beneficiary is
fraudulent.

Under an accessory guarantee, the guarantor must pay only when
the principal is in fact in breach of the guaranteed obligation. Such
accessory guarantees are referred to in national laws by terms such as
"suretyship", "cautionnement", "garantia", and "Burgschaft". The
guarantor must, before paying a claim, ascertain whether the underlying
obligation was breached in order to establish whether the claim is
justified, and the guarantor is normally entitled to invoke all the
defences that the principal could invoke against the beneficiary.

The discussion in the legal frame is limited to independent
guarantees, without thereby implying a preference for this type of
guarantee. Generally, independent guarantees are used to support
obligations set out in the countertrade agreement. While principals tend
to prefer accessory guarantees, beneficiaries are normally reluctant to
accept such guarantees because of the possible delays involved in
obtaining payment. Moreover, guarantors, in particular banks, tend to
prefer independent guarantees because they do not wish to investigate
the performance of the underlying obligation. While the various legal
regimes governing accessory guarantees are well-established,
independent guarantees, essentially a creation of banking and
commercial practice, are not yet firmly established in the various legal
systems and there is no uniformity as regards the extent to which
independent guarantees are recognized.

In some countries banks issue "stand-by letters of credit", which are the functional equivalent of independent guarantees. Accordingly, the discussion in the legal guide on guarantees for security for performance by the principal applies to stand-by letters of credit.

Guarantee Provisions in Countertrade Agreement

When the parties decide to use a guarantee to support the countertrade commitment, they should include in the countertrade agreement certain basic provisions concerning the issuance and terms of the guarantee. The parties may also wish to consider appending to the countertrade agreement a form of a guarantee to be followed by the issuer in establishing the guarantee. In formulating the terms of the future guarantee in the countertrade agreement, the parties should be sure that the agreed formulation would be accepted by the guarantor.

Typically it is the party committed to purchase whose commitment is supported by a guarantee. In many cases this is because the primary objective of that party in agreeing to a countertrade commitment is to secure a sale, rather than to obtain goods from the other party. When the party committed to purchase goods has a particular interest in obtaining the goods, the supplier's commitment to conclude a contract for the supply of the agreed goods may be supported by a guarantee. In some cases, the countertrade agreement may require both the purchaser and the supplier to obtain guarantees to support their commitments. When the parties to the countertrade agreement foresee that a third person may assume the countertrade commitment, the parties may wish to consider whether the guarantee should be procured by the party originally committed to purchase or supply the goods or by the third person.

When the guarantee supports the principal's obligation under a liquidated damages or penalty clause, the question whether a payment under the guarantee would free the principal from liability for fulfilment of the countertrade commitment would be settled by the term of the liquidated damages or penalty clause and the rules applicable to the clause. When the guarantee does not support a liquidated damages or penalty clause and the parties intend, as is sometimes the case, that payment under the guarantee would have the effect of freeing the principal from the countertrade commitment or from liability for any damages exceeding the amount paid under the guarantee, they should state their intention in the countertrade agreement. Without a provision to this effect, it cannot be assumed that payment under the guarantee would free the principal from the countertrade commitment or from liability for damages.

Choice of Guarantor

The parties may wish to specify in the countertrade agreement a guarantor who would be acceptable to both parties. That would enable the beneficiary to be satisfied that the guarantee would be issued by a guarantor that had the necessary financial reserves and that was otherwise acceptable. The identification of the guarantor could be useful to both parties in that it would limit subsequent disagreements and enable the parties to know the cost of the guarantee at the outset.

If the guarantor is not identified at the time of the conclusion of the countertrade agreement, the parties may provide that the guarantor be a first class bank, be agreeable to the beneficiary or be an institution from the home country of one of the parties.

A beneficiary may wish to have the guarantee issued by an institution in its home country because enforcement of a claim for payment against such an institution could be easier than against a foreign institution. However, requiring the use of a local guarantor may be disadvantageous to the extent that the principal is prevented from using a guarantor with whom it has an established relationship and who may provide the same guarantee at a lower cost.

In some legal systems, mandatory rules applicable to the beneficiary provide that a guarantee may be accepted only if it is issued by a financial institution in the country or a financial institution authorized to issue guarantees involving payment in a foreign currency or if the selection of the guarantor is approved by the competent authority.

There have been instances where an undertaking to pay a sum of money termed a "guarantee", supporting the countertrade commitment or the payment of related liquidated damages or penalties has been made by the party whose countertrade commitment is to be guaranteed. The effect of such a "guarantee" is that the party-guarantor promises to pay the other party under the term of the guarantee without raising any defence that could not have been raised by a third-party guarantor, and that it is up to the party-guarantor to sue for reimbursement of the funds paid if it is claimed that the underlying obligation had not been breached. Such a guarantee might be acceptable to the beneficiary if the guarantee is independent from the underlying transaction and is issued by a trading party whose commercial integrity and financial adequacy are regarded by the beneficiary as being beyond doubt. However, it is not clear that such a guarantee gives the beneficiary legal rights in addition to those arising from the obligation being guaranteed.

Conditions for Obtaining Payment Under the Guarantee

The countertrade agreement should clearly set forth the conditions that have to be fulfilled in order for the guarantor to be obligated to pay, in particular, as to any documents that have to be submitted in support of a claim for payment. Disputes may arise from uncertainty as to whether the documents presented by the beneficiary conform to the term of the guarantee.

The terms of an independent guarantee may provide that a demand for payment alone would suffice or that the demand would have to be accompanied by beneficiary's statement concerning the breach. A general declaration to that effect may be sufficient. Alternatively, the beneficiary may be required to state more details, such as the nature of the principal's breach, that the beneficiary is entitled to payment of the claimed amount and that the amount has not yet been paid. In addition to the demand for payment, the beneficiary may be required to present documents issued by a third person relating to the default by the principal, such as an arbitral award or court decision stating that the default has occurred. The guarantee may provide that the requirement of a third-person statement would be obviated if the principal makes an admission of default in writing. In all these cases, the guarantor merely ascertains whether the documents conform on their face to the requirements of the guarantee and is not to inquire into the underlying transaction. In particular, the guarantor is not to investigate whether the statements contained in a document are founded.

Sometimes the parties agree that the beneficiary must notify the principal of the intention to call the guarantee and that the claim cannot be made before the expiry of a specified period of time following the notice. The purpose of such a notice requirement is to provide an opportunity to the principal to cure a breach or to settle a disagreement. A corollary guarantee term would require the beneficiary to submit with the demand for payment documentary evidence that notice had been given to the principal.

Where the guarantee supports the payment obligation under a liquidated damages or penalty clause, the parties may wish to stipulate that among the payment conditions would be a requirement that the beneficiary provide a statement that payment under the liquidated damages or penalty clause is due.

In addition to documentary conditions, a guarantee will usually specify requirements that do not pertain to the performance of the underlying obligation. Such requirements, which do not involve the presentation of a document, most frequently concern the time period within which a claim can be made, the amount of the guarantee, and the office of the guarantor where the claim is to be submitted.

It is advisable that the countertrade agreement, in addition to setting out the agreement of the parties as to the guarantee, provide that the beneficiary is entitled to claim under the guarantee only if there is in fact a failure to fulfil the commitment. Such a provision might facilitate recovery by the principal of losses suffered in the event a claim has been paid without there having been a breach of the underlying obligation.

Amount of Guarantee and Reduction of Amount

The parties should agree on the amount of the guarantee, as well as the currency in which it is to be denominated and payable. The amount of the guarantee is expressed as a specified amount or as a percentage of the value of the outstanding commitment. If the guarantee is supporting payment under a liquidated damages or penalty clause, the guarantee clause in the countertrade agreement may call for payment of the entire amount of the liquidated damages or penalty or a portion thereof. The liquidated damages or penalty may itself be a certain percentage of the unfulfilled countertrade commitment.

In determining the amount of the guarantee, or of the liquidated damages or penalty covered by the guarantee, the parties would take into account factors such as the extent of the losses expected to be suffered in the event of non-fulfilment and the risk of failure to fulfil, as well as the limits which guarantors would usually observe in respect of similar contracts. Another factor may be the ease with which payment of a claim under the guarantee can be obtained. In this respect, the beneficiary generally has a trade-off to make. The closer the terms of the guarantee approach that of a simple demand guarantee and the easier it will be to obtain payment, the less willing the principal will be for the guarantee to cover a high percentage of the countertrade commitment. On the other hand, if the documentary conditions are more difficult to meet when the principal has not breached the commitment, when an arbitral or court decision must be presented, the principal may be willing to agree on a higher amount for the guarantee.

The parties may wish to include in the terms of the guarantee a mechanism to reduce the amount of the guarantee as fulfilment of the countertrade commitment progress. Reduction of the guarantee amount would have the advantage of reducing the exposure under the guarantee and possibly the cost of the guarantee. If the guarantee secures payment of liquidated damages or a penalty, the provisions on the reduction of the guarantee should be consistent with any reduction mechanism for the sum of the liquidated damages or penalty.

It is advisable that the reduction mechanism operate on the basis of the presentation to the guarantor of specified documents evidencing fulfilment of the countertrade commitment, without the guarantor being obligated to verify the degree to which the countertrade commitment has been fulfilled. These documents may include shipping documents, copies of supply contracts, purchase orders, letters of release or other documents recording fulfilment. The parties may also find it useful to stipulate the issuer of the documents and the party responsible for forwarding them to the guarantor. Where the fulfilment period is divided into subperiods, the parties may wish to provide that the guarantee will be reduced by the amount allocated for each subperiod and not claimed within the agreed period of time.

Time of Providing Guarantee
At Entry into Force of Countertrade Agreement or Shortly Thereafter

The parties are advised to agree on the point of time when the guarantee is to be issued. It may be agreed, that the guarantee should be issued to the beneficiary when the countertrade agreement enters into force or shortly thereafter, thirty days after entry into force of the countertrade agreement. The parties may obtain assurance that the guarantee would be procured at the agreed time by providing that the countertrade agreement would not enter into force without procurement of the guarantee or that the principal would be deemed to have breached the countertrade commitment if the guarantee was not procured within the agreed period of time.

When a contract in one direction (export contract) is concluded together with the countertrade agreement, the parties could agree that the issuance of a guarantee supporting fulfilment of the countertrade commitment is a condition for the entry into force of the export contract. Such a provision would assure the importer of not being bound under the export contract before issuance of a guarantee to support the countertrade commitment.

Later in Fulfilment Period

The parties may agree that the guarantee does not have to be procured until a certain date later in the fulfilment period provided that at the time fulfilment of the commitment has not been completed. The agreed date may be. for example, three months before the end of the fulfilment

period or three months before the end of each yearly segment of a
multi-year fulfilment schedule. This approach has the advantage that the
amount of the guarantee could be calculated as a percentage of the then
outstanding countertrade commitment. By making the amount of the
guarantee dependent on the outstanding balance rather than on the entire
countertrade commitment and by limiting the length of time during
which a guarantee is in effect, the extent of exposure under the
guarantee as well as the cost of the guarantee are likely to be reduced.

Since such an approach exposes the beneficiary to the risk that the
guarantee will not be procured, the parties may wish to agree on the
beneficiary's rights in the event the guarantee is not procured as agreed.
It may be agreed that the beneficiary would be permitted to regard the
countertrade commitment as breached and to claim payment under a
liquidated damages or penalty clause. Furthermore, it might be agreed
that the beneficiary would be entitled to deduct the amount of the
liquidated damages or penalty from any amounts becoming due under
the export contract after the failure to procure the guarantee.

Duration of Guarantee
Expiry Date

It is advisable for the parties to agree in the countertrade agreement on
the length of time the guarantee is to remain in force. One possible
approach would be to provide for an open-ended guarantee that would
terminate only when fulfilment of the commitment is deemed to be
achieved or the committed party is otherwise released from the
commitment, "Fulfilment of countertrade commitment". Another
approach would be to provide a fixed expiry date. It should be noted that
most guarantors may be willing to issue guarantees only if the expiry
date is fixed. Furthermore, the Uniform Customs and Practice for
Documentary Credits (1983 Revision, Publication No. 400 of the
International Chamber of Commerce), under which stand-by letters of
credit may be issued, calls, in its Article 46, for the stipulation of an
expiry date for presentation of documents.

It is advisable that the expiry date of the guarantee fall after the end
of the period for the fulfilment of the countertrade commitment. A
period of time between expiry of the fulfilment period and expiry of the
guarantee (thirty days) would allow the beneficiary to await the
conclusion of supply contracts until the close of the fulfilment period
without foregoing the possibility of claiming payment under the
guarantee. Furthermore, the beneficiary, at its discretion, would be able
to allow minor delays attributable to the principal in the fulfilment of
the countertrade commitment without foregoing the possibility of

claiming payment under the guarantee. At the same time, a relatively short interval would allow the liability of the guarantor to be resolved relatively soon after the alleged non-fulfilment of the countertrade commitment has taken place. The parties may also wish to apply such an approach in relation to guarantees covering subperiods of a fulfilment period.

If the security takes the form of a stand-by letter of credit, it should state expressly that it is irrevocable. The need for such a statement arises because Article 7(c) of the Uniform Customs and Practice for Documentary Credits (1983 Revision, Publication No. 400 of the International Chamber of Commerce), which will often be applicable, provides that a credit is deemed to be revocable in the absence of an express indication that it is irrevocable.

Return of Guarantee Instrument

In some legal systems a guarantee may remain in force even after the expiry date if the guarantee instrument is not returned by the beneficiary. The countertrade agreement should therefore obligate the beneficiary to return the guarantee promptly upon fulfilment of the guaranteed obligation. However, the obligation to return the guarantee should be drafted so as not to imply that if the guarantee is not returned it remains in force even after the expiry date.

Extension

For various reasons, the time period for fulfilment of the countertrade commitment may be extended and as a result continue beyond the expiry date of the guarantee. "Fulfilment of countertrade commitment", concerning extension of the fulfilment period. The countertrade agreement might provide that, if the fulfilment period is extended, the principal would be obligated to arrange within a reasonable period of time a corresponding extension of the guarantee. Alternatively, the guarantee might provide for an automatic extension to cover any extension of the underlying fulfilment period agreed to by the parties. However, such a provision might not be acceptable to a guarantor who does not wish to be bound by a guarantee whose duration depends on an agreement to which the guarantor is not a party.

With respect to the cost of extending the period of validity of the guarantee, the parties may wish to agree that the party responsible for the extension of the fulfilment period will be obligated to bear the costs of the extension of the guarantee period.

Modification or Termination of Countertrade Agreement

In legal systems that recognize the agreement of the parties to establish an independent guarantee, an independent guarantee would remain in effect as stipulated regardless of changes in the underlying commitment. If the change in the underlying contract affects the possibility to obtain the documents in support of the payment claim under the independent guarantee it should be ensured that the change in the underlying contract be reflected by a corresponding modification of the guarantee terms.

Under some legal systems that do not fully recognize an independent guarantee, an alteration of the underlying commitment may result in the release of the guarantor; under other such systems, the guarantee may be deemed to cover only the commitment of the principal existing at the date of issuance of the guarantee. With a view to avoiding undesired consequence, the parties may provide that the guarantee would remain in force despite modifications of the countertrade agreement.

The modification of the countertrade agreement may extend the liability of the principal beyond the amount of the guarantee. The parties may wish to provide in the countertrade agreement that in those cases the principal would be obligated to ensure that the amount of the guarantee would be modified accordingly.

Guarantee for Imbalance in Trade

The parties may agree that goods will be shipped in exchange for goods and that the shipments in each direction will not be paid for in money. This type of transaction may be based on a barter contract, "Contracting approach", or on the set-off of countervailing claims for payment, see "Payment". In such cases a supplier runs the risk that the value of its shipments may exceed the value of goods received from the other party and that this surplus is not liquidated, either by supplies of goods or through payment in money. In order to address this risk, the parties may use guarantees to secure liquidation of an imbalance that may develop in the flow of trade.

The amount of the guarantee should be linked to the amount of the imbalance in the flow of trade, with an upper limit. This upper limit for the guarantee could be set at the level of imbalance permitted under the countertrade transaction. It may be agreed that the amount that could be claimed under the guarantee would cover less than the full extent of the imbalance (80 per cent). The purpose of such an approach would be to discourage the calling of the guarantee except as a last resort. A beneficiary who cannot recover the full amount of the imbalance by calling the guarantee would have a greater incentive to achieve the agreed balance in the flow of trade through ordering goods from the other party.

Guarantee for Shipment in One Direction

Where a particular sequence of shipments in the two directions is stipulated, the countertrade agreement may provide that the party scheduled to receive goods first must provide a guarantee supporting the obligation to ship goods in return. This guarantee would cover the risk taken by the party that ships first, that the return shipment fails to take place by the agreed date of is not of the agreed value or quantity. When the first shipment is to take place in stages, it may be agreed that with each partial shipment a separate guarantee is to be provided corresponding to the value of that shipment; alternatively, the guarantor may agree to increase the amount of the guarantee upon the presentation of documents evidencing additional shipments.

With respect to the timing of the issuance of the guarantee, the countertrade agreement may provide that the guarantee is to be handed over to the beneficiary in exchange for the shipping documents relating to the first delivery. Such a procedure would safeguard against the possibility that the party scheduled to ship first obtains the guarantee but fails to ship. In order to ensure that the beneficiary of the guarantee (the party that has shipped first) would not be in a position to claim payment under the guarantee once the principal (the party shipping second) has fulfilled its obligation to ship goods, the countertrade parties may agree that the beneficiary of the guarantee would obtain documents of title to the second shipment only upon surrender of the guarantee instrument.

Guarantees may be used in a similar fashion in multi-party countertrade transactions. When the parties link deliveries in such a fashion that the importer, in exchange for goods received from the exporter, ships goods to a third-party counter-importer, the third-party counter-importer pays the exporter, see "Payment". The guarantee, provided by the importer, would support the obligation to counter-export after receiving the export goods. When the exporter is to be paid by the counter-importer upon shipment of the export goods, the counter-importer would be the beneficiary of the guarantee. Such a guarantee would cover the risk taken by the counter-importer in paying the exporter prior to receiving goods from the counter-exporter. When, however, the counter-importer is to pay the exporter only upon receipt of the counter-export goods, the exporter would be the beneficiary of the guarantee. Such a guarantee would cover the risk that the exporter, having shipped goods, failed to be paid by the counter-importer because the counter-export did not take place.

A similar guarantee may be used when the exporter, instead of being paid by the importer, receives goods from a third-party counter-exporter, who in turn is paid by the importer see "Payment". In this case, it may be agreed that the exporter would be given a guarantee covering the risk that, having shipped first, the exporter failed to be compensated by a shipment of goods from the counter-exporter.

A guarantee may be employed in a similar fashion when both the counter-importer and the counter-exporter are separate parties from the exporter and the importer see "Payment". It may be agreed that the importer must provide a guarantee to the exporter to support the importer's obligation to pay the price of the export goods. When the exporter is to receive payment from the counter-importer upon shipment of the export goods, the beneficiary would be the counter-importer. This would protect the counter-importer against the risk of paying the exporter without receiving goods from the counter-exporter. When, however, the counter-importer is to pay the exporter only upon shipment of the counter-export goods, the beneficiary of the guarantee would be the exporter. This would protect the exporter against the risk of shipping goods without being paid.

Mutual Guarantees

When the parties agree to exchange goods for goods, they may do so without stipulating a particular sequence in which the shipments in the two directions should take place. This is particularly likely when multiple shipments in each direction are envisaged. In such stipulations, both parties encounter the risk of an imbalance in the flow of trade which needs to be redressed either through the shipment of goods or through the payment of a sum of money. To address this risk, it may be agreed that each party is to provide a guarantee to secure liquidation of an imbalance in favour of the other party.